ACTIVE VOICES

ACTIVE
VOICES

Women in Jewish Culture

Edited by

MAURIE SACKS

UNIVERSITY OF ILLINOIS PRESS
Urbana and Chicago

© 1995 by the Board of Trustees of the University of Illinois
Manufactured in the United States of America
1 2 3 4 5 C P 5 4 3 2 1

This book is printed on acid-free paper.

Library of Congress Cataloging-in-Publication Data

Active voices : women in Jewish culture / edited by Maurie Sacks.
    p.   cm.
    Includes bibliographical references and index.
    ISBN 0-252-02154-1 (cloth). — ISBN 0-252-06453-4 (pbk.)
    1. Women in Judaism. 2. Jewish women—Religious life. 3. Jewish
women—Folklore. 4. Jewish women in literature. I. Sacks, Maurie.
BM729.W6A28   1995
296'.082—dc20   94-30759
                                                    CIP

Contents

IV · RITUAL VOICES

V · FOLK VOICES

VI · AN ANTHROPOLOGICAL VOICE

Acknowledgments

This volume began with a conversation I had many years ago with Rabbi Neil Gillman of the Jewish Theological Seminary, who urged me to publish my ideas on the value of the *presence* of women in Judaism. I am grateful for his encouragement and for reading and commenting on an early version of the introduction. Shalom Staub, editor of the *Jewish Folklore and Ethnology Review* at the time of my special issue on women in Judaism, provided invaluable support and help during my maiden voyage as guest editor.

Barbara Kirshenblatt-Gimblett has supported this work through conversations, advice, and finally through two fine critical readings from beginning to end, and I am deeply indebted to her, as I am to Riv-Ellen Prell, who also provided critical comments that helped us strengthen the volume considerably.

Judith McCulloh, at the University of Illinois Press, has nurtured, nudged, encouraged, and been incredibly patient with me during the long process of putting this book together. If she had ever lost faith, I probably would have, too.

I would like to thank my many colleagues—at the Association for Jewish Studies, the American Folklore Society, the American Anthropological Association, and the Melton Center for Jewish Studies at Ohio State University—for sharing their data, ideas, and friendship, all of which are reflected in these pages, over the years.

Gratitude is due to Montclair State University, which has supported different phases of this project with Career Development grants for released time from teaching. The work simply could not have been done without this relief.

To my long-suffering authors who have written, revised, refaxed pages I misplaced, and never once let me down—you know this book would not *be* without you. Although the long process of preparing this book has resulted in our not having references to some important new publications, we are speaking in the timeless ethnographic present, and I hope you are as proud as I am to have a part in the final product.

I am indebted to my children, Cem and Lisa, who have always had faith in me, even when my own confidence has sometimes flagged. Deep appreciation is also due to William Batkay, who has critically edited and discussed my work with me for many years, and who read early drafts of the introduction and made helpful comments. And Kenneth Pletter, who read the introduction and several chapters with a sensible nonacademic eye and offered useful criticism as well as a loving environment in which to complete this work, has my heartfelt gratitude.

I dedicate this volume to my grandmother, Jeannette Seymans, and her daughters, Teddy, Wilma, Etta, and Debby, who never let me doubt the value, abilities, and power of Jewish women.

ACTIVE VOICES

Introduction

MAURIE SACKS

Background

This book represents the scholarly efforts of several writers to recognize the long-ignored voices of Jewish women. It began as a special issue on women of the *Jewish Folklore and Ethnology Review,*
a publication of the Jewish Section of the American Folklore Society.[1] This work's organizing principles, including its interdisciplinary
approach and its particular feminist perspective, are functions of my
own life experiences, which include my years as a member of a
Muslim family in Turkey and my anthropological training. To offer
a better understanding of this collection of essays, I will explore these
issues briefly.

My sojourn as a daughter-in-law in a Muslim family in Turkey,
an experience that spanned the late sixties and early seventies, inspired my interest in the issues treated in this collection. Having
grown up in the 1950s, I was much surprised to discover in the patriarchal Turkish social milieu that women valued women and their
support and companionship more than that of men. This was at a
time when many American women were meeting in consciousness-
raising groups to discover their common interests and the value of
sisterhood. Unlike so many of their American counterparts, few
women among my Turkish acquaintances felt marginalized or lacking in self-love.

My learning of Turkish womens' strong sense of self led me to
pose several questions: If Turkish Muslim women did not suffer from
the "feminine mystique" and the failure of self-esteem first set out
for American women by Betty Friedan in 1963,[2] could there not also
be Jewish women who experienced their roles in Judaism as meaningful and fulfilling? Is the malaise of the contemporary American

Jewish feminist an artifact of Jewish patriarchy itself, as many authors have suggested, or a result of the specific conditions of *American* Jewish women of a particular class and political persuasion? What did Judaism look like from the point of view of the women whose voices had not been recorded, women of earlier periods, women of third-world Jewries, even some contemporary American women who have chosen to experience their Judaism in an Orthodox model? I turned to anthropology to find the answers to these questions, which were very uncomfortable to be asking during the early seventies, the years in which the radical-liberal feminist discourse of NOW demanded that women achieve their rightful place in society by assuming roles historically assigned to men. This approach was considered "correct thinking" for an educated, middle-class white American woman, and my concerns were thought to be impertinent, if not downright antifeminist.

In pursuit of a feminist social science that recognizes women's roles in constructing society and culture, anthropology offers three useful approaches to the study of human behavior: ethnography, wholism, and critical anthropology. Ethnographic research has only very recently been applied to the study of Jewish women's lives.[3] Documenting Jewish women's "voices" through qualitative ethnographic research methods like interviews, life-histories, and participant observation in women's gendered activities, as represented in this volume, is an important strategy for ending the age-old "silence" of Jewish women cited in Jewish feminist literature of the 1970s.[4] Ethnographic knowledge of Jewish women is further enhanced through ethnohistorical scholarship that employs analysis of heretofore unexamined documents to throw light on women's roles in constructing Jewish society and culture. Weissler's work on *tehines,* or women's vernacular prayers, and the construction of female selves and roles in the sixteenth through nineteenth centuries[5] offers a major contribution along these lines, while in this volume the work of Berkowitz and Nadell and Simon represent this strategy.

For Jewish feminist studies, the wholistic approach that anthropology brings to the study of society and culture addresses the same issue raised recently by Paula Hyman at an American Anthropological Association meeting, where she noted that some Jewish scholars jokingly refer to their own work as the study of texts talking to texts.[6] Anthropology insists that no subarea of culture, such as religion or written texts no matter how aged or respected, can be isolated from any other in the pursuit of ethnographic knowledge. From this perspective, a socioscientific understanding of Jewish women's power and significance in the historical enterprise of Jewish culture cannot be divorced from knowledge of the material conditions of life, social structure, and folk culture. Textual evidence alone, whether religious or more comprehensively historical, cannot illuminate sufficiently for anthropological purposes the meaning of Jewish women's lives. Whether written within the discipline of anthropology or not, many of the chapters in this volume transcend conventional knowledge about women's roles in Judaism. They examine meaning in women's lives in the broader context of Jewish society and culture, rather than limit inquiry to those behavior clusters commonly known as "religion."

Finally, critical anthropology meshes with other postmodern lines of inquiry, such as feminist criticism, that question the nature of how we know what we know. During the 1970s a genre of feminist ethnography appeared that questioned and contradicted the masculine texts and even some of the tenets of male-dominated science.[7] The very existence of this feminist discourse required a reexamination of the assumptions upon which the discipline of anthropology was based, and a literature addressing these issues was soon forthcoming.[8]

If the "scientific" model of anthropology, proposed by scholars like Boas during the first half of the twentieth century, supposed a positivistic approach to "reality," then the discovery of women's worlds posed a challenge to this view. The very concept of "objectivity" in social science, and of the nature of the gendered scientist as data collector, came under scrutiny.[9] Reflection on the biased nature of the gendered researcher called for "constant examination of [our] assumptions and motivations."[10] Ardener, in 1975, suggested that we need to question the very idea that social discourse is consistent across gender lines, that we can know all we need to know about a society by asking any member. He argued that, at least in some societies, males and females may experience quite different cultures and have divergent cosmological views.[11] Gendered power relations were also cast in a new light by anthropologists such as Annette Weiner, Beverly Chiñas, and Jane Goodale,[12] who examined different definitions of power and looked at patriarchal cultures from a female point of view. Weiner argued that women's power can be experienced only when the concept "power" is defined to include women's influential behavior in reproducing the relationships that constitute society.[13]

These new explorations in anthropology paralleled developments in feminist theory by the French feminists Hélène Cixous and Luce Irigiray and by feminist literary critics such as Elaine Showalter. Cixous and Irigiray, working from Lacan's ideas, proposed that the very discourse of Western culture is male-centered.[14] Concepts such as dominance and subordination, it follows, are artifacts of Western notions of power developed mostly by male thinkers and must therefore be questioned by feminist theorists. Deconstruction of male concepts that have been long accepted as "given" elements of Western culture opens the way for the demystification of patriarchy and legitimizes serious investigation of a female way of being. Showalter believes that this process is revealed in the "female" phase of women's writing that frees itself of "both imitation [of] and protest [against male discourse]—two forms of dependency—and turn[s] instead to female experience as the source of an autonomous art."[15]

Chava Weissler, in her research on Ashkenazi Jewish women's religion, has tried to clarify these various approaches to the analysis of women's culture. She identifies three strategies for the feminist study of religion:

(1) those that add an account of women's religious lives to an already existing history of Judaism
(2) those that consider women's Judaism within the framework of other groups usually omitted from the history of Judaism and
(3) those that seek to transform our understanding of Judaism through the incorporation of the perspective gained from the study of women's religion.[16]

Although Weissler specifically limits herself to considering the "study of Jewish religion," her analysis can be applied to a much broader spectrum of behaviors, that is, Jewish society and culture. Judaism, as embodied in Jewish cultures, transcends the subcluster of behaviors called "religion." By freely exploring women's self-expression in both religious and nonreligious areas of Jewish life, this collection addresses, particularly, Weissler's types one and three, filling in the "holes" in the record, where women's history and ethnography ought to have been and transforming our understanding of Judaism by incorporating the study of women's behavior into the study of Judaism.

Critical anthropologists and feminist theorists have both proposed investigation of a female experience not necessarily dependent upon male constructs. It is therefore useful, as Weissler suggests, in "transforming our understanding of Judaism," to bring to the fore women's experiences and relegate men's Judaism to the background.[17] Insights derived from such thinking have informed my choice of materials for presentation here.

My particular anthropological training at Columbia University (in the early seventies) further influenced the organization of this book, leading me to formulate the kinds of questions the volume is designed to address. I had the good fortune to study with the late Professor Robert Murphy, who had a way of turning culture inside-out in order to understand it better.[18] Murphy always seemed to be studying the world as if looking at photographic negatives rather than positive prints of sociocultural systems. His influence on me has doubtless fueled my desire to study an avowedly patriarchal society such as Judaism from the point of view of women—persons who "were not there," who have not, in the past, been generally recognized as significant movers in Jewish culture.[19] Does not the negative produce the positive when passed through the process of photographic development? By analogy, then, might not looking at women's Judaism produce an enhanced understanding of the cultural process through which the whole of Judaism has developed?

Although here we take a multidisciplinary approach, the anthropological framework establishes a systemic and a critical orientation for these essays. A systemic approach demands that we set aside both the concepts derived from the history of Western thought like dominance and subordination and the concepts defining Jewish women that appear in the rhetoric of Jewish texts and public practice. We examine gendered behavior as it functions in a total Jewish sociocultural environment, not just in the domain called "religion." It is the critical aspect of this undertaking that requires us to question the "scientific" applicability of our own culturally determined concepts like dominance and subordination to our subject of inquiry, in this case women's place in Jewish society. In fact, our critical stance makes it possible to redefine "Judaism" to include, within a single framework, rabbinical texts, folk culture, historical, sociological, literary, and ethnographic materials that are usually studied in isolation from one another. In isolation, most studies presuppose what is Jewish and fail to relate the religious, folkloric, or historical focus to the broader, contextual nature of Jewish societies and cultures. The present anthropological perspective informs a choice of chapters that address women as agents *within Jewish cultural systems*.

Structuring this collection as a discourse across disciplinary boundaries (framed anthropologically) differentiates it from other new readers on Jewish women.[20] Scholars writing from the perspectives of anthropology, sociology, family therapy, history, folklore, literary criticism, women's studies, religious studies, and ethnomusicology address here similar interests but use somewhat different research methods. While these scholars usually do not have the opportunity to speak to one another,[21] they appear here in juxtaposition. The result of this design is a multifaceted collection that explores a broad spectrum of scholarly approaches to the study of women in the context of Jewish society and culture.

Finding Jewish Women's Voices

Although volumes about Jewish women are appearing in increasing numbers, with few exceptions[22] socioscientific and historical documentation of Jewish women's lives is a relatively recent phenomenon. These works are part of the "explosion of discourse" on women licensed by the postmodern trend in intellectual development in which Jewish feminists have hastened to make their voices heard.[23] Jewish women, assimilated as many are among middle-class Western intellectuals, can be found in the vanguard of those claiming legitimacy for contemporary political and intellectual feminist criticism. Additionally, feminists have turned their attention to Judaism itself, examining its texts, religious practices, and finally the sociocultural systems that have generated, guarded, and passed Jewish religion and culture on through the ages. Feminist discourse that appeared in a radical and programmatic criticism of the misogynistic elements of "traditional Judaism" in 1973 also provided a fertile environment for inquiry into actual lives of Jewish women. Many of them, it turned out, had transcended patriarchal notions and did not regard themselves as "marginal" nor their spirituality as inferior to that of men.[24]

The question, then, arises: How do we deal with the discrepancy between some of the findings produced by research on real women through examination of heretofore unconsidered historical documents and contemporary ethnography and the expectations many feminists have concerning women's status in patriarchal society? Here, it is helpful to refer back to Showalter's concept of the "female" experience, in which reality is perceived through women's eyes, as opposed to the "feminine" construct, which accepts an androcentric definition of women. Both contrast with the "feminist," worldview that protests the patriarchal construction of gender. While the "female" is entirely women-centered, feminine and feminist differ in their submission and opposition to perceptions of gender that are entirely male focused.

The female experience, as so eloquently documented by Sered, among others,[25] pertains to an everyday Judaism in which women play powerful and focal roles. This Judaism is not well represented either in the religious texts or in the formal Judaism of the synagogue and house of learning. While it is beyond the scope of this introduction to define "religion" as opposed to "society" and "culture," we must be aware of the problem posed by the disjuncture between these concepts as we explore the relationship between cultural representations of Jewish women and their actual lives. If Judaism is *only* the male-dominated religion of halakah[26] (and its local interpretations) that relegates women to places out of sight of the focal Torah Service, discourages them, or even prohibits them, from learning the holy words, and assigns women, but not men, to helpless roles like that of *agunah*,[27] then it deserves to be characterized as "misogynistic." However, if we examine the wider social and cultural aspects of Jewish life it is possible to emancipate ourselves from patriarchal categories. We can then bring to the fore a richer and subtler panoply of female experience than is manifested in the texts and traditional public practices, the focus, until now, of most Jewish Studies research.

Scholars writing in this volume have captured Jewish women in various times and places engaged in active, assertive behaviors. These are Jewish women who defined themselves as persons in their own right, with powers to construct their own lives and to pass on to future generations a Judaism they helped to create. Except for Baskin, the authors beg the question of female subordination and investigate women's self-images and their active roles in producing and reproducing Jewish culture.

Preview

This book is divided into several sections. First, Baskin's essay presents some "men's voices" so that readers can later compare what they read with these more expected assertions. This collection thus addresses the problem of understanding the active, assertive lives of women portrayed in these essays within the context of a Judaism dominated by rabbinical views of Jewish women. Chapters are arranged in sections analyzing public, literary, ritual, and folk voices. Sered's concluding "anthropological voice" is a clarion call to empower women's voices in Judaism by learning to value what women say.

Since men have dominated text-writing and text-keeping throughout Jewish history, they have obviously been influential in establishing the images and models that we (literate twentieth-century text-readers) have of Jewish women through the ages. In her article, Baskin provides a sampling of rabbinical texts revealing representations of women commonly thought to be central to traditional Jewish religious discourse. Part of this discourse, however, presented a dilemma even for the rabbis: since women are defined as "other," hence unknown and potentially threatening, they must be controlled by men; but there is no true "human-ness" without the merging, through marriage, of man and woman. Man is dependent upon woman to complete his human self. If the self also represents society, woman cannot therefore be marginal to Jewish society, because she is integral. But what, then, is her role?

The other contributors in this volume address the issue of women's "otherness" by bringing it to the fore, making women's experiences the focus of inquiry. In fact, by taking the "female" point of view, these authors relegate male-centered Judaism to the margins. When the researcher looks directly at women as full-fledged persons and productive members of a culture-bearing community, the male view revealed in the religious texts does not occupy center stage.

Women are observed defining Judaism, too, as they define themselves. The power to construct their self-image culturally is an indicator of the presence of the independent spirit of Jewish women. It is important, as Sered asserts, that the reader not predetermine that women's Judaism only takes up spaces not filled by men.

In "Public Voices," Berkowitz and Nadell and Simon treat women acting as organizers of Jewish communal institutions. Berkowitz's essay portrays European Zionist women of the late nineteenth and early twentieth centuries constructing and disseminating images of Palestine as they would like it to be known, and creating institutions capable of funding the early *yishuv*.[28] Nadell and Simon, contradicting earlier work on Jewish Sisterhoods, believe that women's synagogue auxiliaries did, in fact, have a major impact in modeling and structuring women's roles as we know them today in American Reform Jewry. Both of these essays make the point that women's organizations are not merely supplementary to those of men, but take an active role in *constructing* the aspect of Judaism that they address, be it Zionism or Reform sectarianism.

"Literary Voices" treats two genres, the Victorian novel and belles lettres defining the Holocaust experience, from womens' perspectives. Both Ashton and Goldenberg portray women in the act of constructing selves through their documents. Ashton's Grace Aguilar, in her novels, assertively creates an image of the middle-class Anglo-Jewish woman as a Victorian lady of high sensibility and spirituality. Of course, Aguilar finds this woman in her own self, and through her writing projects this image to the world, as well as to other Jewish women, for consideration. This construction of Jewish womanhood is especially accepted in America, and Nadell and Simon document its influence on the Sisterhood movement in Reform Judaism in the twentieth century.

Goldenberg's painful essay documents Jewish women in the most horrifying and degrading of circumstances, in the Nazi death camps. Even here, women actively, through their stories and testimony, portray an assertive and nurturing self, to themselves and each other and for posterity. They understand that self-definition is part of their effort to survive and cope with the tragedy of the Holocaust.

The three essays in the section called "Ritual Voices" depict three different approaches to Jewish women's ritual behavior. While Adelman describes contemporary American women creating ritual that meets their feminist needs, Davis elucidates the managerial role Jewish women have always controlled in respect to family ritual, and Kaufman explores how some contemporary women reinterpret Orthodox ritual to make it meaningful in today's feminist context.

Adelman takes care to indicate that women constructing new ritual have first become learned in Jewish religious and historical texts, which they reinterpret and utilize in creating an expanded psychoreligious space where they can function spiritually within a Jewish symbolic system. Davis, in contrast, considers women's roles in more traditional, male-dominated Jewish contexts. Even here she shows that a look from a fresh perspective reveals women not downtrodden by patriarchal institutions, but actively participating in the organization and interpretation of Jewish tradition in ways that can only be described as instrumental and self-assertive. Kaufman's essay, derived from narratives collected from newly Orthodox Jewish women (*ba'alot teshuvah*), explores how unobservant women who choose to adopt Orthodox practice literally reinvent themselves, as well as their Judaism. Their discourse describes traditional Jewish ritual imbued with positive feminine values that they find more satisfying than the misogyny they experienced in secular "liberal" American culture. Although Kaufman's sample is limited to women who have "returned" to Orthodoxy and married, and does not purport to speak for all *ba'alot teshuvah,* the discourse in which these women engage represents at least one approach that self-actualizing women have taken to Jewish tradition.

"Folk Voices" contains three contrasting essays analyzing women's roles in folk performance—an area recognized by scholars as an important expression of cultural style and values. Schely-Newman's storyteller demonstrates the function of folktales and the folktale-teller in reconciling social change with tradition. Cohen's Sephardic musicians go one step further and adapt their performance to the folk music market as the traditional context for their genre disappears through migration and modernization of familial roles. Charnow's Orthodox high-school girls are unexpectedly the most radical of all, for they take an entirely secular American art-form, the class play, and turn it into a Jewish expression of tension between Orthodox values and American aspirations.

Schely-Newman's storyteller assertively holds on to her self-image as wife and mother. She has experienced traumatic cultural displacement and adapts her concept of the cosmos to her new environment, yet stubbornly remains the woman with whom she is most comfortable. In Cohen's article, Sephardic women pass on images of themselves and their communities in their repertories. These images sometimes reflect patriarchal values, but the women control them while playing roles as performers within social settings of their own making. As the context of Sephardic women's performance changes, Cohen's informants also create new active roles as preservers and purveyors of their culture. They become producers and scholars of Sephardic folk tradition, as well as public performers.

Charnow's unique essay about an Orthodox girls' performance indicates that even pious, Orthodox-trained young women take an active hand in creating their own self-image. Despite religious prohibitions to the contrary, they do not refrain from portraying themselves as men as well as women. To continue the theme, Charnow's girls, like Schely-Newman's storyteller, maintain perceptions of themselves as traditional Jewish women while still incorporating into their self concepts education, professional career goals, and roles as writers, performers, and producers of scripts. While Charnow's girls perform publicly, within the context of their female community, Cohen's Sephardic singers have moved out of the context of household and family ritual and joined, along with some male performers, the show business world of the folk music circuit, creating new social roles like that of the "insider performer" as well as the musical entrepreneur. While it is not unusual to find Jewish women in the marketplace, it is interesting to note that some Jewish women are aware that their *traditions* have marketable value.

Finally, Sered, in her examination of Middle-Eastern Jewish senior citizens in Jerusalem, shows how these elderly, illiterate women have formulated their own approach to Jewish public ritual. Their interpretation of their synagogue experiences are quite different from those treated in the writings of Jewish-American feminists. In her essay Sered bravely calls for a new approach to Jewish feminist studies—one that, following the lead of her senior informants, does not accept the revealed wisdom of androcentric Judaism as the yardstick by which to measure women's status in Jewish society and culture. This idea returns to the concept of women constructing female selves and a female Judaism that Sered would recognize as being equal in value to male Judaism.

All together, the chapters in this volume utilize various feminist approaches to Jewish studies to illustrate the idea that Judaism is not a religion existing only in the texts and male-dominated institutions such as the synagogue and house of learning with women a necessary appurtenance, on the sidelines, looking in. Judaism is, and always has been, a culture (or many cultures) passed along from generation to generation by male *and* female members of Jewish societies. To discuss gender roles in Judaism without taking into account the social context of the religion does injustice to women, since women's forte in Jewish communal life has most often been outside the realm of the male-centered institutions.

Women's work in producing and reproducing the communities that, through the ages, have supported Jewish patriarchal institutions cannot be disregarded if we wish to have a balanced record of "Judaism." It is only by adopting a limiting androcentric view of the Jewish religion, where text and text study are the *one* dominant value, that one becomes encumbered with the idea that subordination and humiliation represent the fundamental condition of Jewish women. By taking broader historical and social-scientific perspectives and critically asking questions concerning the gendered nature of Judaism—where we thought answers had already been provided—it is possible to retrieve a rich documentation of generations of assertive, active Jewish women. Often Jewish women have had healthy self-esteem and no particular sense of being limited in their choices, any more than men, by the nature of traditional gendered social systems, have been limited in theirs.

If we choose to draw practical or political conclusions from the work presented here,[29] then these would encompass recognition that Jewish women have always enjoyed a dialogue with Judaism, a dialogue in which female voices can be heard, if only we know how to listen. Listening to women's voices as represented in Jewish society and culture can only empower Jewish women to continue to shape Judaisms that meet their needs.

NOTES

1. The American Folklore Society is a century-old association of scholars interested in investigating vernacular culture. The presence of a Jewish Section in the AFS is testimony to the extent to which Jewish-Americans have

gravitated to certain kinds of scholarly endeavors, and also to the extent to which the AFS as a whole recognizes Jewry as a significant category for study. The readiness of this society to sponsor journal issues devoted to women's studies is a function of the degree to which this particular society acknowledges feminist inquiry to be legitimate. See the *Journal of American Folklore* 100, no. 398 (1987), a special issue on women's folklore that includes two articles on Jewish women, and the *Jewish Folklore and Ethnology Review* 12, nos. 1–2 (1989), a combined special issue on Jewish women.

2. Betty Friedan, *The Feminine Mystique* (New York: Norton, 1973).

3. To date most ethnographies of Jewish communities concentrate on male institutions or ignore gender issues entirely. For example, see Frida Kerner Furman, *Beyond Yiddishkeit: The Struggle for Jewish Identity in a Reform Synagogue* (Albany: State University of New York Press, 1987); Samuel C. Heilman, *Synagogue Life: A Study in Symbolic Interaction* (Chicago: University of Chicago Press, 1973); William Toll, *The Making of an Ethnic Middle Class: Portland Jewry over Four Generations* (Albany: State University of New York Press, 1983). An exception would be Riv-Ellen Prell, *Prayer and Community: The Havurah in American Judaism* (Detroit: Wayne State University Press, 1989); see also Prell, "Laughter That Hurts: Ritual Humor and Ritual Change in an American Jewish Community," in Jack Kugelmass, ed., *Between Two Worlds: Ethnographic Essays on American Jewry* (Ithaca: Cornell University Press, 1988), pp. 192–225, and "Sacred Categories and Social Relations: The Visibility and Invisibility of Gender in an American Jewish Community," in Harvey Goldberg, ed., *Judaism Viewed from Within and from Without* (Albany: State University of New York Press, 1987), pp. 171–95.

4. Chava Weissler, "The Religion of Traditional Ashkenazic Women: Some Methodological Issues," *AJS Review* 12, no. 1 (1987): 73–94. For this point of view, see also Rachel Adler, "The Jew Who Wasn't There: *Halakah* and the Jewish Woman," in Susannah Heschel, ed., *On Being a Jewish Feminist: A Reader* (New York: Schocken Books, 1983), pp. 12–18; Paula Hyman, quoted in "Lilith Interview: After a Decade of Jewish Feminism the Jewry Is Still Out," *Lilith* 11 (1983): 20–24.

5. Chava Weissler, "Prayers in Yiddish and the Religious World of Ashkenazic Women," in Judith R. Baskin, ed., *Jewish Women in Historical Perspective* (Detroit: Wayne State University Press, 1991), pp. 159–81, and "'For Women and for Men Who Are Like Women': The Construction of Gender in Yiddish Devotional Literature," *Journal of Feminist Studies in Religion* 5, no. 2 (1989): 7–24.

6. Paula Hyman commenting on the panel "Jewish Women: Spirituality, Politics, and Identity" at the American Anthropological Association meetings in San Francisco, December 1992.

7. For example: Annette Weiner, *Women of Value, Men of Renown: New Perspectives in Trobriand Exchange* (Austin: University of Texas Press, 1976); Jane Goodale, *Tiwi Wives* (Seattle: University of Washington Press, 1982); Beverly Chiñas, *The Isthmus Zapotecs: Women's Roles in Cultural Context* (New York: Holt, Rinehart & Winston, 1973).

8. Shirley Ardener, ed., *Perceiving Women* (New York: Halstead Press, 1975); Rayna Reiter, *Toward an Anthropology of Women* (New York: Monthly Review Press, 1975); Susan Rogers, "Woman's Place: A Critical Review of Anthropological Theory," *Comparative Studies of Society and History* 20, no. 1 (1978): 123–62; Michele Zimbalist Rosaldo and Louise Lamphere, eds., *Women, Culture, and Society* (Stanford: Stanford University Press, 1974); Peggy Sanday, "The Reproduction of Patriarchy in Feminist Anthropology," in M. M. Gergen, ed., *Feminist Thought and the Structure of Knowledge* (New York: New York University Press, 1988), pp. 49–68.

9. Tony L. Whitehead and Mary Ellen Conaway, eds., *Self, Sex, and Gender in Cross-Cultural Fieldwork* (Urbana: University of Illinois Press, 1986).

10. Polly Young-Eisendrath, "The Female Person and How We Talk about Her," in Gergen, ed., *Feminist Thought*, pp. 152–72.

11. Edwin Ardener, "Belief and the Problem of Women," in Ardener, ed., *Perceiving Women*, pp. 1–18.

12. Chinas, *Isthmus Zapotecs*; Goodale, *Tiwi Wives*; Weiner, *Women of Value*.

13. Annette Weiner, "Trobriand Kinship from Another View: The Reproductive Power of Women and Men," *Man* (n.s.) 14 (1979): 328–48.

14. Hélène Cixous, "Laugh of the Medusa," *Signs* 1, no. 4 (1976): 875–93; Luce Irigaray, *Ce sexe qui n'en est pas un* (Paris: Editions de Minuit, 1977).

15. Elaine Showalter, *The New Feminist Criticism: Essays on Womens' Literature and Theory* (New York: Pantheon, 1985), pp. 137–38.

16. Weissler, "Traditional Ashkenazic Women," p. 73.

17. Ibid.

18. Robert F. Murphy, *The Dialectics of Social Life: Alarms and Excursions in Anthropological Theory* (New York: Basic Books, 1971).

19. Adler, "Jew Who Wasn't There."

20. Baskin, *Jewish Women*; Susan Grossman, ed., *Daughters of the King* (Philadelphia: Jewish Publication Society, 1992); Ellen Umansky and Dianne Ashton, eds., *Five Centuries of Jewish Women's Spirituality* (Boston: Beacon Press, 1991).

21. In the academic world professional associations and pressure to

publish in journals in one's field tend to keep apart scholars who happen to be trained in different disciplines, even if their substantive interests are similar. One reason for this is difficulties trained scholars have with other disciplines' methodologies. For example, historians may question the legitimacy of the folklorist's analysis of textual collections that are not based on examination of original texts, while anthropologists might look askance at historians who retrieve history from obscure documents, but do not analyze their material in broad social contexts. Interestingly, the academic structure of Jewish Studies, by its nature interdisciplinary, does allow scholars at the annual meetings of the Association for Jewish Studies to talk across disciplines.

22. For well-known examples, see the biblical books of Esther and of Ruth and Marvin Lowenthal, trans., *The Memoirs of Gluckel of Hameln* (New York: Schocken, 1977).

23. Of course, the postmodern era is not the first to spawn feminist movements or Jewish feminism. See, for example, Marion Kaplan, *The Jewish Feminist Movement in Germany: The Campaigns of the Juedischer Frauenbund, 1904–1938* (Westport, Conn.: Greenwood Press, 1979).

24. For example, compare Paula Hyman, "The Other Half: Women in Jewish Tradition," in E. Koltun, ed., *The Jewish Woman: New Perspectives* (New York: Schocken Books, 1976), pp. 105–13, and quotes from "Lilith Interview," in which Hyman deplores Jewish patriarchy, with C. Baum, P. Hyman, and S. Michel, *The Jewish Woman in America* (New York: Dial Press, 1976), in which the authors document the lives of vigorous and assertive women in American Judaism.

25. See Susan Sered, *Women as Ritual Experts: The Religious Lives of Elderly Jewish Women in Jerusalem* (New York: Oxford University Press, 1992).

26. Halakah is Jewish legal tradition.

27. An *agunah* is a woman unable to wed or even take a lover because her husband will not issue her a bill of divorce (*get*) or because her husband's death has not been properly witnessed according to the law, so that, although he is missing, the rabbis presume him to be alive.

28. *Yishuv* refers to the early twentieth-century migrations from Eastern Europe to Palestine.

29. This is not meant to devalue the changes in the allocation of power in Judaism, such as rabbinical ordination in the Reform, Conservative, and Reconstructionist branches, and somewhat increased representation of women in upper management in Jewish institutional life, achieved by the women's movement in America. These changes have revitalized Judaism for many American Jewish women and may be the only hope for passing on

Jewish identity and practice for many American Jews who would otherwise go the way of total assimilation. My claim is that much of the rhetoric instigating these changes renders silent the voices of Jewish women through the ages.

·I·
MALE
VOICES

· 1 ·

Silent Partners:
Women as Wives in
Rabbinic Literature

JUDITH R. BASKIN

Rabbinic Judaism, which recorded its literary traditions in the first six centuries of the Common Era, is the basis of all contemporary forms of Jewish religious practice. Its interpreters and expositors were men, and the ideal human society they imagined was decidedly oriented toward their sex. With few exceptions, female voices are not heard in rabbinic literature, and when they are, they are usually mediated through the male assumption that women differ from men in intellectual, spiritual, and social capacities, as well as in legal obligations and status. As Susan Sered notes in connection with the "mystification" of written texts, the rabbinic literary tradition assumes that male Judaism is "official" Judaism.[1] Women's understandings of their lives and experiences, and their specifically female spiritual practices, what Sered calls "the little tradition," are all but impossible to discover from these androcentric writings. Thus, an examination of rabbinic laws and traditions pertaining to wives reveals only men's perceptions of the marital state, and of how their spouses should behave. From the perspective of rabbinic social legislation, as opposed, perhaps, to actual social life in rabbinic times, married women are silent partners.[2]

Rabbinic Judaism considered marriage as natural for all adults and regarded women as men's foreordained and essential counterparts. Moreover, in a system of theological imagery that envisioned human marriage as the closest approximation of the intimacy that can exist between human and divine, the relationship between wives and husbands had particular significance. In my essay, reflecting the voice of male tradition, I discuss the rabbis' views of the roles and functions of wives in order to demonstrate the contexts and boundaries within which rabbinic Judaism recognized and sanctioned female activities. Halakic (legal) and aggadic (nonlegal) traditions are considered separately since they yield different kinds of data. The legal formulations of the halakah present a comprehensive, if idealized, program for marital relations, while the anecdotal and personal nature of the aggadah may better reflect actual practices, attitudes, and female-male interactions.

The Wife as Other in Rabbinic Judaism

The basic literary documents of rabbinic Judaism are the Mishnah, a compilation of legal rulings organized by subject matter, whose editing was completed in the land of Israel in the early third century C.E., and its voluminous commentary, the Gemara, produced in the rabbinic academies of Iraq. The Mishnah and Gemara were combined to form the Babylonian Talmud sometime in the sixth century C.E.[3] The male sages who produced these texts apportioned separate spheres and separate responsibilities to women and men, and these separations continue within some forms of traditional Jewish life and practice up to the present day. Modern scholars have taken a number of approaches in their efforts to understand what the rabbis mean when they say that "women are a separate people"[4] whose place in the cosmos is profoundly different from their own. Jeremy Cohen writes that according to the rabbis, free and unblemished Jewish males "were the only full-fledged partners of God in his divine covenant."[5] Since entry into this covenant (b'rit) is solemnified by the circumcision of the male infant's penis, a ceremony known as b'rit milah, women are disqualified simply by virtue of their anatomical difference from men. As Howard Eilberg-Schwartz points out, "Since circumcision binds together men within and across generations, it also establishes an opposition between men and women. . . . Only the bodies of men can commemorate the promise of God to Abraham."[6]

To explain the general rabbinic exclusion of women from participation in religious obligations such as communal prayer and study, and their relegation to home-based roles, anthropological distinctions, such as public vs. private domain and culture vs. nature, have been usefully invoked. Such dichotomies are reflections of the relative status of men and women in a society, for as the anthropologist Michelle Zimbalist Rosaldo explains, in cultures where a strong separation between public and private arenas of activity exists, and where women are isolated from each other and placed under a single man's authority in the home, they are valued least; and real power and societal prestige lie beyond the household.[7] This effect appears to be the desired intent of rabbinic social policy, which fosters women's procreative and nurturing qualities by placing them under the aegis of a protective husband, far removed from the culturally esteemed activities of the public domain.

Rosaldo also recognizes that in virtually all societies women have tended to be defined almost exclusively in terms of their biologically based female characteristics, a perception that sheds light on rabbinic Judaism's anxiety to circumscribe, defuse, and control the sexual attributes of the female within marriage or protective male guardianship. Moreover, the conviction that contact with a *niddah,* a menstruating or postpartum woman, will render persons and objects ritually impure is fundamental to the rabbinic separation of women, for the *niddah* is a potential source of danger to male holiness.[8] Shaye Cohen observes that such attitudes, expressive of folk piety as much as legal formulation, confirm "the marginality of all women, menstruating or not, in the organized, public expressions of Jewish piety." As he writes, "In Judaism (at least until recently) public sacred space is male space, and the exclusion of menstruants from that space confirms that women, because they are women, are not its natural occupants."[9]

More than one interpreter has agreed with Jacob Neusner that rabbinic Judaism's exponents viewed women with deep ambivalence and unease. In his study of Nashim, the Mishnah's division of legal tractates concerned with women, Neusner calls particular attention to the theme of woman as anomaly, or aberration, noting that in the ideal society imagined by the Rabbis, "man is normal and woman is abnormal."[10] Nashim, which is primarily concerned with the contracting and dissolving of marriages, intends to keep women subject to men and to establish rules that shift authority over a woman from her father to a husband. As Neusner writes, "The regulation of the transfer of woman is Mishnah's way of effecting the sanctification of what, for the moment, disturbs and disorders the orderly world that Mishnah deems desirable." Thus, the goal and purpose of Nashim is "to bring under control and force into stasis all the wild and unruly potentialities of sexuality." The anomaly of woman's "otherness" can only be resolved by assigning her specific roles submissive to male authority.[11]

Yet, in her detailed study of the status of women in the Mishnah, Judith Romney Wegner argues that legal definition varies with context: the Mishnah perceives of woman as chattel only when the context is control of her sexual and reproductive function; in other contexts women are full persons. The Mishnah treats the woman as belonging to the man in all matters that affect his ownership of her sexuality. "When by contrast, no man has a legal claim on a woman's sexuality, the system always treats her as a person, both in sex-related and other matters."[12] The autonomous woman, who is not a minor daughter, wife, or Levirate widow,[13] has control over her personal life. Wegner goes on to emphasize, however, that while the autonomous woman has some latitude in the private domain, Mishnaic rules governing women's relationship to the public domain tell quite a different story, systematically excluding all women from the life of the mind and spirit, which is perceived as belonging to men. In rabbinic Judaism's system of oppositions, then, it is male wariness of woman's manifest difference from men, together with fear of her sexuality, and her polluting potential, that renders her an ever present threat to the realms of purity, order, and public value.

Contradictions abound in rabbinic Judaism's vision of the role of gender in the ideal ordering of human society. The sexes must be separated as much as possible, yet marriage is essential for everyone, for procreation and as a channel for sexual energies. A solution, of sorts, is the assigning of wives to domestic roles, providing for their husband's needs, nurturing children, and participating in family-based economic endeavors. That women may have been deeply fulfilled by their marriages, that more than a few found ways of exerting power within the home, and that many may have derived spiritual and social satisfaction within groups made up of other women,[14] is not to be denied; but unfortunately women within the purviews of rabbinic Judaism were not able to record their experiences for posterity. We may be able to imagine their traditions and rituals, but we cannot know them with any certainty.

All this is not to say that the rabbinic vision of how wives should be treated is negative. There is considerable honor and respect for the spouse who fulfills her domestic roles. Rabbinic literature is full of praise for the supportive, resourceful, and self-sacrificing wife, and there is no lack of consideration for her physical and emotional needs and welfare.[15] Indeed, rabbinic Judaism takes for granted that marriage is the natural state for both women and men, and it is full of praises for the institution, finding scriptural support from the divinely attributed rationale for woman's creation: "It is not good that the man should be alone" (Gen. 2:18). Thus, the Talmud states that "any man who has no wife lives without joy, without blessing, and without goodness" (B. Yeb. 62b). In these texts, of course, all approbation of wives is predicated on their participating in sanctioned activities under male control.

Halakic Tradition

The Mishnah (M. Qid. 1:1) views marriage as a legal transaction initiated when a man betroths a wife in one of three ways: "by money, by deed, or by intercourse," ratified by a statement of espousal. The view of the woman as property, with authority over her sexual function being transferred from guardian to husband, is expressed by M. Ket. 4:5: "She continues within the control of her father until she enters the control of the husband at marriage." As Wegner notes, this impression is "highlighted by the unilateral nature of the espousal ceremony in which the man recites a formal declaration to which the woman makes no reply."[16] In this statement the man declares that the woman is "set apart" for him alone.

Still, marriage is also seen as a contract, entered into with the consent of both parties (B. Qid. 2a), and it is a covenant that imposes rights and obligations, financial and otherwise, on both sides. In rabbinic times the husband's commitments to his wife, within the marriage and in the event of its dissolution by divorce or death, were often written in a *ketubah* (marriage settlement detailing a husband's financial obligation to his wife). Even if no written *ketubah* existed, however, his responsibilities would be enforced by a court.[17] These ten traditional obligations include a husband's providing his wife with food, appropriate clothing (M. Ket. 5:8), and conjugal rights.[18] He is to ransom her, provide for her support after his death, and guarantee that her property passes from him to her heirs. He must also give her sufficient money to cover her minor expenses, and if he does not, the wife may keep the proceeds of her work in wool, which normally belong to her husband (M. Ket. 5:9). Should a man take more than one wife, as he is permitted to do, he is required to fulfill his obligations to each wife in an equitable way. Moreover, a wife still maintains certain degrees of independence, particularly in the economic sphere. She maintains title to property she brings into her marriage, although her husband is entitled to any profit it yields. She has the power to sell the property, and her husband cannot sell it against her will (M. Git. 5:6). From these and other similar provisions, it is clear that the wife was expected to be a significant part of the family economic unit, contributing her earnings, generally gained through weaving and needlework. Her business transactions, as all economic functions before the modern period, are considered to be activities belonging to the domestic/private realm in which women are able to function independently. In certain situations, in fact, a wife may undertake to totally support her husband.[19]

The duties incumbent upon the wife are enumerated in M. Ket. 5:5: "The following are the kinds of work which a woman must perform for her husband: grinding corn, baking bread, washing clothes, cooking, suckling her child, making ready his bed and working in wool. If she brought him one bondwoman she need not do any grinding or baking or washing. If she brought two bondwomen, she need not even cook or suckle her child. If three, she need neither make ready his bed nor work in wool. If four, she may lounge in an easy chair." The Mishnah goes on to note, however, that Rabbi Eliezer objected to this easy life for the wealthy woman: "even if she brought him a hundred bondwomen he may compel her to work in wool; for idleness leads to unchastity. And she should, nevertheless fill for him his cup, make ready his bed and wash his face, hands and feet." Rabban Simeon b. Gamaliel concurred, noting that idleness leads to lowness of spirit (M. Ket. 5:5). The Talmud, in its explication of this passage, states that the halakah is in agreement with Rabbi Eliezer (B. Ket. 61a–b); no matter the extent of her wealth, a woman must engage in worthwhile activities and must fulfill her husband's personal needs.

Although in some situations a wife can petition the court to compel her husband to divorce her for specified causes (M. Ket. 7:1–5,

10), she has no power to unilaterally end her marriage. This is the right of the husband alone, and the sources make clear that he may divorce his wife for any reason (M. Git. 9:10), provided that he returns the monetary settlement specified by her *ketubah*. Indeed, this postbiblical requirement of financial restitution did offer women a certain amount of protection, constituting a strong financial disincentive to a divorce-inclined husband and providing an economic basis on which a second marriage might be built for a cast-off wife.[20]

A wife forfeits her marriage settlement if she violates Jewish law or ritual, or refuses conjugal relations with her spouse. Offenses include preparing untithed food, ignoring dietary regulations, breaking the rules of menstrual separation, or immodest behavior. Moreover, a wife is expected to have been honest in saying she was not bound by any vows and was without physical or moral flaw before her marriage. Discovery of either of these conditions is also grounds for divorce without her marriage portion (M. Ket. 7:6–7). As Wegner point out, "responsibilities as much as rights mark an individual as a person. A woman no less than a man must abide by the law and must keep her personal commitments, otherwise she will be liable for breach of duty just like a man."[21]

Indeed, rabbinic legislation does endow a wife with a high degree of personhood. Her legal rights as a property holder are protected; she is assigned rights and privileges that are denied to the non-Israelite male. On the other hand, she is also her husband's possession, at least as far as her sexuality is concerned. The case of the wife suspected of adultery offers an example of the legal duality implicit in the wife's ambiguous role. As a sexual chattel, a wife suspected of infidelity (*sotah*) can be put through a barbaric ordeal without evidentiary proof, but as the owner of a valuable marriage settlement she cannot be deprived of her property without due process. Similarly, the rabbinic acceptance that in certain cases a wife is morally entitled to a divorce reveals an analogous paradox. As Wegner has pointed out, the notion of a wife's legitimate right to a divorce recognizes her as a person, yet the formalities require urging her husband to use a procedure that treats her like a piece of property. In this instance, the Mishnah treats the wife as person and chattel at once.[22]

The situation is similar in the area of conjugal relations, where the married woman is not simply a sexual object but is treated as a person with rights as well as obligations. In particular, the rabbinic sources believe that a woman possesses the absolute right to intercourse with her husband. This is based on the Mishnaic interpretation of the difficult biblical term *'onah* (Exod. 21:10) to mean that a husband must provide his wife with regular conjugal visits, in addition to providing her with food and clothing. In fact, the Mishnah provides detailed guidelines for fulfillment of this matrimonial duty, based on the husband's occupation and the amount of time he spends at home (M. Ket. 5:6).[23] However, the husband's legal duty to have intercourse with his wife is matched by her corresponding obligation to consent. Each spouse incurs daily financial penalties for noncompliance, but the wife's penalty is more than twice as heavy as her husband's (M. Ket.5:7). As Wegner notes, "this reciprocal network of sexual entitlements and obligations places the spouses in a complementary relationship, though not on a precisely equal footing,"[24] since the sages, in penalizing the rebellious wife more severely, value the woman's rights below those of a man. This tension between the view of a wife as a sexual possession and as an independent entity remains unresolved in the rabbinic halakah.

Aggadic Traditions

A significant body of aggadic or homiletical material is devoted to the theme of marriage as the prerequisite for achieving fully human status for both males and females. The interconnectedness of man and woman is expressed in the maxim that "Any man who has no wife is no proper man" (B. Yeb. 62b), based on a homiletic interpretation of Gen. 5:2: "Male and female He created them and He called their name Adam." Underlying it is a rabbinic midrash that the first human being created by God was both male and female at once: "When the Holy One, blessed be He, created the first *adam,* He created it androgynous, as it is written, 'Male and female He created them, and He called their name Adam.'" Rabbi Shmuel bar Nachman said, "When the Holy One, blessed be He, created the first *adam,* He created him with two faces, then split him and made him two backs—a back for each side" (Gen. Rab. 8:1). Thus, the midrash teaches that only when the male and female are united are they truly *adam,* that is, truly human. In a similar vein, Rabbi Hama b.

Hanina is said to have stated that "as soon as a man takes a wife his sins are buried; for it is said in the book of Proverbs, 'Whoever finds a wife finds a great good and obtains favour from the Lord' (Prov. 18:22)" (B. Yeb. 63a).

Indeed, rabbinic folklore underscores the personal and societal value of matrimony by its vision of marriages as foreordained; so crucial is this conviction that several sources describe matchmaking as God's principle occupation since the completion of creation.[25] Other traditions, too, emphasize that when it comes to marriage nothing is left to chance. One midrash relates that forty days before the embryo is formed, a heavenly voice goes forth and says: "The daughter of so and so for so and so" (B. San. 22a). Although it is clear that aggadic traditions see marriage as necessary and foreordained for both men and women in a patriarchal society in which unprotected women were at risk, and where there also may have been a shortage of males, it is not surprising to find a strong feeling that women are more desirous of being married than men (B. Yeb. 113a). As the sage Resh Lakish stated: "It is preferable to live in grief, that is, with a bad husband, than to dwell in widowhood" (B. Qid. 7a; B. Ket. 75a). Rabbi Papa observed that even though her husband might follow a very humble profession, his wife is proud to call him to the threshold and sits down at his side. Rabbi Ashi said, "Even if her husband is unattractive, she requires no lentils for her pot" (B. Ket. 75a). And when it comes to the husband's qualities, Rabbi Joshua says, "A woman prefers a poor husband who makes love to her, to a wealthy one who ignores her" (M. Sotah 3:4).

The rabbis' asymmetrical views of men and women are revealed in the opinion of Samuel b. Unya, who taught that before marriage a woman is a shapeless lump. It is her husband who transforms her into a useful vessel. In fact, the parallel is drawn that just as God formed the character of the people of Israel, so does a husband shape the personality of his wife. "'For thy maker is thy husband'"; says the prophet Isaiah, "'the Lord of Hosts is his name' (Isa. 54:5)" (B. San. 22b). Nor is the divine metaphor unusual; both in the Hebrew Bible and throughout later Jewish literature, the relationship between a man and a woman is often understood metaphorically as signifying the intimate bonds between God and human beings. Traditional rabbinic interpretation of the Song of Songs, for example, has always assumed that the biblical book's love poetry between a man and a woman is an allegory detailing the passion between God and the people of Israel.[26]

Rabbinic tradition is irresolute about the qualities that should be sought in a wife. Thus Rabbi Hiyya holds that "a wife should be taken mainly for the sake of her beauty; and mainly for the sake of children. She must not be treated as a bondwoman doing heavy work like grinding which would impair her beauty or adversely affect her pregnancies; rather she should work in wool in return for the maintenance her husband allows her" (B. Ket. 59b). Elsewhere, he states that "it is sufficient for us that they rear up our children and deliver us from sin [by providing a sexual outlet]" (B. Yeb. 63a). Other sages believed that the ideal wife is one who provides her husband with empathy and emotional support; one passage advises, "If your wife is short, bend down to hear her whispers" (B. Ber. 17a).

According to B. Shabbat 25a, Rabbi Akiba lauds the man whose wife is "comely in deeds." Rabbi Akiba's wife, Rachel, is, in fact, famous for her loyalty and devotion, having forfeited a rich inheritance from her father in order to marry Akiba when he was a destitute and illiterate shepherd. She sent him away to study for twelve years and then another twelve, and when he returned with thousands of students, he lauded her before them, declaring that all his learning rightly belonged to his wife (B. Ned. 50a). In rabbinic terms Rachel's acts are praiseworthy because they serve as a model of what is expected of the wife of the scholar. She garners cultural esteem through enabling the men of her family to pursue their studies, even though this may mean family deprivation and a husband's absence for long periods of time. Indeed, according to the Talmud, this is precisely how wives earn merit: "By sending their children to learn [Torah] in the synagogue, and their husbands to study in the schools of the rabbis, and by waiting for their husbands until they return from the schools of the rabbis" (B. Ber. 17a). According to the aggadah (B. Ned. 50a), Rachel expresses satisfaction with her choices; having sacrificed the status of wealth for love of a poor but talented man, she sacrifices her own needs for many years in order that her husband may earn higher status for both of them as a result of his learning. In the end, she regains as well the approbation of the father she had defied. We cannot know the authenticity of this story; we can only know that it expresses sentiments of which the male tradition approves.

Such an androcentric vision of a wife's functions extends not only to how a wife's actions serve her husband's needs, but to a consideration of how her behavior reflects on his status and piety. In the following text food provides a convenient metaphor for marital relations:

> R. Meir used to say: As men differ in their treatment of their food, so they differ in their treatment of their wives. Some men, if a fly falls into their cup, will put it aside and not drink it. This corresponds to the way of Papus b. Judah who used, when he went out, to lock his wife indoors. Another man, if a fly falls into his cup, will throw away the fly and then drink the cup. This corresponds to the way of most men who do not mind their wives talking with their brothers and relatives. Another man, again, if a fly falls into his soup, will squash it and eat it. This corresponds to the way of a bad man who sees his wife go out with her hair unfastened and spin cloth in the street with armpits uncovered and bathe with the men. (B. Git. 90a–b)

It is a religious duty, the rabbis continue, to divorce such a wife, and they warn that anyone who marries this wicked woman after her divorce courts death. Women, then, warrant watching, whether strict or moderate, and according to this view it is the uncontrolled woman who is a source of societal disruption and of danger to her husband. As Raba remarks, "[If one has] a bad wife it is meritorious to divorce her, for it is said, 'Cast out the scoffer, and contention will go out; yea, strife and shame will cease' (Prov. 22:10)" (B. Yeb. 63b).[27]

In rabbinic times, divorce remained a ready expedient for unhappy marriages. From the rabbis' patriarchal point of view, the fault was generally with the women. Thus, Raba states, "Come and see how precious is a good wife and how baneful is a bad wife. How precious is a good wife, for it is written (Prov. 18:22), 'Whoso findeth a wife findeth a great good' but how baneful is a bad wife, for it is written 'And I find more bitter than death the woman' (Ecclesiastes 7:26)" (B. Yeb. 63a); and several sages lament the dreaded fate of a bad wife, "the amount of whose *ketubah* is large, and who is too expensive to divorce" (e.g., B. Yeb. 63b).

In fact, rabbinic literature contains a number of what might be called "bad wife" stories. In one, for example, poor Rab is said to have been constantly tormented by his wife. Her rebellions were on a small scale: "If he told her, 'Prepare me lentils,' she would prepare him small peas; and if he asked for small peas, she prepared him lentils" (B. Yeb. 63a). In some instances women are castigated for their efforts to avoid normal sexual intercourse, no doubt in order to prevent conception in an era with few other reliable forms of birth control. Once more, the food/sex metaphor comes into play: "How is one to understand the term a 'bad wife'? Abaye said: One who prepares for him a tray and has her mouth also ready for him. Raba said: One who prepares for him the tray and turns her back upon him" (B. Yeb. 63b).

It must be noted, however, that when it is the husband who demands sexual variety, his wife has no judicial support for any reluctance she may feel, for according to B. Ned. 20b, "Just as meat may be cooked according to preference, so a man may do as he pleases with his wife." Another story of a "bad wife" also illustrates the very shaky position of a rebellious woman in a society that allowed her husband to divorce her at will:

> R. Jose, the Galilean, had a bad wife who despised him in the presence of his disciples: They said to him, "Divorce her." One day R. Jose and R. Elazar b. Azarya were sitting and expounding the Law. When they had finished, the disciples said to R. Jose, "Let the master pay heed to us, and now we will go to your house." He said to them, "Yes." When they got there, his wife lowered her face in anger at these unexpected guests and went out. He looked into the pot upon the stove and called to her and said, "Is there anything in the pot?" She said, "There are bread crumbs and vegetables, [hoping to deter the visitors.]" R. Elazar b. Azarya went and opened the lid and found in it chickens. So he knew that she did not behave well to her husband. When they sat down to eat, R. Jose said to her, "Did you not say that there were vegetables in the pot, and we have found chickens in it?" She said, "It is a miracle." When they had eaten, R. Elazar said, "Divorce your wife: she does not act to your honor." He said, "Her marriage portion is too great for me: I cannot divorce her." They said to him, "We will provide the marriage portion and then do you divorce her." They did so. They provided the marriage portion and he divorced her, and they made him marry another wife, who was better than the former one.

The passage continues with the suffering that now befalls the discarded wife as a consequence of "her sins"; in her moment of deepest humiliation she is forced to accept the charity of her former husband, perhaps the cruelest punishment of all.[28]

In these stories women are at a grave disadvantage, as they were in rabbinic society in general. Their minor rebellions indicate their limited arenas of power. In fact, these stories are intended to be didactic: to delineate for men the boundaries of female freedom, and to demonstrate to women potential penalties for their attempts to exceed them. Still, it is important to point out that while divorce was legally easy to obtain (if sometimes financially painful), ethically it was not approved by most of the sages. This conflict between legal privilege and ethical responsibility is closely argued in the conclusion of the talmudic tractate, Gittin, following the legal ruling that a man is at liberty to divorce his wife for any reason:

> "For a hateful one put away" (Malachi 2:16): R. Judah said: [This means that] if you hate her you should put her away. R. Johanan says: It means, he that sends his wife away is hated. There is really no conflict between the two, since the one speaks of the first marriage and the other of the second, as R. Eleazar said: If a man divorces his first wife, even the altar sheds tears, as it says: "And this further you do, you cover the altar of the Lord with tears, with weeping and with sighing, in so much that he regards not the offering any more, neither receives it with good will at your hand. Yet you say, Wherefore? Because the Lord has been witness between you and the wife of your youth, against whom you have dealt treacherously, though she is your companion and the wife of your covenant" (Malachi 2:13–14). (B. Git. 90a–b; see also B. San. 22a)

This admonition to value the wife of one's youth should be seen in the context of a polygynous society that attached no reproach to a man's having more than one wife. While taking a second wife is understood by some of the rabbis to be an appropriate punishment for a difficult spouse, following Raba who advised that "a bad wife, the amount of whose *ketubah* is large, [should be subdued by] a rival at her side" (B. Yeb. 63b), this was not always the case. For an older woman in an established marriage the humiliation of becoming a co-spouse was likely preferable to the shame and probable financial disaster of divorce.[29]

A basic purpose of marriage is the birth of children, and particular pain must have been felt by the woman in an infertile union.

Childlessness was regarded as a grave misfortune for both men and women. A man's suffering is implicit in his inability to fulfill the commandment of procreation (incumbent only upon men), and leave pious offspring behind him. The barren women suffers, too, for even if she has no religious obligation to meet, she has failed to fulfill the primary expectation of her societal role, and as Gen. Rab. 71:5 remarks, in the name of Rabbi Ammi, it is children who secure a woman's position in her home.[30] The barren wife doubtless felt great shame, and endured reproach for disappointing her husband at home and in the eyes of the world. There can be no doubt that the position of the barren wife was most unpleasant, and that the rabbis viewed it with compassion.

According to rabbinic teachings, only men are legally obligated to procreate; in the case of ten years of childless marriage a husband must take a second wife, or he and his first wife are to be divorced, so that they may try their luck with other spouses (M. Yeb. 6:6). Yet even in this case, the aggadic tradition very strongly deprecates the dissolution of a stable marriage, pointing out that barrenness is never more than a presumption, and relating tales of loving couples whose longtime infertility was ultimately rewarded with children after many years of prayer.[31] Such aggadic stories must be read as offering an ethical and humane rebuttal to the halakic option of divorce, and they constitute another extralegal expression of concern both for women and for preserving meaningful human relationships.

Conclusion

Suspended between halakah and aggadah, the rabbinic vision of women as wives is complicated and unresolved, as in any area where ideal norms collide with experienced reality. Still, one must conclude that rabbinic Judaism was determined to localize wives' activities in the domestic sphere of family and family-based economic activities, where they could facilitate the more "important" religious, intellectual, and communal endeavors of their husbands. While a few unusual women of the rabbinic elite may have had some expertise in the "official" learning of Judaism, the tradition tends to remark negatively on those few gifted females who attempt to offer opinions on legal issues.[32] We have no testimony from these learned women about their own situations, activities, and aspirations, while women's "unofficial" teachings and traditions are not preserved in rabbinic literature at all because they were not valued by the "official" halakic enterprise. It must be left to the other essays in this volume to detail the active roles women have always undertaken in Jewish culture.

NOTES

Abbreviations Used in Text and Notes

B.	Babylonian Talmud
Ber.	Berakot
Deut.	Deuteronomy
Gen.	Genesis
Gen. Rab.	Genesis Rabbah
Git.	Gittin
J.	Jerusalem Talmud
Ket.	Ketubot
Lev. Rab.	Leviticus Rabbah
M.	Mishnah
Qid.	Qiddushin
San.	Sanhedrin
T.	Tosefta (collection of legal rulings contemporaneous with, but not codified in, the Mishnah)
Yeb.	Yebamot

1. Susan Sered, "Toward an Anthropology of Jewish Women: Sacred Texts and the Religious World of Elderly, Middle-Eastern Women in Jerusalem," in this volume; and see also Sered, *Women as Ritual Experts: The Religious Lives of Elderly Jewish Women in Jerusalem* (Oxford: Oxford University Press, 1992).

2. For information on the Greek-speaking culture of the Jewish Diaspora of late antiquity, which appears to have offered women quite different options from the rabbinic model, see Bernadette J. Brooten, *Women Leaders in the Ancient Synagogue* (Chico, Calif.: Scholars Press, 1982); Ross S. Kraemer, "Jewish Women in the Diaspora World of Late Antiquity," in Judith R. Baskin, ed., *Jewish Women in Historical Perspective* (Detroit: Wayne State University Press, 1991), pp. 43–67; and Kraemer, *Her Share of the Blessings: Women's Religions among Pagans, Jews, and Christians in the Greco-Roman World* (New York: Oxford University Press, 1992).

3. The process of rabbinic legislation did not end with the completion of the Talmud but continues up to the present era in several different forms. On the rabbis and the rabbinic period, see Eliezer Diamond, "The World

of the Talmud," in Barry W. Holtz, ed, *The Schocken Guide to Jewish Books* (New York: Schocken Books, 1992), pp. 47–69. Other major texts of rabbinic Judaism include the Jerusalem Talmud (or Talmud of the Land of Israel), which combines the Mishnah with a less voluminous Gemara reflecting teachings current in the land of Israel rather than Babylon, and midrash collections, which preserve halakic and aggadic exegeses of biblical books, usually organized by the order of the biblical text, rather than by subject matter.

4. B. Shabbat 62a. For analyses of the role of women in rabbinic Judaism, see Judith R. Baskin, "The Separation of Women in Rabbinic Literature," in Y. Y. Haddad and E. B. Findly, eds., *Women, Religion, and Social Change* (Albany: State University of New York Press, 1985), pp. 3–18; Judith Romney Wegner, "The Image and Status of Women in Classical Rabbinic Judaism," in Baskin, *Jewish Women;* and Judith Hauptman, "Images of Women in the Talmud," in R. R. Ruether, ed., *Religion and Sexism: Images of Women in the Jewish and Christian Traditions* (New York: Simon and Schuster, 1974), pp. 184–212, who writes that in rabbinic texts, "A woman's prime function in life is to concern herself with man's welfare and to provide for his physical comfort" (197).

5. Jeremy Cohen, "Be Fertile and Increase, Fill the Earth and Master It," *The Ancient and Medieval Career of a Biblical Text* (Ithaca: Cornell University Press, 1989), p. 162.

6. Howard Eilberg-Schwartz, *The Savage in Judaism: An Anthropology of Israelite Religion and Ancient Judaism* (Bloomington: Indiana University Press, 1990), p. 171.

7. Michelle Zimbalist Rosaldo, "Woman, Culture, and Society: A Theoretical Overview," in Michelle Zimbalist Rosaldo and Louise Lamphere, eds., *Women, Culture, and Society* (Stanford: Stanford University Press, 1971), pp. 17–42 (quote is on p. 36).

8. Ibid.; and see Baskin, "Separation of Women," pp. 8–12. Rabbinic Judaism regards ritual purity as a religious ideal, while ritual uncleanness necessitated a separation from the Divine. On the basis of Leviticus 11–17, the main sources of ritual impurity were leprosy; the dead bodies of certain animals, and particularly, human corpses; and issue from sexual organs. See Rachel Biale, *Women and Jewish Law: An Exploration of Women's Issues in Halakhic Sources* (New York: Schocken Books, 1984), pp. 147–74, for laws applying to the menstruating woman (*niddah*).

9. Shaye J. D. Cohen, "Purity and Piety: The Separation of Menstruants from the Sancta," in Susan Grossman and Rivka Haut, eds., *Daughters of the King: Women and the Synagogue* (Philadelphia: Jewish Publication Society, 1992), pp. 112–13.

10. Jacob Neusner, "Thematic or Systemic Description: The Case of

Mishnah's Division of Women," *Method and Meaning in Ancient Judaism* (Missoula, Mont.: Scholars Press, 1979), pp. 79–100 (quote is on p. 97); and see Mary Douglas, *Purity and Danger: An Analysis of the Concepts of Pollution and Taboo* (London: Routledge & Kegan Paul, 1966), p. 53, who writes concerning the similar case of the dietary laws in Leviticus that in this legislation holiness is exemplified by completeness and that holiness means keeping distinct the categories of creation to avoid improper contacts.

11. Neusner, "Thematic or Systemic Description," pp. 97, 100.

12. Judith Romney Wegner, *Chattel or Person? The Status of Women in the Mishnah* (Oxford: Oxford University Press, 1988), p. 19.

13. Ibid. A levirate widow (*yebamah*) is a woman whose husband has died without male issue. Following Deut. 25:5–10, the Mishnah requires her to marry her husband's brother (*levir* in Latin), unless he agrees to release her from this obligation (*halitzah*). See Wegner, *Chattel or Person?* pp. 97–113; and Biale, *Women and Jewish Law,* pp. 113–20.

14. Rosaldo, "Women, Culture, and Society," pp. 22. Wegner, *Chattel or Person?* p. 232n.142, notes that the Mishnah (Sotah 6:1) speaks of women who gossip together while spinning their yarn by moonlight and elsewhere rules that a man may not unreasonably prevent his wife from attending wedding and funeral gatherings in other women's home. "But the notion of women meeting together in organized groups for some cultural or intellectual purpose is specifically precluded by the prohibition of female commensal fellowship groups (M. Pesahim 8:7)."

15. See Hauptman, "Images of Women," pp. 197–208, for praise of worthy wives.

16. Wegner, *Chattel or Person?* p. 44; and see Isaiah Gafni, "The Institution of Marriage in Rabbinic Times," in David Kraemer, ed., *The Jewish Family: Metaphor and Memory* (Oxford: Oxford University Press, 1989), pp. 13–30.

17. See *Encyclopaedia Judaica* (1972), s.v. "husbands and wives," for the full particulars of spousal rights and duties, both as laid out in rabbinic literature and as interpreted and modified in the rabbinic tradition of the medieval and early modern periods. A written *ketubah* for all marriages became the norm in medieval times.

18. Wegner, *Chattel or Person?* p. 71. These obligations are discussed in ibid., pp. 71–75. Gafni, "Institution of Marriage," pp. 15–17, notes that there was always room for individual flexibility in negotiating these provisions.

19. See Gafni, "Institution of Marriage," p. 16, who cites T. Ket. 4:7 and J. Ket. 5:2, 29b, for a case in which "Yehoshua, son of R. Akiba married a woman and stipulated with her that she would feed and support and teach him Torah." "Teaching him Torah" implies that she would financially support his Torah studies.

20. See Wegner, *Chattel or Person?* pp. 80–84; Biale, *Women and Jewish Law,* pp. 70–101 (esp. pp. 84–89); and *Encyclopaedia Judaica* (1972), s.v. "divorce."

21. Wegner, *Chattel or Person?* pp. 84–85. Certain legal improvements (*takkanot*) in women's marital status were instituted by medieval Jews living in Christian lands. These *takkanot,* attributed to Rabbi Gershom of Mainz (960–1028), provide that women cannot be divorced against their wills and that a man must practice monogamy. See Biale, *Women and Jewish Law,* pp. 49–52; and Ze'ev W. Falk, *Jewish Matrimonial Law in the Middle Ages* (Oxford: Oxford University Press, 1966). On Jewish marriage in the Muslim sphere, see Mordechai A. Friedman, "Marriage as an Institution: Jewry under Islam," in Kraemer, *Jewish Family,* pp. 31–45.

22. Wegner, *Chattel or Person?* p. 176.

23. M. Ket. 5:6 specifies: "The duty of marriage enjoined in the Law is: every day for those that are unoccupied; twice a week for laborers; once a week for ass-drivers; once every thirty days for camel-drivers; and once every six months for sailors."

24. Wegner, *Chattel or Person?* p. 79.

25. B. Sotah 2a; Lev. Rab. 8:1.

26. On this topic, see Arthur Green, "Bride, Spouse, Daughter: Images of the Feminine in Classical Jewish Sources," in Susannah Heschel, ed., *On Being a Jewish Feminist: A Reader* (New York: Schocken Books, 1983), pp. 248–60; Moshe Idel, "Sexual Metaphors and Praxis in the Kabbalah," in Kraemer, *Jewish Family,* pp. 197–224; and David Biale, *Eros and the Jews: From Biblical Israel to Contemporary America* (New York: Basic Books, 1992).

27. On the folklore tradition that some women are sources of death to men, see Mordechai A. Friedman, "Tamar, a Symbol of Life: The 'Killer Wife' Superstition in the Bible and Jewish Tradition," *Association for Jewish Studies Review* 15 (1990): 23–62.

28. Lev. Rab., "Behar" 34, 143; and see J. Ket. 11:3, f. 34b, line 61, for an even more punitive ending.

29. Gafni, "Institution of Marriage," points out the importance of external factors in the frequency of Jewish polygyny in rabbinic times, noting that Palestinian rabbinic sources appear to imply a predominantly monogamous Jewish society, perhaps under the influence of the monogamous atmosphere of Roman society, together with a similar emphasis in Christian practice, while the situation in Sassanian Babylonia, where polygyny was generally common, was quite different (pp. 21–23).

30. See Judith R. Baskin, "Rabbinic Reflections on the Barren Wife," *Harvard Theological Review* 82, no. 1 (1989): 101–14, for a more thorough discussion of this topic.

31. Ibid., pp. 111–14.

32. Among the learned women mentioned in rabbinic literature, the most prominent is B'ruriah, the wife of Rabbi Meir, who is said by medieval Jewish sources to have ended as an adulterous wife and a suicide. On B'ruriah, see Wegner, "Image and Status of Women," p. 76; and Rachel Adler, "The Virgin in the Brothel and Other Anomalies: Character and Context in the Legend of Beruriah," *Tikkun* (Nov.–Dec. 1988): 28–32, 102–5. On other learned women in rabbinic sources, see Hauptmann, "Images of Women," pp. 197–208.

· II ·
PUBLIC
VOICES

· 2 ·

Transcending
"Tzimmes and Sweetness":
Recovering the History of
Zionist Women in Central and
Western Europe, 1897–1933

MICHAEL BERKOWITZ

From the rise of Theodor Herzl in Central and Western Europe around 1897, to the time when the "Jewish Question" changed beyond recognition, around 1933, the Zionist movement in Europe, west of the Pale of Settlement, was a predominantly and self-consciously male affair.[1] To be sure, Zionism was beholden to the European order out of which it was born, the endemic paternalism of Jewish life, and the governments its adherents wished to emulate. The women who took part in the movement were, therefore, a marginal element in a marginal force. Although Zionism proclaimed its openness toward women, Zionist women had a difficult time making their voices heard once they were within the movement. This contradiction apparently refutes part of the enduring legacy of women in Zionism: the image of a strong, assertive woman in the worldwide organization, in the social landscape of the incipient Jewish nation in Palestine, and later in the State of Israel.[2] Nevertheless, women's impact on the Zionist movement, while different from their male counterparts', was real and significant and unfortunately has long been ignored. We will see that organized Zionist women in Central and Western Europe distinctly influenced the course of Zionism and particularly its reception among Western Jews. Especially due to their experience in social service, Central and West European Zionist women helped instill and disseminate the notion that modern social welfare was integral to the formative Jewish state and the movement's developing sense of nationalism.

The "invisibility" of Western Zionist women in most Zionist histories partially derives from the difficulty of writing the history of Zionism in general.[3] The movement operated simultaneously on a number of levels, in vastly different locales (in several languages), without a clear-cut chain of command, and with numerous overlapping functions. Its organizational structure was notorious for being incomprehensible even to those inside it. In addition, Zionism does not fit into the conventional boundaries of national or regional histories, and the connections between Diaspora Jews and those in Eretz Israel (the Land of Israel) make it even more enigmatic: it is difficult to determine the precise relationship between Zionists in the Diaspora and those in Palestine. Paradigms based on colonialism applied to the Jews' experience in Palestine, which are favored by commentators fundamentally opposed to the Zionist project, usually fail to capture the paramount goal of Zionism—the creation of an independent sovereignty. Such a model implies the deliberate installation of a center-periphery model, in which the periphery (Israel) is "exploited" by the center (Britain).[4]

Few scholars of Zionism, even those concerned with incorporating the history of women and strategies of the "new history," have managed to transcend these problems. In the histories of German and Austrian Zionism, with the notable exception of the works of Marsha Rozenblit and Harriet Freidenreich on Vienna, one is hard pressed to find a basic chronology of the establishment, main activities, and demise of Zionist women's organizations. By comparison, the history of British Zionist women is more accessible, but largely from commemorative volumes produced expressly for the membership of the Women's International Zionist Organization, known as WIZO.[5]

Yet to neglect the history of these women strips European Zionism of a vital strand that affected its multifaceted character, and in turn influenced the overall movement. It also diminishes the fact that several thousand Jewish women identified, to varying degrees, with Zionism.[6] Although it is important to make known the specific contributions of women to Zionism, there is more at stake than "to correct or supplement an incomplete record of the past," as Joan Scott writes in *Gender and the Politics of History*. There also is a need "to critically understand how history operates as a site of the production of gender knowledge."[7] A gender-conscious study of European Zionist women leads to rethinking segments of the narrative and analysis of the Zionist movement. Simultaneously, it can provide new insight about the relationship of gender to the European cultures of which Jews were a part, the persistence of old structures in the quest for a better order, variations in concepts of social responsibility, perceptions and realities of power relations, and the possibilities—as well as the limitations—of personal and collective renewal through participation in Zionism. In addition, such an approach may illuminate the process of fabricating myths and symbols that are centered on women, and the consequences wrought by the emergence of new mythologies.

At first glance, it is tempting to rebuke the historians of Zionism for not considering European Zionist women. Yet given the best intentions to include women in one's study, the reconstruction or even recovery of their history according to the criteria of academic history, is a frustrating task. This is partly due to the fragmentary nature of the sources, and to an unusual amount of undated and unsigned material. The meticulousness with which Zionist men kept their letters and documents stands in stark contrast to the general absence of evidence concerning the organized women's role. We are reminded that it was a period in which Zionist men tended to overestimate themselves as the makers of history, while most women and men in Europe accepted the maxim that the most virtuous woman is the one least spoken of.[8] The East European women who reached Palestine, however, believed it imperative to record and relate their stories and have therefore left an extensive and richly textured account—including art, photographs, poetry, and memoirs.[9] Simultaneously, the Europeans acceded to the greater significance of the pioneers in the *yishuv* (the Jewish settlement in Palestine) from the very beginning, which helped push the organized European women to the furthest recesses of the movement's memory.[10]

What follows is an attempt to render these women "visible." First, I will show that women were seriously involved in Zionism, despite the emphasis on producing "manly men" that might have excluded them; second, I will discuss the differences between their participation and that of Zionist men; and last, I will argue that such differences had an important impact on the history of Zionism. In part, the luster of Zionism derived from its claim to have created an equitable order between Jewish men and women. It is no surprise that this myth does not hold up to scrutiny, regarding the movement in Europe or the *yishuv*. What usually comes to mind in any discussion of women in Zionism is the image of the Jewish woman worker, engaged in manual labor—so-called man's labor—on her own "native soil" in Palestine. This arose in contrast to the typically conservative use of women as national symbols in England, France, and Germany.[11] The significance of the Jewish woman as worker certainly should not be undervalued, and it needs thoughtful explication. But the woman engaged in social welfare work, as an aspect of the reality and mythology of Zionism, has rarely been placed in a comparative, historical, and critical context.

Women and Men in Zionism

Admittedly, Zionist women appeared and operated within the world of Zionist men. Starting around 1896, Zionist men initiated systems of attracting and recruiting their like-minded coreligionists, cultivated an image of statesmanlike respectability, established fundraising mechanisms akin to a mass-based charity, and exercised some control over selected institutions in Jewish Palestine. In promotional materials about the *yishuv*, the Zionist Organization wished to highlight the "new man" created through Zionism, who found harmony with nature as pioneer-farmer and had attained some semblance of a normal national existence despite grave adversity. Theodor Herzl, the movement's founder, had envisioned Zionism as a means by which Jews could "become real men." His attitude, shared by most early Zionists, was a disavowal of the anti-Semitic stereotype of Jewish men as unmanly, and it affirmed the European-wide equation of manliness and rightful membership in the nation. The way to a "new Jewish existence" could be reached through participation in a "society of friends," or "a special type of comradeship" that was possible for Jewish men only through Zionism.[12] The self-conscious effort of Zionist men to assert themselves as men is an aspect of the movement that has rarely been explored.

Obviously, this side of Zionism could not have provided much of an impetus for women to join the ranks. The limited existing literature acknowledges that many of the women who entered the movement were the wives, sisters, or daughters of Zionist men.[13] A concomitant assertion is that Zionist women were primarily motivated by an ardent commitment to realizing Jewish nationhood. I have found that along with an ideological identification with the movement, Jewish women came to Zionism through their backgrounds and interests in social service. My research also indicates that the women's movement in general and the Jewish feminist movement in particular were crucial in preparing the way for a separate women's culture within Zionism. It was the convergence of these Jewish-national, feminist, and social welfare streams that accounts for the specific programs and spirit they brought to Zionism.

Their ideology and practice was a counterpoint to the ideal that a nation is founded primarily through the struggle of "pioneers," or isolated, albeit collective, enclaves. Also important for Zionism's acceptance among middle-class Jews: the women's vision and programs could exist independent of the nascent state socialism or revolutionary socialist ideas prevalent in the *yishuv*. Nevertheless, that the Zionist mission of these women was assimilated almost immediately into the movement suggests the degree to which it coalesced with the reigning ideology in Jewish Palestine and melded with existing Jewish communal patterns.

In the central body of the movement, a dozen women were among the two hundred plus delegates to the First Zionist Congress, which met in Basel, Switzerland, in 1897. Their presence was officially noted and "appreciated" by Herzl, but they were not given full voting rights until the Second Congress in 1898.[14] They were decidedly lower-rank citizens; women rarely rose to positions of leadership in the chief institutions of the World Zionist Organization, or in the local and national organizations of Central and Western Europe before 1933. Nevertheless, not all efforts by women to influence the center stage—Zionist Congress politics in early Zionism—were confounded. In the eleven congresses before World War I, the most comprehensive and impressive address by a woman was that of Miriam Schach, at the Tenth Congress of 1911. She attempted to impart a countermyth against what she saw as Zionism's perception and self-apprehension as a society of men, and against its portrayal and placement of women in subordinate positions. The sister of a German

Zionist leader, Fabius Schach, she felt representative of a group that had been overlooked as a great source of potential for the movement.[15]

Miriam Schach was an active Zionist in Paris, which was no easy assignment; the Parisian Jews were perhaps the least receptive of all the major European Jewish communities to the movement. Schach co-founded the French Zionist weekly *L'Echo Sioniste* and remained active in Zionist affairs throughout her life. By 1911, women had delivered a few speeches in earlier congresses, thoughtful articles had appeared about women in official publications, women had worked side-by-side with men in students' groups, and numerous Zionist women's organizations had been founded, probably the best known of which was the Juedisch-nationale Frauenvereinigung (the Jewish-National Women's Organization) in Germany.[16]

Part of Schach's 1911 speech responded to Zionism's figurative representations of women. In the movement's first decade, women had been symbolically illustrated as "the personification of Zionism"—such as in Fredrich Beer's medal given to delegates at the First and Second Zionist Congresses, and in the postcards from the Sixth and Seventh Congresses. They were shown as indistinct, passive figures, pointing the way to Zion. In some other Zionist products, though, such as the *Juedischer Almanach* (1902) and the anthology *Juedischer Kuenstler* (1903), biblical women were frequently depicted as commanding figures.[17] Pictures of contemporary women in the same volumes, however, usually in domestic scenes, were closer to their assigned role in European society and Zionism until this time—solid supports for their husbands and children.

At any rate, Schach's speech was probably the first time that the matriarchs were presented before the entire movement as Zionist heroines, as models for Jewish women, new Zionist women. Furthermore, Schach announced that it was time to "call Zionist women from the kitchen" and allow them to embark on serious cultural work; hitherto they had been asked to dispense "tzimmes" and "sweetness." The same Zionism must be imbued in women as in men, she implored; and when meaningful, rather than passive symbolic and supportive roles were assigned to women, the movement could expect far greater results.[18] But no matter how enthused and inspired she may have left her audience, the onset of World War I in the next years severed the links between Zionists in the warring nations and dampened their sputtering efforts. The war also stranded most Zionist enterprises in Palestine and helped assure that Schach's proposals remained hanging in the air.

German and Austrian Organizations

In the German-speaking world, as early as November 1898, the Wiener zionistische Frauenverein (the Zionist Women's Organization of Vienna) was established and its statutes published in the Zionist organ *Die Welt*. Members of this organization were deeply impressed by Herzl's request for them to participate in an overtly *"political* venture." Marsha Rozenblit informs us that in Vienna in 1896, a group of young women calling itself Miriam was founded to support Jewish colonization in Palestine, and another proto-Zionist group, Moria, directed itself to strengthening Jewish-national consciousness by promoting "the study of Jewish history, literature, and the role of women in the Jewish past." In Berlin, the Juedisch-nationale Frauenvereinigung also expressed interest in illuminating the role of women in Jewish history and literature.[19] Of greatest significance, though, was the Verband Juedischer Frauen fuer Kulturarbeit in Palaestina (Jewish Women's Group for Cultural Work in Palestine) founded in 1907, which was also known as the Kulturverband fuer Frauenarbeit. To discern the origins of the latter group, we must look beyond the exclusively Zionist women's organizations to the role of Jewish women in social service in Germany and Austria. It will be shown that there were similar influences on Zionist women's groups in Great Britain.

In the late nineteenth century, when social and economic changes and immigration from Eastern Europe prompted adjustments and growth in the social service structure, Jewish women began to enter the field of social service in Jewish communities as volunteers and professionals. The aim of social service was revised during this period, toward rooting out the causes of maladjustment and assisting the needy individual in regaining their economic footing. In sum, "charity gave way to organized scientific philanthropy."[20]

Also beginning in the mid- to late nineteenth century, the German feminist movement had a devoted following among Jewish women, many of whom became its leaders. In large part the movement was directed to "social betterment through political activity," with the reorganization of the intellectual and technical training of girls and women as one of its basic demands. And whatever one might have felt about socialism, there is little doubt that increased social democratic agitation helped stimulate German Jewish women toward seeing Zionism as a possible forum for social and political action.[21]

The women who come together in auxiliaries of the newly established branch of the B'nai B'rith probably also had an impact on the formative Zionist women's organizations. B'nai B'rith women imitated newly devised programs in vocational and technical training, health care, nutrition, and education for specifically Jewish welfare activities. Their efforts also comprised an attempt to arouse "a Jewish mass-consciousness" and to make the notion of caring for one's coreligionists "socially fashionable." This was accomplished through combining fund-raising functions, lectures on social welfare, and work projects with more purely social functions, such as banquets, teas, parties, and concerts. The allure of such activities was abetted by the bourgeois injunction that "a privileged woman has a moral duty to be benevolent." The B'nai B'rith, therefore, might be seen as an institution that inspired and legitimized Jewish solidarity and sociability—for children, adolescents, men, and women—in a secular setting.[22]

As detailed by Marion Kaplan, the inauguration of the Juedischer Frauenbund (JFB) (Jewish Women's Organization) in Germany in 1904, under its extraordinarily gifted and charismatic leader, Bertha Pappenheim, had a much weightier impact. Pappenheim was most crucial in fusing and publicizing Jewish, feminist, and social welfare concerns, and in creating a nexus for mutual support. The JFB program of comprehensive social services and political agitation included "a wide ranging journal, institutes and lectures on various aspects of Jewish culture," and most important, as a model for Zionists, "schools for farming and the household arts."[23]

The biographies of women Zionists demonstrate the extent to which their Zionist activities were fired in a Central European social welfare crucible. Siddy Wronsky and Anitta Mueller-Cohen were leading figures among social workers and, later, Zionist women. Wronsky wrote extensively on social work in Germany and in other countries, and on the Jewish communal achievements in this field. She directed relief efforts for foreign Jews and helped establish the Bund zionistischer Frauen (Zionist Women's Organization) in the interwar years. Anitta Mueller-Cohen founded a mutual aid society bearing her name. She ran kindergartens, soup and tea kitchens for thousands of local poor as well as Jewish war refugees, and vocational schools where trades were taught to refugee women; Mueller-Cohen also marketed the wares produced by these women. For Rahel Straus in Munich, the way to Zionism was through her work in public health, as a physician.[24]

It was from this background that efforts to support the Jews of Palestine were initiated by the Kulturverband; often, they ran a parallel course with relief efforts for refugees in Germany and Austria. With varying degrees of success, these programs were grafted onto the *yishuv*, principally under the auspices of the Anglo-centric Women's International Zionist Organization, which subsumed the germinal Central European groups in 1919.[25]

Vowing to combat "the exploitation of women," the Kulturverband originally was concerned with the lace-making workshops that had been established by Sarah Thon in Jerusalem, Safed, and Jaffa. By 1913 some four hundred women worked in the craft shops, most of whom were born in Palestine or had migrated from other parts of the Ottoman Empire. There is some indication that the German women had intended these workshops for girls from Eastern Europe, but their self-selected clientele turned out to be overwhelmingly Sephardic. The Kulturverband also sponsored women's agricultural training farms, a school for home economics, public kitchens, and health facilities for women and children; it partially financed and supervised kindergartens and Shaare Tzedik Hospital in Haifa. The Kulturverband was the first women's group to send a nurse to the *yishuv*, which, along with its other work in the health field, inspired Hadassah's mission in Palestine.[26] Above all, though, it was the chief support for the institution that would become the most significant link between European Zionist women and their Palestinian counterparts before and during World War I: the Girl's Training Farm in Kineret. It was especially from this institution that the image and myth of the working woman pioneer was propagated.

But the Central European women also sought to mitigate the revolutionary and feminist fervor embraced by many of the women immigrants in Palestine. The professed goal was to transform immigrant women into productive workers and ideal mothers; they also wished to replace "idleness" with productive work, along with literacy in

Hebrew, and to inculcate "a positive national identification" with Palestine. It was important to the women of the middle class that the Chaluzot (women pioneers) learn "the value and delight of order, cleanliness, and good taste." They feared the emergence, or even the appearance, of women in the Jews' incipient nation as a shade too "red" for polite society. This sentiment also revealed the ambivalence of many Zionist women, even ardent activists, toward the idea of complete equality, and their fear of its possible consequences.[27]

To a certain extent, the modifications of the Kulturverband anticipated the shape the Zionist movement would assume in seeking to enlist the sympathy of greater numbers of assimilated Jews. The promotions of the Kulturverband made a point, almost from the outset, of trying to draw into their orbit all Jewish women of Germany, whether Zionist or not. In this regard a leader of the Juedisch-nationale Frauenvereinigung, Edith Lachmann, suggested a need for more "neutral" student and girls' organizations in order to provide a common meeting ground for all Jewish youth. She also suggested that the movement sponsor separate organizations for girls to encourage their independence, because girls tended to be intimidated by boys in the usual settings; to be on their own would enable them to speak and act for themselves.[28] After the Balfour Declaration (1917), it was from the British women's camp that the strongest message was relayed that the "building-up of the Jewish national home was a reality, whether one had wished for it or not," and now every Jew was responsible for it proceeding in the best and most constructive manner possible.[29]

Organized Zionist Women in Great Britain

With the Allied powers' victory in World War I and the rise of Chaim Weizmann as a Zionist leader, England became the center of the movement in Europe. Certainly, part of the reason why the German and Austrian women's groups have received scant attention is that they were later brought under the control of WIZO. In Great Britain, the Federation of Women Zionists (FWZ) was established in 1918, but sporadic Jewish-national societies, and committees dedicated to resettling Jews in Palestine, began in the late 1880s. Among the earliest known groups was the Western Women's Tent, which saw itself as adjunct to the efforts of the Hovevei (or Hibbat)

Zion (Lovers of Zion). Scattered groups related to Hovevei Zion were formed in the wake of intensified Russian persecutions in 1881; these were primarily interested in supporting the revival of Hebrew and colonization efforts to serve the incipient secular-Jewish community in Palestine. In 1910, an organization emerged called the Zionist Pioneer Women, which coalesced from the earlier bodies. One of their members actually immigrated to Palestine after joining the group—with a ticket purchased from the club's treasury. This was a highly unusual course for a woman from such an organization in the prewar years. In the limited files of these groups, there are very few inquiries from prospective pioneers, or immigrants to Palestine, from their home nations of Great Britain, Germany, or Austria.[30]

A public "struggle for an equal and separate place" for women in the movement officially commenced in 1909, at the first Conference of Jewish Women's Organizations in Manchester, because, as one of their leaders admitted, "equal rights on paper did not necessarily bring them in reality."[31] Among the well-known women in the Manchester circle were the wife of Chaim Weizmann, Vera, and the Marks sisters (of Marks and Spencer fame), wives of Israel Sieff and Harry Sacher. Vera Weizmann had been involved in social welfare work as a physician: her communal activities provided valuable contacts for her husband's Zionist endeavors. From a more expressly political perspective, Rebecca Sieff had been deeply influenced by the suffragette movement, an experience she also applied to Palestine. In 1917 these women, along with Henrietta Irwell, a child welfare worker, formed the core of the Ladies Committee of the English Zionist Federation, which included a dozen women's groups. The male-dominated federation urged the women to concentrate on "recruitment," a task that they resisted in favor of a more comprehensive role. "Recruitment" implied raising funds through membership subscriptions, which would go into the central body's coffer.[32] With surprising candor for this genre, one of the chroniclers of WIZO relates that

> It took many years for the relationship between the English Zionist Federation and the Federation of Women Zionists to settle down: from its inception, with all the goodwill in the world, the situation was a slightly uneasy one. There are still many men, and indeed, some women too, who think the vast and complex task

of the Zionist movement calls for complete unity; that the splitting away of the feminine workers can only weaken the whole. Especially in fund-raising work there are those who still condemn any activity which they think might divert money from the major funds. . . . The fruits of their co-operation have been far more numerous, as well as valuable and significant, than the many minor, often merely technical, points of difference.[33]

Shortly before World War I, several women's groups in England and elsewhere in Western Europe were associated with the Kulturverband of the German Zionist women. After the war, "Mrs. Paul Goodman re-established connections with the Kulturverband branches in Germany, Poland, Holland, and Moscow as well as in Palestine, and succeeded in arousing their interest and sympathy in the plans for an international body of Zionist women."[34] This sentiment materialized as a conference in July 1920, calling WIZO into being, while the British Federation of Women Zionists was maintained in a somewhat truncated state. One WIZO account infers that in 1927, the ascension of Mrs. Robert Solomon as chairman of the FWZ initiated an important shift. Until this time, among women and men, the Zionist movement's following had largely been from "newer immigrants from Europe," that is, Jews of the lower classes—despite the middle-class outlook of many in their ranks. The leadership, on the other hand, was mostly from the assimilated bourgeoisie. Mrs. Solomon's profession of Zionist sympathies was said to "broaden [the] base" of the movement considerably. It could now draw in many more wealthy and highly assimilated Jews who had earlier scorned Zionism.[35]

Coordinated Efforts

As the *yishuv* developed and demanded increasing financial support, organized Zionist women were painstakingly concerned that the audience of their promotions visualize the work that was being done in Palestine—through photographs and narratives in slick flyers and booklets, and through exhibitions, including scale models of their facilities, examples from workrooms, and even a film entitled *Heldinnen des Aufbaues* (Heroines of the *Yishuv*). They were very aware that these images must be presented in both an aesthetically pleasing and realistic manner, and for the most part they succeeded in fulfilling their intentions. All of this helped make Jewish Palestine, and above all the women's part in its re-creation, a "living reality" to the Zionist faithful and the wider Jewish audience.[36]

The European women's organizations also showed Palestine as the bastion of new cultural creativity for women, as a complement to their newly found productive labor, and as rooted in their ancestral soil. This was especially apparent in the British and German organs of WIZO, which featured literature, poetry, drama, and art of the *yishuv* women.[37] These works contained an occasional radical reinterpretation of Judaism and Jewish history from a feminist perspective. In a 1933 article, "Earth—Mother of all Living," Ada Fishman wrote, "In days long since past, indeed thousands of years ago, even before primitive man . . . woman was the first to discover the secrets of the soil on which she lived and to turn the richness and strength hidden in it to the use of mankind for his bodily sustenance and strength"; Zionist women were re-creating "that bond of union between Woman and the soil which was first established by [their] primitive ancestresses."[38] Evidence suggests as well that the British and German organizations began to perceive the cultural fruits of Zionist women living in Europe as having a distinctive value, ethic, and voice.[39]

Although the Hebrew literature produced by men at this time included a tendency to be starkly critical and challenge many of the prevailing mythologies of the movement, the men at the helm of Zionism were not as ready as the women to spread such literature as part of official promotions. European women Zionists seemed more comfortable with exposing the caveats and contradictions of a movement that pretended to solve the frustrations of the Jews.[40] "In spite of the revolution in the life of the Jewish people," relates a WIZO booklet, "their conception of the woman [has] not fundamentally changed, even among the most progressive circles."[41] In one retrospective view, from a compilation of reports that appeared before 1934, the central myth of the emergence of the new woman is torn asunder: the texts proclaimed the Zionist woman "as a type does not yet exist." It was admitted that "the composition of Jewish womanhood in Palestine is a truly reflected image of the incongruity of the *yishuv*. Differences of education, social standards, upbringing, and countries of origin present enormous difficulties in any attempt to unite women for a common aim and task. Even within the same social class, interests vary. An abyss seems to separate the Yemenite woman or the Orthodox housewife from the woman worker of Russian origin or the professional woman from Eastern Europe."[42]

Yet, even as they were more critical and attuned to realities of life in Palestine than the men, European Zionist women fostered a sort of unreflective detachment from the Zionist project. In what might be seen as the underside of their legacy, European Zionist women, along with Zionist men, promoted the notion that a Jew in the Diaspora could be fully integrated into the incipient Jewish nation simply by donating money to the cause—which helped lead to a patronizing style of "Diaspora Zionists." This elicited predictable negative responses from the object of their charity, the so-called pioneers in Eretz Israel, and reverberates to this day in the tension between Jews in the United States and the State of Israel. European Zionist women championed the categorization of Zionists as "pioneers and helpers," praising Martin Buber for providing the theoretical underpinning for this idea. The implications of such divisions, whether called pioneers and helpers, Diaspora and Palestinian Jews, or givers and spenders, suggests a dichotomy that Zionist historiography has chronically ignored. Women, too, helped inaugurate a system that combined sentiments and elements of nationalism, charity, guilt, recriminations, and dependency, resulting in problems that have yet to be resolved.[43]

From the social service, charitable, and home economic underpinnings of most European women's Zionist work, it is understandable that their brand of nationalism would be relatively inclusive, tending to appeal to a broader spectrum than the narrowly defined Zionist faithful. European women, followed by American women, were the first to press for the so-called de-politicization of Zionism, to make it more appealing to the greatest number of Jews. Interestingly, European and American Zionist women also allowed for a deeper sensitivity to the plight of Palestine's Arabs and expressed an interest in reaching out to Arab women earlier, and in a more pronounced manner, than their male counterparts.[44]

By the time that Zionism came to be seen as one of the few avenues of survival for all of Europe's Jews, European Zionist women had succeeded in posing a widely admirable model of a modern, independent Jewish woman, skilled in the sciences of home economics, hygiene, and education. Undergirding their efforts was a commitment to the specific needs and potentialities of women and children. To a great extent, however, they consciously or unconsciously accepted the male-centeredness of the movement. This is also true of the women who participated in the left wing of the movement in Central Europe, and women from Mizrachi, the religious camp of Zionism, who formed their own organization in 1925.[45]

As becomes apparent even at the initial stage of recovering the history of European Zionist women, they were not simply just like men, nor were they merely better at men's tasks when they were given the chance.[46] Despite their self-consciously created myths extolling their unanimity with Zionist men, in many important respects organized Zionist women of Central and Western Europe came from a different world than their husbands and brothers. Even at that time, some women activists noted that a significant difference in "mentality" helped account for the varying Zionist outlooks and practices between women and men. They sought to transform the reality of the *yishuv,* and its transmission to the Jews of Europe along the lines of their own middle-class virtues and values, according to a cultural framework with which they were familiar and believed to be most efficacious.[47] In their minds' eyes, and on the ground in Palestine, they engendered a different order from that of the men. They endowed Zionist nationalism with the image, idea, and praxis that public kitchens, infant welfare centers, and the physical, intellectual, and spiritual well-being of women are essential building blocks in the founding of a nation—which helped make it possible to assert that "Zionism is the social conscience in Jewry."[48] History may ultimately reveal the Zionist women of Central and Western Europe, though limited by the constraints of their time, as embodying an even more remarkable and creative humanitarian strategy than that which emerged from their longest-lasting myths.

NOTES

Research for this study was made possible by grants from the Lucius N. Littauer Foundation, the Monkarsh Fellowship of the University of Judaism, and St. Lawrence University in Canton, New York. In the Central Zionist Archives in Jerusalem, Dr. Michael Heymann, Pinchas Selinger, and Reuven Koffler provided generous and essential assistance. I would also like to thank Deborah Rozansky, Leila Rupp, Derek Penslar, Marsha Rozenblit, Shmuel Almog, George Mosse, Eli Shibi-Shai, Shoshana Gershonzohn, Miriyam

Glazer, Steven Lowenstein, Carol Selkin, David Harari, Rabbi Laura Geller, and the Jewish Feminist Research Group of the Center for the Study of Women and Men in Society at the University of Southern California.

1. The problem is alluded to in: George L. Mosse, *Nationalism and Sexuality: Respectability and Abnormal Sexuality in Modern Europe* (New York: Howard Fertig, 1985), p. 42; Lesley Hazleton, *Israeli Women: The Reality behind the Myths* (New York: Simon and Schuster, 1977), p. 95; and Jay Y. Gonen, *A Psychohistory of Zionism* (New York: Meridian, 1976), p. 141. The works in progress of David Biale, John Hoberman, and the author portend a more comprehensive treatment of the subject; see also Michael Berkowitz, *Zionist Culture and West European Jewry before the First World War* (Cambridge: Cambridge University Press, 1993).

2. For the larger context of the development of Zionism see David Vital, *The Origins of Zionism* (Oxford: Oxford University Press, 1975), *Zionism: The Formative Years* (Oxford: Oxford University Press, 1982), and *Zionism: The Crucial Phase* (Oxford: Oxford University Press, 1987); Stuart A. Cohen, *English Zionists and British Jews: The Communal Politics of Anglo-Jewry, 1895–1920* (Princeton: Princeton University Press, 1981); Jehuda Reinharz, *Fatherland or Promised Land* (Ann Arbor: University of Michigan Press, 1975); Jehuda Reinharz, ed., *Dokumente zur Geschichte des deutschen Zionismus, 1882–1933* (Tuebingen: J. C. B. Mohr, 1981); Paula Hyman, *From Dreyfus to Vichy: The Remaking of French Jewry, 1906–1939* (New York: Columbia University Press, 1979), pp. 153–78. See also Women's International Zionist Organization, "General Report," *Report for the Period 1923–25 for the Third International Zionist Conference* (London), p. 3; letter from Helena Weissberg, 15 July 1912, Z3/983, Central Zionist Archives, Jerusalem (hereafter cited as CZA); Edith Lachmann to Z.Z. [Zionistische-Zentralcomite], 23 Nov. 1913, Z3/983, CZA; Otto Warburg to Arthur Ruppin, 22 Apr. 1914, L1/20, CZA; Hazleton, *Israeli Women*, pp. 15–37; and cf. Rachel Katznelson-Rubashow, ed., *The Plough Woman Records of the Pioneer Women in Israel*, trans. Maurice Samuel (New York: Nicholas L. Brown, 1932); *Pioniere und Helfer* 2 (Nov. 1928): 10; Lina Wagner Tauber, 14 Aug. 1912, Z3/983, CZA.

3. See David Vital, "The History of the Zionists and the History of the Jews," *Studies in Zionism* 6 (Autumn 1982): 159–70.

4. Sarah Graham-Brown, *Images of Women: The Portrayal of Women in Photography of the Middle East, 1860–1950* (New York: Columbia University Press, 1988), pp. 26, 29–30, 140, 233.

5. Paula Hyman, "The History of European Jewry: Recent Trends in the Literature," *Journal of Modern History* 54, no. 2 (June 1982): 303–19; Hyman, *From Dreyfus to Vichy*, pp. 153–78; Marsha L. Rozenblit, *The Jews*

of Vienna, 1867–1914: Assimilation and Identity (Albany: State University of New York Press, 1983), p. 163; and Harriet P. Freidenreich, *Jewish Politics in Vienna* (Bloomington: Indiana University Press, 1991), pp. 59, 236. Margalit Shilo provides the most comprehensive treatment of early Zionist women in "The Women's Farm at Kinneret, 1911–1917: A Solution to the Problem of the Working Woman in the Second Aliya," *Jerusalem Cathedra* (1981): 246–83. Yehuda Eloni, *Zionismus in Deutschland: Von den Anfaengen bis 1914* (Gerlingen: Bleicher, 1987), pp. 144–48, briefly traces only one of three organizations, the Juedisch-Nationale Frauenvereinigung. Women Zionists are mentioned in passing in the leading work on German-Jewish women, Marion A. Kaplan, *The Jewish Feminist Movement in Germany: The Campaigns of the Juedischer Frauenbund, 1904–1938* (Westport, Conn.: Greenwood Press, 1979); see also Edward J. Bristow, *Prostitution and Prejudice: The Jewish Fight against White Slavery, 1870–1933* (New York: Schocken Books, 1983); Linda Gordon Kuzmack, *Women's Cause: The Jewish Women's Movement in England and the United States, 1881–1938* (Columbus: Ohio State University Press, 1990), pp. 5–6; Rosalie Gassman-Sherr, *The Story of the Federation of Women Zionists of Great Britain and Ireland* (London: Federation of Women Zionists, 1968); Fay Grove-Pollak, ed., *The Saga of a Movement: WIZO, 1920–1970* (n.p.: Department of Organization and Education of WIZO, n.d.).

6. By 1928 there were at least twenty-five thousand members of the Women's International Zionist Organization from thirty-three countries, and this figure does not include women in the general organization who were not specifically WIZO members. "Uebersicht ueber die Institutionen der Weltorganisation zionistischer Frauen (WIZO) in Palaestina," *Palaestina-Fragen* (Zurich: WIZO, 1929), p. 66.

7. Joan Wallach Scott, *Gender and the Politics of History* (New York: Columbia University Press, 1988), p. 10.

8. Miriam Scheuer and Wera Levin, eds., *Women in the Zionist World* (n.p.: Women's International Zionist Organization Instruction and Information Center, n.d.), p. 17.

9. Katznelson-Rubashow, *Plough Woman Records,* p. v.

10. Until I began research for this project at the Central Zionist Archives in Jerusalem (in the summer of 1989), there were no more than three small, separate files from organized European Zionist women. Now, the archivists are starting to mark or separate such sources, which will help facilitate the investigation of Zionist women, or at least heighten the awareness that European Zionist women constitute a subject worthy of attention.

11. Mosse, *Nationalism and Sexuality,* pp. 90–113; Lynn Hunt, *Politics, Culture, and Class in the French Revolution* (Berkeley: University of California Press), pp. 61–66, 93–95.

12. Nahum Goldmann, *Erez Israel* (Frankfurt a.M.: Voigt and Gleiber, 1914); Jesias Press, *Die juedischen Kolonien Palaestinas* (Leipzig: J. C. Heinris'sche Buchhandlung, 1912); Davis Trietsch, *Bilder aus Palaestina* (Berlin: Orient, n.d.), and *Palaestina Handbuch* (Berlin-Schmargendorf: Orient, 1910); Israel Cohen, ed., *Zionist Work in Palestine* (Leipzig: T. Fischer Unwin, 1911); Yaakov Benor-Kalter, *Photographs of the New Working Palestine* (Haifa: S. Adler, 1935)—although published in Palestine, the photographs were printed in Vienna; Alex Bein, Hermann Greive, Moshe Shaerf, and Julius H. Schoeps, eds., *Theodor Herzl Briefe und Tagebuecher*, vol. 2 (Berlin: Propylaeen, 1983), p. 57; Hans Kohn, "Geleitwort," *Vom Judentum: Ein Sammelbuch Herausgegeben vom Verein juedischer Hochschuler Bar Kochba in Prag* (Leipzig: Kurt Wolff, 1913), p. v; Elias Auerbach, *Pionier der Verwirklichung* (Stuttgart: Deutsche Verlags-Anstalt, 1969), p. 131. See also Max Nordau, *Stenographisches Protokoll der Verhandlungen des X. Zionisten Kongresses in Basel vom 9 bis inklusive 15 August 1911* (Berlin: Juedischer Verlag, 1911), p. 20; *Jewish Chronicle* (London), 12 Sept. 1913, p. 18; Martin Buber, "Theodor Herzl and History," in Martin Buber and Robert Weltsch, *Theodor Herzl and We*, trans. Chaim Arlosoroff (New York: Zionist Labor Party, 1929), p. 12, and "Maennerlied," *Juedische Turnzeitung* 7/8 (1901): 101.

13. See, for example, *Who's Who in WIZO, 1966–1970* (Tel-Aviv: Department of Organization and Education of WIZO, n.d.).

14. "Of course, the women are very honored guests, but they cannot take part in the voting" (Herzl, *Zionisten-Congress in Basel Officielles Protocoll* [Vienna: "Erez lsrael," 1898], p. 115). See also *Jewish Chronicle*, 3 Sept. 1897, p. 10; Vital, *Origins of Zionism*, p. 357.

15. *Encyclopaedia Judaica*, s.v., "Fabius Schach"; there is no separate entry for Miriam.

16. Emma Gottheil, in *Stenographisches Protokoll der Verhandlungen des IV. Zionisten-Kongresses in London, 1900* (Vienna: "Erez Israel," 1900), pp. 286, 181, and "The Early Days of Zionism," in Tulo Nussenblatt, ed., *Theodor Herzl Jahrbuch* (Vienna: Heinrich Glanz, 1937), pp. 255ff.; Rozia Ellman, in *Stenographisches Protokoll der Verhandlungen des II. Zionisten-Kongresses gehalten zu Basel vom 28, bis 31, August 1898* (Vienna: "Erez Israel," 1898), pp. 239ff., 48; Rosa Pomeranz, "Die Bedeutung der zionistischen Idee im Leben der Juedin," in Lazar Schoen, ed., *Die Stimme der Wahrheit: Jahrbuch fuer Wissenschaftlichen Zionismus* (Würzburg: Philippi, 1905), pp. 329–33, and Marta Baer-Issachar, "An unsere Frauen," in ibid., pp. 334–40; Maurice Friedman, *Martin Buber's Life and Work: The Early Years, 1878–1923* (New York: Dutton, 1981), p. 51; Israel Klausner, *The Opposition to Herzl* (in Hebrew) (Jerusalem: Achiever, 1960); Miriam Schach, in *Stenographisches Protokoll der Verhandlungen*

des X. Zionisten-Kongresses in Basel, vom 9, bis inklusive 15, August 1911 (Berlin: Juedischer Verlag, 1911), pp. 219ff.

17. Herzl "personality" file and medals collection, CZA; "Die Congress-Medaille," *Die Welt,* 5 Aug. 1898, p. 5; Berthold Feiwel and E. M. Lilien, eds., *Juedischer Almanach* (Berlin: Juedischer Verlag, 1902); Martin Buber, ed., *Juedische Kuenstler* (Berlin: Juedischer Verlag, 1903).

18. Miriam Schach, in *Stenographisches Protokoll der Verhandlungen des X: Zionisten-Kongresses,* pp. 219ff.

19. *Die Welt,* 18 Nov. 1989, p. 12; Scheuer and Levin, *Women in the Zionist World,* p. 3; Rozenblit, *Jews of Vienna,* p. 163; *Statuten der Juedisch-nationalen Frauenvereinigung zu Berlin,* n.d., CZA.

20. Else Rabin, "The Jewish Woman in Social Service in Germany," in Leo Jung, ed., *The Jewish Library,* vol. 3 (New York: Jewish Library, 1934), pp. 271–72.

21. Ibid., pp. 276; *Protokoll* der gemeinsamen Vertreter-Versammlung des Bundes zionistischer Frauen und des Verbandes juedischer Frauen fuer Kulturarbeit in Palaestina, vom 12, November 1929, p. 12; Rabin, "Jewish Woman in Social Service," p. 272; "Notiz," Organisation der zionistischen Arbeit unter den Frauen, 1911–1917, Z3/983, CZA.

22. Rabin, "Jewish Woman in Social Service," pp. 296–98; Bonnie S. Anderson and Judith P. Zinsser, *A History of Their Own: Women in Europe from Prehistory to the Present,* vol. 2 (New York: Harper & Row, 1988), p. 176. See also Dennis B. Klein, *Jewish Origins of the Psychoanalytic Movement* (Chicago: University of Chicago Press, 1985), pp. 72–84; announcements, Juedisch-nationale Frauenvereinigung, May 1914, 21 Feb. 1911, 3/1/2/5, CZA.

23. Betty Lescyesky to Sarah Thon, 16 May 1911, L2/257II, CZA; Rabin, "Jewish Woman in Social Service," p. 303.

24. Announcement, Bund Zionistischer Frauen, 16 Sept. 1925, 3/1/2/ 5, CZA; Rabin, "Jewish Woman in Social Service," pp. 306–7; Rahel Straus, "The Importance of Our Work for the Promotion of Health in Palestine," *Report of the Jewish Women's League for Cultural Work in Palestine for 1913,* CZA; Straus, *Wir lebten in Deutschland: Erinnerungen einer deutschen Judin, 1880–1933* (Stuttgart: Deutsche Verlags-Anstalt, 1962).

25. Announcement, Juedisch-nationale Frauenvereinigung, June 1915, CZA; announcement, Bund zionistischer Frauen in Deutschland Ortsgruppe Berlin: Juedisch Nationale Frauenvereinigung, 12 Jan. 1926, CZA; Grove-Pollak, *Saga of a Movement,* p. 67; Nanny Margulies-Auerbach, *Frauenarbeit und Volksbewegung* (Vienna: KKL [Keren Kayemet l'Israel], 1920), pp. 29–32; Betty Lisczinski to Otto Warburg, 14 July 1911, L1/20, CZA; Gassman-Sherr, *Story of the Federation of Women Zionists,* p. 18.

26. Thon's husband, Jacob, was the assistant director of the Palestine

Office of the Zionist Organization, under Arthur Ruppin. See Shilo, "Women's Farm," p. 256; Scheur and Lewin, *Women in the Zionist World,* p. 17; "Uebersicht ueber die Institutionen," p. 66; Grove-Pollak, *Saga of a Movement,* p. 66; Rose G. Jacobs, "Beginnings of Hadassah," in Isidor S. Meyer, ed., *Early History of Zionism in America* (New York: Arno, 1977), p. 233.

27. Nadia Stein, *Women in Eretz Israel,* trans. D. C. Adler Hobman (London: Women's International Zionist Organization, 1927), p. 5; *Pioneers and Helpers* 3 (May 1928): 6; Arlosoroff-Goldberg, *Palaestina-Fragen,* pp. 5ff.; Marie Syrkin, "Preface," in Ada Maimon, *Women Build a Land,* trans. Shulamith Schwarz-Nardi (New York: Herzl Press, 1962), pp. 13–14; Shilo, "Women's Farm, p. 272; Mrs. Otto Warburg to Arthur Ruppin, 15 Apr. 1914, L2/771, CZA; Bette Lesczynsky to Sara Thon, 2 Jan. 1914, A 148/37, CZA; Gordon Craig, *The Germans* (New York: G. P. Putnam's Sons, 1982), p. 147, in reference to the general history of women in Germany; Miriam Schach, *Those with Whom I Walked* (Hebrew) (Tel-Aviv: Dvir, 1951).

28. "Bericht VJFKP," n.d., 3/1/2/5, CZA; "Programm fuer zionistische Fraunvereine," n.d.[1911?], Z3/983, CZA; announcement, Juedisch-nationale Frauenvereinigung, May 1914, 3/1/2/5, CZA; undated later from Edith Lachmann to Heinrich Margulies, A 392/2, CZA; Arthur Handtke to Edith Lachmann, 4 Dec. 1913, Z3/983, CZA; Jenny Blumenfeld, "Referat," 12 Nov. 1929, Berlin, 3/1/2/5, CZA; *Korrespondenzblatt des Verbandes juedischer Frauen fuer Palaestina Arbeit,* n.d., pp. 3ff., 3/1/2/5, CZA; *Palaestina-Aufbau und Frauenarbeit* (London: Weltorganisation zionistischer Frauen, n.d.), p. 19; Lachmann to Margulies, 14 Mar. 1914, A 392/2, CZA.

29. Blumenfeld, "Referat."

30. Gassman-Sherr, *Story of the Federation of Zionist Women,* p. 5; Rachel Gruenspan to Sara Thon, 23 July 1913, L2/258/I, CZA.

31. Gassman-Sherr, *Story of the Federation of Zionist Women,* p. 7.

32. *In Memorium: Henrietta Irwell* (published privately, n.d.); Gassman-Sherr, *Story of the Federation of Zionist Women,* p. 16.

33. Gassman-Sherr, *Story of the Federation of Zionist Women,* p. 10.

34. Ibid., p. 17.

35. Ibid., p. 21.

36. Frau Dr. Maisel Schochat, "Frauenarbeit in Palaestina," *Volk und Land* (6 Feb. 1919): 162–70, and "Eine Rede an junge Zionistinnen," *Volk und Land* (3 May 1919): 562–66; WIZO, *Report for the Period 1923–1925,* pp. 4–5; *Pioniere und Helfer* 2 (Nov. 1928): 10; WIZO, *Taetigkeitsbericht 1929–31 an die VI. Konferenz in Basel, 22–28 Juni 1931,* p. 14; promotional booklets, Verband juedischer Frauen fuer Kulturarbeit in Palaestina, 3/1/2/5, CZA; announcement, "Was will der Verband juedischer Frauen

fuer Kulturarbeit in Palaestina?" Jan. 1922, CZA; Scheuer and Levin, *Women in the Zionist World,* p. 17; *Protokoll* der gemeinsamen Vertreter-Versammlung des Bundes zionistischer Frauen und des Verbandes juedischer Frauen fuer Kulturarbeit in Palaestina, vom 12, November 1929, p. 12; "Woman Marches On," *Pioneer and Helpers* 1 (Jan. 1931): 15; WIZO, "Welfare Work for Women and Children in Palestine," n.d.

37. *Arbeiterinnen Erzaehlen: Kampf und Leben in Erez Israel* (Berlin: n.p., 1935); "Literarisch Sondernummer," *Pioniere und Helfer* 1 (Jan. 1929); *Pioneers and Helpers* 3 (Feb. 1932): 13; *Protokoll* der gemeinsamen Vertreter-Versammlung des Bundes zionistischer Frauen und des Verbandes juedischer Frauen fuer Kulturarbeit in Palaestina, vom 12, November 1929, p. 7; Martha Hofmann, "Culture and Propaganda," in *WIZO: Report of the 5th Biennial Conference in Zurich, July 1929,* p. 33.

38. Ada Fishman, "Earth—Mother of All Living," *Pioneer and Helpers* 4 (May 1932): 14; Shoshanah Bogen, in Katznelson-Rubashow, *Plough Woman Records,* p. 219.

39. "Juedische Frauenkundgebung Programm," postcard announcement of Bund zionistischer Frauen in Deutschland, 15 May 1926, CZA.

40. See, for example, Jeffrey Fleck, *Character and Context: Studies in the Fiction of Abramovitsh, Brenner, and Agnon* (Chico, Calif.: Scholars Press, 1984), pp. 60–85; "Woman Marches On," p. 15; Katznelson-Rubashow, *Plough Woman Records,* pp. 141–45, 150–51, 180, 189, 193, 212; Mrs. I. M. Sieff, in *WIZO: REPORT of the 5th Biennial Conference in Zurich, July 1929,* p. 37.

41. Scheuer and Levin, *Women in the Zionist World,* p. 11.

42. Naomi Ben-Asher, *Great Jewish Women throughout History: Course of Study in Seven Outlines* (New York: Education Department–Hadassah, 1954), p. 40; Scheuer and Levin, *Women in the Zionist World,* p. 7.

43. "Juedische frauen!" announcement, Verband juedischer Frauen fuer Kulturarbeit in Palaestina, May 1924, 3/1/2/5, CZA; "Kennen Sie das Programm unseres Verbandes?" Verband juedischer Frauen fuer Kulturarbeit in Palaestina, 3/1/2/5, CZA; "Bericht VJFKP," n.d., 3/1/2/5, CZA; *Pioneers and Helpers* 4 (Oct. 1928): 19; David Vital, *The Future of the Jews* (Cambridge: Harvard University Press, 1990), p. vii; "Ein Brief zum Geleit," *Pioniere und Helfer* 1 (Jan. 1927): 1. On the contemporary ramifications, see Eliezer D. Jaffe, *Givers and Spenders: The Politics of Charity in Israel* (Jerusalem: Ariel, 1985).

44. Scheuer and Levin, *Women in the Zionist World,* pp. 6–7; Henrietta Szold, "Familiar Letter No. 5," May 1921, "Familiar Letter No. 5," Dec. 21, 1921, Hadassah, 3/1/2/1, CZA.

45. 15. Bericht des Verbandes juedischer Frauen fuer Kulturarbeit in

Palaestina, 3/1/2/5, CZA; Bath-Shewa Saslawsky, "Aufgaben der Wander-lehrerin," in Arlosoroff-Goldberg, ed., *Palaestina-Fragen,* pp. 53ff.; founding announcement of the Verband juedischer Frauen fuer Kulturarbeit in Palaestina, "VJFKP—Aufruf!" 3/1/2/5, CZA; Betti Lesczynsky, "Abschrift eines Briefes an die Vertauens und Vostandesbande," 2 Apr. 1911, L2/257/ I, CZA; announcement, Juedische-Nationale Frauen Vereinigung, 3/1/2/5, CZA; "Fragments—from the letters and notebooks of Shoshanah Bogen," in Katznelson-Rubashow, *Plough Woman Records,* pp. 216–17; *Der Neue Weg: Monatsschrift der juedischen Sozialdemokratischen Arbeiter-Organisation Poale Zion in Deutschland* (Dec. 1924–Aug. 1925); D.D. (D'vrai D'fus collection), 3/1/2/8, CZA; "25 Years—Dedicated to Building Israel in the Spirit of the Torah," Mizrachi Women's Organization, 1950.

46. Cf. Israel Sieff, *Memoirs* (London: Weidenfeld and Nicolson, 1970), p. 123.

47. "Sokolow Month" speeches: Romanna Goodman, "Women in the Zionist Organization," 1931, D.D., A 2/3/4/1/4, CZA; *Korrespondenzblatt des Verbandes juedischer Frauen fuer Palaestina Arbeit,* n.d., pp. 3ff.; Hedwig Gellner, "Programm," in Arlosoroff-Goldberg, *Palaestina-Fragen,* pp. 7ff.; Lina Wagner Tauber, 14 Aug. 1912, Z3/983, CZA; *4. Bericht des Verbandes juedischer Frauen fuer Kulturarbeit in Palaestina, Berlin, January 1912,* pp. 7, 10.

48. Betti Lescinski to Arthur Ruppin, 15 Dec. 1911, L1/20, CZA; Katznelson-Rubashow, *Plough Woman Records,* pp. 141–43, 156; Gellner, "Programm," p. 8; Ada Fischman, *Die Arbeitende Frau in Erez-Israel: Geschichte der Arbeiterinnenbewegung in Palaestina, 1904–1930* (Tel-Aviv: WIZO, 1930), pp. vi, 129, 164; S. Bernstein, *Zionism: Its Essential Aspects and Its Organization* (Copenhagen: Office of the Zionist Organization, 1919), p. 50.

· 3 ·

Ladies of the Sisterhood: Women in the American Reform Synagogue, 1900–1930

PAMELA S. NADELL
RITA J. SIMON

Hostesses of coffee and tea, organizers of meals for the bereaved, planners of "Jewish Home Beautiful" pageants, outfitters of synagogue kitchens, fund-raisers for schools and scholarships, diners at mother-daughter banquets, and discussers of great Jewish books— these were the customary roles of sisterhood women in mid-twentieth-century American Reform, Conservative, and Orthodox synagogues. In the eyes of their members, then, such activities and the parameters they established for Jewish women's behavior within their temples seemed to have been set from time immemorial. When the rabbi appealed to sisterhood women to staff the Sunday school, when they planned Sisterhood Sabbath, or when they studied the rabbinic text "Ethics of the Fathers,"[1] sisterhood women were following what they presumed to be well-established patterns of what women had always done in and for their synagogues.

Yet, an examination of the emergence of Reform synagogue sisterhoods in the early twentieth century and of the founding, in 1913, and programs of the national organization of Reform synagogue sisterhoods, the National Federation of Temple Sisterhoods (NFTS), reveals how recently women had assumed these roles. It also suggests that the early history of women's religious organizations can serve as an example of how, as the historian Paula Hyman notes, women "created a female culture and constructed a community different from the organized community of Jewish men."[2] In this case women shared the space and institutional structure of the synagogue and the values and aspirations of Reform Judaism with their husbands and brothers. But through organized communities of women, they created a culture that enabled them to change the expectations of their proper behavior within its portals and expand Jewish women's public religious roles.[3]

By the end of the second decade of the twentieth century Jewish women's associational life had blossomed into an array of national organizations. In the United States women had organized for their self-education and for social welfare in the National Council of Jewish Women (1893), for Zionism in Hadassah (1912), and for the synagogue in Reform Judaism's National Federation of Temple Sisterhoods (1913) and Conservative Judaism's National Women's League of the United Synagogue of America (1918). Jewish women, in essence, created a "volunteer army" dedicated to serving their community.[4] Yet this efflorescence of women's national organizational activity masks a long history of Jewish women's local activism.

In small Jewish communities across the United States as early as the 1830s, German Jewish immigrant women had begun to band together in Hebrew ladies benevolent societies. Possibly modeled on German Jewish female associations, called Frauen Vereine, from which some took their names, they enabled Jewish women to render aid to one another and social welfare to those less fortunate. Collectively and publicly fulfilling the Jewish commandment of *tzedakah,* the ladies of the benevolent societies aided the sick, sewed for the poor, helped the unemployed, and buried their dead. While many of the associations were communally based, some, espousing that women give personal service to the cause of Judaism and not just to needy Jews, became synagogue auxiliaries. Through bazaars, strawberry festivals, and even oyster suppers, these women raised money to build local synagogues. And once built, their synagogues depended upon them to raise funds to sustain them. Together the women of the ladies' auxiliaries bought chairs and organs, papered Sunday school classrooms, and arranged flowers to decorate the sanctuary.[5] Thus like American women in their churches, they too began to exercise influence in their communities by extending accepted middle-class female roles—sustaining their families, nurturing their children, and beautifying their homes—to their community in the public spaces of their synagogues.[6]

But by the 1900s, as the historian William Toll writes, "the benevolent societies were undergoing an eclipse as . . . the concept of general nurturant benevolence was being replaced by more specialized institutions."[7] As synagogues proliferated, rabbis in some places and their wives in others organized sisterhoods as the successors to the Hebrew ladies benevolent societies.

The founding of the sisterhood of Washington Hebrew Congregation, today with twenty-eight hundred family and individual memberships, the leading Reform congregation in the nation's capitol, was typical. In 1905, a year after her husband, Abram, became the synagogue's first ordained rabbi, Carrie Obendorfer Simon founded the Ladies Auxiliary Society of Washington Hebrew Congregation. Its goals were "for congregational work, pure and simple, and to endeavor to establish a more congenial and social congregational spirit." Sisterhood lore recalls that fifty women attended the founding meeting, pledged themselves to ten cents dues, promised to raise money to pay off the mortgage, and then promptly recessed to polish the doorknobs. In its first years the sisterhood sponsored bazaars and concerts to reduce the temple's Sinking Fund, presented a gavel to the board and a memorial tablet to the congregation, and gave the children Chanukah candles. These roles, then, fit well within the already accepted patterns of synagogue sustenance, beautification, and nurturance pioneered by the Hebrew ladies benevolent societies.[8]

However, Carrie Simon had higher hopes for women in the temple. She envisioned a national union of women organized specifically for religious work. The historian Jacob Marcus has suggested that the National Federation of Temple Sisterhoods emerged to "counter and rival the National Council of Jewish Women."[9] Founded in 1893 as the first Jewish equivalent of the women's club, the National Council of Jewish Women had originally been interested in both the religious lives of its members and social welfare work. But as Ellen Sue Levi Elwell has demonstrated, by the end of the first decade of the twentieth century, the council had largely shifted its priorities from religious to philanthropic concerns.[10] Possibly troubled by the decline of National Council of Jewish Women's interest in the synagogue and religious affairs, Simon persuaded Reform leaders, like Rabbi David Philipson, of the merit of a national union of sisterhoods within the Reform movement.[11] Working with Rabbi George Zepin, the director of Synagogue and School Extension for the Union of American Hebrew Congregations, Reform's national association of synagogues, Carrie Simon helped bring 156 delegates from fifty-two sisterhoods to Cincinnati in 1913. There she became the founding president of the National Federation of Temple Sisterhoods, then seen as the feminine counterpart of the union and an organization that would "forge a mighty weapon in the service of Judaism."[12]

While women in their local sisterhoods continued to raise funds, take charge of the decor, and concern themselves with the education of their children in their synagogues, the national organization, with its biennial conferences, annual executive board meetings, nationwide correspondence with individual sisterhoods, and printed accounts of many of these, offered to the women of Reform Judaism possibilities for expanding their roles within the synagogue. In his opening address at the founding convention, Rabbi David Philipson, speaking on "Woman and the Congregation," recognized this aspect of the fledgling organization's agenda. First, he enumerated the many steps Reform Judaism had taken to ameliorate women's status within Judaism. Next, he highlighted Reform's introduction of the family pew, which did away with the seclusion of women in their own gallery, the replacement of bar mitzvah with confirmation for boys *and* girls, and the counting of women in the minyan, the quorum of ten adults required for communal worship. He then proposed that "the last word in woman's relation to the congregation will not be spoken until she is received into full membership if she so desires, on the same footing as man."[13] That may have been the most revolutionary reform David Philipson envisioned sisterhood women would achieve. However, over the course of a bit more than the next decade, the women of NFTS would discover that together they could expand old avenues and open up new ones for their participation in synagogue life that Rabbi Philipson had not even imagined.

Not surprisingly, through NFTS, sisterhood women continued their, by then, well-established roles of sustaining and beautifying their synagogues. In addition, almost every sisterhood remained highly involved with the religious education of its children. Sisterhood women raised money to buy furniture and equipment and decorate schoolrooms. They arranged entertainments and refreshments to celebrate holidays. Some organized parents meetings to help bring what was taught in the school into the home. In small communities, where there was often neither a rabbi nor trained teachers, sisterhood women not only sponsored the schools but also taught in them. In so doing, they drew not from the Jewish tradition of the past but rather from the American milieu, which over the course of the second half of the nineteenth century had seen women move in ever greater numbers into teaching. In larger communities they ran free religious schools for the children of the poor and organized teacher training programs to help staff them. In both, sisterhood women created the first synagogue libraries,[14] thereby playing pioneering roles in shaping the emerging American synagogue as an educational center for Jewish youth.

The national organization also enabled women to extend their philanthropic activities. Collectively as NFTS, sisterhood women raised funds for much larger projects than they could undertake as women organized in individual communities. Just as sisterhood women cared for the education of the youth of their congregations, they now expanded their concern to the "boys of the College." In 1921 NFTS pledged to build a dormitory at Hebrew Union College, Reform Judaism's rabbinical seminary in Cincinnati, and appointed Carrie Simon to take charge of the nationwide fund-raising.[15] The National Federation of Temple Sisterhoods gave the women of Reform Judaism a sense of sorority that allowed them to extend their public participation in Reform Judaism beyond their established roles as nurturers and philanthropists. Concerned with religion, with the rites and rituals of Judaism, its ceremonies and services, sisterhood women sought influence over their own religious lives. Through its National Committee on Religion, NFTS was in contact with women throughout the United States interested in religious life in the home and the synagogue. Its reports reveal the range of sisterhoods' religious activities and how sisterhood women, surely working in concert with their rabbis and their rabbis' wives, raised their voices to help shape Reform Judaism. Determined to revive Jewish ceremonials Reform had previously abandoned, NFTS women reclaimed traditions they viewed as too hastily dismissed. Recalling the custom of *shalach mones,* the ritual of giving gifts on Purim, they collected food, clothing, and money for local charities. Concerned with Passover, they hosted communal seders and also celebrated the returning of the seder to the home.[16] In so doing, sisterhood women broadened their participation in Jewish religious life.

The most striking changes, however, occurred in the extension of women's roles in the public religious spaces of Reform Judaism. Because sisterhood women wanted to foster worship, they conceived of the "novel innovation" of providing babysitting at services to allow the mothers of young children the leisure to pray. Not only did the sisterhoods do all they could to enable and encourage attendance at public worship—sometimes even canvassing house-to-house to convince people to come to services—but through the collective of NFTS they came to articulate definite ideas about those services. They called for the reintroduction of congregational singing. They championed the "free pew" movement so that wealth no longer determined where one sat in the congregation. They helped revive the synagogue holiday of Simchat Torah. Citing their own desire for "a book of prayer suitable for every day of the year," they tried to prod the Reform rabbinical association, the Central Conference of American Rabbis, into publishing one. Upset by the fact that, when rabbis vacationed, services were irregular at best, a number of sisterhoods took charge of conducting and leading summer services. In fact, in a striking example of a new idea filtering its way down from the top, the chair of the National Committee on Religion reported that no letter had ever received more response than the one she sent about sisterhoods organizing summer services.[17]

Quickly NFTS came to demand public recognition of women's contributions in an annual Sisterhood Sabbath. Originally, this was conceived as the day when a woman would deliver a "message" to the congregation, that is, speak from the pulpit. In some synagogues, by the early 1920s, it had become the one day outside the summer when women conducted the entire service. In others, women read parts of the service and the rabbi preached a sermon appropriate for the day.[18] By increasing Reform Jewish women's avenues for participation and even religious leadership within their synagogues, the National Federation of Temple Sisterhoods helped change the expectations of the proper female roles within Reform Judaism.

Perhaps recalling David Philipson's remarks at the founding convention, sisterhood women thus continued to champion the emancipation of women within their temples. NFTS reports noted, with satisfaction, that several congregations had admitted married women to full membership and that more temples were admitting women to their boards.[19]

The women of Reform Judaism were by no means unaware of

the extent of the transformation made through sisterhood. On NFTS's silver jubilee in 1938 Carrie Simon reflected, "The Ladies Aid Society Grows Up." She noted how the early Hebrew ladies benevolent societies had pioneered new roles for women with their "insistence that women have a place in the practical life of the congregation." But she also stated, "Where formerly the women of the Aid society did not get beyond the threshold of the Temple, recent years . . . have found them within its very sanctum."[20] Understanding the changes in women's roles that had occurred within Reform Judaism, she wrote elsewhere: "In the past we have considered the Jewish woman as a follower. Within recent years she has become a participant. Does the next step lie in her becoming a leader, religiously speaking?"[21] Thus from her position as the founding president of the National Federation of Temple Sisterhoods, Carrie Simon called for women's ordination, the final barrier to the achieving of full emancipation by women within Reform Judaism.

Quickly, the new avenues for women's activities in Reform synagogues, orchestrated through NFTS, became a comfortable status quo. By the middle of the 1920s Reform sisterhoods' creative "feminist" period was over. The roles first described as indicative of mid-twentieth-century sisterhoods were set. What had once been pioneering new activities for women in the synagogue, such as women leading summer services and speaking on occasion from the pulpit, had apparently, within a bit more than a decade, become accepted venues of women's behavior.

Several factors may account for the acceptance of the shifting boundaries of woman's sphere in the synagogue that occurred within the first decade of the founding of NFTS in 1913. Surely, the first lies within Reform Judaism's pioneering stance on women's equality. As Michael Meyer's penetrating study of Reform Judaism has shown, Reform, influenced by Immanuel Kant's ideas of rationally viable faith, came to assert: "The idea that pure religious faith is essentially moral rapidly became the theoretical basis and the practical operative principle of the Reform movement."[22] Because women's inequality within Judaism tested its morality, especially according to nineteenth- and twentieth-century liberal notions of equality of opportunity for all, the amelioration of women's status became a critical test of its theoretical base. Almost from its inception, as David Philipson reminded his audience at NFTS's founding convention, some of the first leaders of Reform Judaism considered it their "sacred duty to declare with all emphasis the complete religious equality of woman with man."[23] As Reform Judaism gained ground in America, Reformers continued to work to improve the position of women within Judaism, despite, as Karla Goldman has carefully documented, real ambivalence about what would happen to gender roles if the full implications of women's emancipation within the synagogue were realized.[24] Hence Philipson's was but another voice in a long tradition of revered Reform leaders calling for women's equality within the synagogue. When NFTS leaders echoed his call, or even daringly, as Carrie Simon did, envisioned a greater emancipation, they stood squarely within Reform's tradition of theoretical equality for women.

Second, NFTS activity must be seen within the larger context of American women's organizational life. Synthesizing twenty years of scholarship in American women's history, William Chafe, in his revision of his path-breaking 1972 study *American Woman,* considers how by the end of the nineteenth century, middle- and upper-class white women had expanded and empowered what had once been a sharply limited "separate sphere" into "more an instrument for political influence than a barrier to freedom." Drawing upon the works of the historians Paula Baker, Suzanne Lebsock, Nancy Cott, and others, he demonstrates how, by the end of the nineteenth century, women's voluntary societies were ubiquitous, that through them women had helped develop the social and educational infrastructures of American life, and that many of these organizations had continued and new ones had emerged to push particular agendas in the 1920s and 1930s.[25] The achievements of NFTS must be viewed as part of this stream. In this case middle- and upper-class Jewish women united in service to the synagogue. In so doing, they forged a community and a culture that enabled them to shift the boundaries of their proper roles there.

Unquestionably, their actions were widely influenced by their intersections with American life and culture. In the 1910s and 1920s that meant the debate about suffrage, the meaning of women's votes, and the emergence of new opportunities for middle- and upper-class women in all spheres—education, the professions, and the labor force. Rabbis and their wives participated in these debates, mutually influencing one another with their ideas about women's roles. Even before 1921 when Martha Neumark, a young student at Hebrew Union College, raised for Reform its first real test case of a woman seeking rabbinic ordination, Carrie Simon's husband, Abram, asserted to his congregation that women had political and social equality and that that should extend to the pulpit.[26] Which came first, his wife's vision of women's emancipation or his, is not clear. But they shared a common stance on the implications of women's emancipation in the wake of the success of the suffrage battle in 1920, one that they carried together to the synagogue. So, too, other rabbis and their wives together paved the way for women's expanded roles within the synagogue.[27]

These debates naturally impacted upon their congregants. NFTS never did endorse suffrage.[28] But as Beth Wenger has revealed, when Stella Bauer of Atlanta's leading Reform synagogue, The Temple, called in 1920 for its board to grant women representation, she did not appeal to Reform's history of ameliorating women's status within Judaism as David Philipson had done. Instead, she justified her call by alluding to "this age of woman's suffrage."[29] Thus at their particular intersection of ethnicity, class, and gender in American life, the women of NFTS extended the sphere of women's roles in the synagogue and allowed their leaders to envision new ones that one day their daughters and granddaughters would champion.

Echoing that earlier period of intense activism, in 1961 Reform sisterhood women, sparked anew by a sense of the changing possibilities for women's lives and prodded by its executive director, Jane Evans, once again took up the call made by its founding president for the ordination of women as rabbis.[30] In so doing, they helped reopen the debate on the women's issue in Reform Judaism at the same time that President John F. Kennedy's Commission on the Status of Women reopened the debate on women's rights that had seemed to close with the passage of the 1920 suffrage amendment. Just when American women began exploring new possibilities for their lives, while high schooler Sally Priesand was planning on becoming a rabbi,[31] the women of the National Federation of Temple Sisterhoods reminded the leaders of Reform Judaism that the time had come for Reform to implement the "complete religious equality of woman with man" that it had championed a century and a half before.

NOTES

Pamela S. Nadell wishes to thank the American Jewish Archives for its Marguerite R. Jacobs Memorial Fellowship for 1988–89, which supported part of this research, and the National Federation of Temple Sisterhoods for its assistance. Earlier versions of this essay were presented as "Sisterhood Ladies and Rabbis: Women in the American Reform Synagogue" at the conference "An Age of Faiths: Religion and Society in the Modern World," University of Maryland (Apr. 1990); and as "The Beginnings of the Religious Emancipation of American Jewish Women," at the Berkshire Conference of Women's Historians, Douglass College (June 1990).

1. Minutes of the sisterhood of the Sons of Jacob Congregation, Waterloo, Iowa (1950–66). This Conservative sisterhood in the only synagogue in the area demonstrates activities typical of sisterhoods at mid-century.

2. Paula E. Hyman, "Gender and the Immigrant Jewish Experience in the United States," in Judith R. Baskin, ed. *Jewish Women in Historical Perspective* (Detroit: Wayne State University Press, 1991), p. 223.

3. For an opposing view of sisterhoods, see Jenna Weissman Joselit, "The Special Sphere of the Middle-Class American Jewish Woman: The Synagogue Sisterhood, 1890–1940," in Jack Wertheimer, ed., *The American Synagogue: A Sanctuary Transformed* (Cambridge: Cambridge University Press, 1987), pp. 206–30. There she concludes, "As forces for change within the American Jewish community, the sisterhoods were negligible factors. In every case, the sisterhood left untouched the basic social structure of the synagogue and, by extension, that of the larger Jewish community" (p. 223).

4. Works on these organizations include Ellen Sue Levi Elwell, "The Founding and Early Programs of the National Council of Jewish Women: Study and Practice as Jewish Women's Religious Expression" (Ph.D. diss., Indiana University, 1982); Faith Rogow, *Gone to Another Meeting: The National Council of Jewish Women, 1893–1993* (Tuscaloosa: University of Alabama Press, 1993). On international women's organizations, see Marion A. Kaplan, *The Jewish Feminist Movement in Germany: The Campaigns of the Juedischer Frauenbund, 1904–1938* (Westport, Conn.: Greenwood Press, 1979); Michael Berkowitz, "Transcending 'Tzimmes and Sweetness': Recovering the History of Zionist Women in Central and Western Europe, 1897–1933," in this volume.

5. "Hebrew Ladies Benevolent Societies, 1857–1912," in Jacob R. Marcus, ed., *The American Jewish Woman: A Documentary History* (New York: Ktav, 1981), pp. 204–19. See also Hasia Diner, *A Time for Gathering: The Second Migration, 1820–1880* (Baltimore: Johns Hopkins University Press, 1992), pp. 86–113.

6. See Dianne Ashton, "Grace Aguilar and the Matriarchal Theme in Jewish Women's Spirituality," in this volume. These roles reveal Jewish women's acceptance of the nineteenth-century "cult of true womanhood," first described by Barbara Welter, "The Cult of True Womanhood, 1820–1860," *American Quarterly* 18 (Summer 1966): 151–74. Believing that women were inherently passive, domestic, pious, and pure, prescriptive literature, politicians, and religious leaders instructed women to use the leisure they had attained as they moved into the middle class to be better wives and mothers. American middle-class women seeking public spaces in which to extend the sway of their moral influence had found that through their churches they could apply the standards of "true womanhood" outside their homes. In fact, as early as the 1780s American women began organizing voluntary, charitable associations within their churches (Sara M. Evans, *Born for Liberty: A History of Women in America* [New York: Free Press, 1989], p. 74). The Hebrew ladies benevolent associations could be considered the Jewish counterpart of this American female phenomenon.

7. William Toll, "A Quiet Revolution: Jewish Women's Clubs and the Widening Female Sphere, 1870–1920," *American Jewish Archives* 61, no. 1 (Spring/Summer 1989): 12.

8. Archives of Washington Hebrew Congregation, Washington, D.C., Box SIS 1, Sisterhood Programs, Minutes of the Washington Hebrew Congregation, 5 May, 3 Nov., 24 Apr. 1907, 5 Apr. 1911; "Fiftieth Birthday Sisterhood Highlights," Feb. 1955.

9. Marcus, *American Jewish Woman*, p. 664.

10. Elwell, "Founding and Early Programs," pp. 136–79. On women's clubs, see Karen J. Blair, *The Clubwoman as Feminist: True Womanhood Redefined, 1868–1914* (New York: Holmes & Meier, 1980). David Philipson notes retrospectively that he was aware of a shift in the objectives of the NCJW (*My Life as an American Jew: An Autobiography* [Cincinnati, 1941], pp. 234–37, cited in Marcus, *American Jewish Woman*, p. 666). While rivalry may have been a motive at the national level, at the local level, as Beth Wenger has shown for Atlanta, the two organizations, with very similar memberships, were seen as complementary. Sisterhood was concerned with the synagogue and NCJW with philanthropy (Beth S. Wenger, "Jewish Women of the Club: The Changing Public Role of Atlanta's Jewish Women, 1870–1930," *American Jewish History* 76 [Mar. 1987]: 321).

11. Philipson, *My Life,* pp. 234–37, cited in Marcus, *American Jewish Woman,* pp. 665–68.

12. American Jewish Archives (hereafter cited as AJA), Cincinnati, Ohio, Nearprint Files, National Federation of Temple Sisterhoods, "We Are the Women of Reform Judaism: Celebrating the 75th Anniversary," 21 Jan. 1988.

13. David Philipson, "Woman and the Congregation," *Proceedings of the National Federation of Temple Sisterhoods* (hereafter cited as *NFTS*) 1 (1913): 15–18.

14. "Report of the Committee on Religious Schools, 1918," *NFTS* 1 (1919): 47–48; "Report of the National Committee on Religious Schools, 1923," *NFTS* 2 (1925): 25–28; "Report of the National Committee on Religious Schools, 1922," *NFTS* 1 (1923): 66–68: Rita J. Simon and Gloria Danzinger, *Women's Movements in America: Their Successes, Disappointments, and Aspirations* (New York: Praeger, 1991), pp. 36–95.

15. "Report of the Special Committee on Hebrew Union College Dormitory, 1922" *NFTS* 1 (1922): 24.

16. "Report of the National Committee on Religion, 1920," *NFTS* 1 (1921): 57–59; "Report of the National Committee on Religion, 1922," *NFTS* 1 (1923): 63–65.

17. "Report of the National Committee on Religion, 1923," *NFTS* 2 (1924): 20–23; Carrie Simon, "The President's Annual Message," *NFTS* 1 (1917): 26; "Report of the National Committee on Religion, 1919," *NFTS* 1 (1920): 20–22; Hattie M. Wiesenfeld, "Report of the President, 1922," *NFTS* 1 (1922): 16–18; "Report of the National Committee on Religion, 1920," pp. 57–59; "Report of the National Committee on Religion, 1921," *NFTS* 1 (1922): 22–24.

18. Wiesenfeld, "Report of the President, 1922," pp. 16–18; "Report of the National Committee on Religion, 1921," pp. 22–24; "Report of the National Committee on Religion, 1923," pp. 20–23.

19. "Report of the National Committee on Religion, 1923," pp. 20–23.

20. AJA, Nearprint Files; Mrs. Abram Simon, "Four Presidents on the N.F.T.S. Silver Jubilee," *Topics and Trends* 4, no. 1 (Jan.–Feb. 1938): 3.

21. AJA, MS #267, 1/3, Abram Simon Collection, Sermons and Addresses O–Y, Untitled, "What Can the Women Do for Judaism?" p. 6. It is exceedingly unlikely that this typed, unsigned, undated sermon was given by Rabbi Abram Simon. In several places (p. 5), it speaks of "us women," "our husbands," and "we women." In addition, a handwritten addition at the end seems to correspond with a sample of Carrie Simon's handwriting located in the archives of the Washington Hebrew Congregation, Washington, D.C. Consequently, we are attributing its authorship to Carrie Simon and would suggest that this may have been a text she used when she spoke from the pulpit on behalf of NFTS. See *Washington Star,* 21 Nov. 1913, p. 1, which reported that she spoke from the pulpit of Temple Israel in Boston on "the call of the Sisterhood"; and her biographical sketch in *Who's Who in American Jewry* (New York: Jewish Biographical Bureau, 1926),

which claims that she "spoke in many pulpits throughout the country in the interest and advancement of Jewish womanhood."

22. Michael Meyer, *Response to Modernity: A History of the Reform Movement in Judaism* (New York: Oxford University Press, 1988), pp. 64–65.

23. David Einhorn, "Report of a Committee on the Position of Women," cited in Philipson, "Women and the Congregation," p. 16.

24. Karla Goldman, "The Ambivalence of Reform Judaism: Kaufmann Kohler and the Ideal Jewish Woman," *American Jewish History* 79 (Summer 1990): 492.

25. William H. Chafe, *The Paradox of Change: American Women in the Twentieth Century* (New York: Oxford University Press, 1991), pp. 5, 9–10, 35–36.

26. *The Evening Star* (Washington, D.C.), 9 Oct. 1920, 4.

27. When, in 1922, Reform rabbis debated the question of women's ordination, they voted to allow their wives to join in the debate ("Resolution on Ordination of Women," *Central Conference of American Rabbis Year Book* 32 [1922]: 51).

28. Women of Reform Judaism, *Index of Resolutions: Adopted by the National Federation of Temple Sisterhoods, 1913–1985* (New York: Women of Reform Judaism, 1988).

29. Cited in Wenger, "Jewish Women of the Club," p. 327.

30. AJA, National Federation of Temple Sisterhoods, Box 73, 5/3, "Resolutions at the 23rd Biennial, 1961," p. 6.

31. In 1972 Sally Priesand became the first woman in America to be ordained a rabbi.

·III·
LITERARY
VOICES

· 4 ·

Grace Aguilar and the Matriarchal Theme in Jewish Women's Spirituality

DIANNE ASHTON

For four centuries, Jewish women have used the biblical tales of the matriarchs as a blank slate on which to write and legitimize their own spiritual understandings.[1] In the first half of the nineteenth century, Jewish women in America and England also used these sacred tales to respond to perceived threats from Christian evangelists.[2] In their writings, Jewish women combined the Bible, folkloric traditions, and their own personal insights to create intricate psychological and spiritual experiences they imagined the matriarchs to have had. The key to understanding the matriarchs was, as one woman put it, to "read the Bible with your heart."[3] In the Jewish and general popular press, Jewish women defended Judaism as the source of their own spirituality and as a religion whose patriarchy went no further than did that of their contemporary Victorian society.

In her writings, the Englishwoman Grace Aguilar (1816–47) described the spiritual pleasures of Jewish women in a manner that brought her readers into a fully Jewish, yet Victorian, femininity. In the Victorian era, literature published both independently and by religious organizations played a key role in developing an ideology about the nature of womanhood.[4] The passionless, pious, self-sacrificing Victorian woman of our imaginations grew out of nineteenth-century literature, art, medicine, and religion, all of which asserted womanly modes of pleasure based on self-control. Bourgeois women themselves further cultivated the pleasures of spirituality based on sensual self-denial in their own relationships and espoused it in their original writings.[5]

Aguilar, the most famous, prolific, and influential nineteenth-century Jewish woman to write in this manner, placed her work in the center of the public debate over which religion best suited women's nature by choosing titles that recalled those of Christian polemicists.[6] All but three of Aguilar's fifteen books deal with either Judaism or the influence of women in the home and convey a sense of Jewish women's moral and spiritual power.[7] Aguilar maintained close personal friendships with many Protestant women[8] and expected her books to be read by her contemporaries, both Protestant and Jewish. Nonetheless, in her introduction to *The Women of Israel,* Aguilar said that her book's purpose was defensive. First, she hoped to convince young Jewish women that the Bible was "a true and perfect mirror of themselves." The biblical women of Israel are worth studying, she wrote, because they are admirable. By implication, Jewish women in the nineteenth century also were admirable, and thus Aguilar hoped to overcome the demeaning caricatures of Jews in the English press and literature, a problem she addressed directly in an essay at the end of *Women of Israel* (1847). In her hands, the matriarchs often had "proper self-esteem," something she hoped to instill in her Jewish readers. Second, she hoped to increase Jewish women's appreciation for and knowledge of the Hebrew Bible. And third, she refuted claims that only Christianity offered women spiritual consolation and immortality and that nineteenth-century women owed their "influence and equality with men" to Christianity.[9]

Aguilar's *Women* described the pleasures of Jewish feminine spirituality based on sensual self-denial, an idea her Victorian world deemed the hallmark of female respectability. Contrasted with the hardy, hard-working, and obedient working-class woman, the "true woman" heralded by the rising middle class exemplified moral authority through spirituality and sacrifice. Aguilar wrote that Jewish women strengthened their families just as did Christian women, and, by extension through their families, she implied that Jewish women could strengthen their countries in a manner similar to Christian women. Her American Jewish readers hoped her tactic would bank the fires of American nativism, which occasionally rose against Catholic and Jewish immigrants. In fact, Aguilar's books found their largest reading public in the United States, and her books linked Victorian Jewish culture on both sides of the Atlantic into the twentieth century. She articulated a Jewish theology that merged Victorian values with popular Jewish beliefs.

One of her best read books, *The Women of Israel,* portrayed biblical Hebrew matriarchs as Victorian women faithful to Judaism. Though her book spoke with a Victorian voice to a Victorian audience, its focus on the matriarchs of the Hebrew Bible participated in an old, popular Jewish tradition that clothed the biblical tales in contemporary garb. In the first century C.E., Josephus reshaped the accounts of the matriarchs so that they conformed to Hellenistic feminine ideals and enhanced respect for Jewish men.[10] Rabbinic midrash also reshaped the lives of biblical women to better conform to their authors' understandings of sacred literature.[11] Aguilar knew both Josephus's work[12] and rabbinic lore. Her close reading of a Hebrew-English Bible translation, which included selected rabbinic midrash in the translator's notes, provided the ground for her imaginative discussions of the matriarchs' psychological, emotional, and spiritual lives. These, in turn, provided the bases for Aguilar's own didactic commentaries about the ways in which Judaism speaks to women.[13]

As early as the sixteenth century, Jewish women were using female biblical figures to create original spiritual devotions. Their works, like Aguilar's later, blended sacred texts with Jewish folklore and their own insights to express and legitimize nonbiblical ideas about religion and religious duties. One early example of devotions based on matriarchal tales are the original supplicatory prayers, written in sixteenth-century Europe in Yiddish, which women recited both in private devotions and in the synagogue. A number of these prayers were written by women and were titled "Prayers of the Matriarchs," because they developed their requests for God's protection by alluding to an event in the lives of Sarah, Rebekah, Rachel, or Leah. In contrast to the Hebrew liturgy recited in the synagogue, which asked God to remember the descendants of Abraham, Isaac, and Jacob, Yiddish prayers by women often asked a matriarch to intercede on her children's behalf before God. These prayers remained popular among Jewish women in Yiddish-speaking communities into the early decades of the twentieth century, and women's matriarchal readings shaped their religious experiences.[14]

Aguilar, a traditionally observant Jew who published during the 1830s and 1840s, defended Jewish tradition. In her blend of Victorian and Jewish spirituality she constructed a Jewish memory according to the fundamentally ahistorical traditional Jewish attitude described elsewhere by Yerushalmi.[15] *Women* ignored the millennia between the first century when the Hebrew Bible was closed and the nineteenth century when Aguilar lived and wrote. Its 578 pages focus solely on the stories of Jewish women who lived before the fall of the Second Temple and the dispersion of the Jews by Rome in 70 C.E. Aguilar reminded Jewish women of what she and Judaism considered their special function in the world: maintaining faith in God so that the messiah will come and ordinary "history" (exile, the period since the fall of Jerusalem) will end in the redemption of the world.[16]

A complex book, *Women* addressed the religious and temporal needs of nineteenth-century Jewish women immersed in a Christian society and an increasingly secular culture. It was a guide to the Victorian life-style designed for Jewish women in case the messiah tarried and Jews needed the full civil rights then being debated in England. From 1830 to 1858, English Jews won the right to be freemen of London, to be called to the bar, to vote in Parliamentary elections, and to sit in the House of Commons.[17] At the same time, by identifying nineteenth-century Jewish women with ancient women of Israel, the book offered its Jewish audience a traditional Jewish faith that viewed secular history as ultimately irrelevant to Jewish life. Aguilar provided Jewish women with an image of family devotion linked to religious piety that resonated with Jewish memory, yet she used the same sentimental rhetoric and terms as did contemporary Christian mentor literature for women.

Aguilar frequently and liberally commented on the biblical characters whom she interpreted in her book. Through Eve, Aguilar defined womanhood as a condition needing God. She explained that woman was uniquely created to both feel happiness herself and to make others happy. Merging happiness with spirituality, she wrote, "Woman['s] . . . hol[y] mission . . . is . . . to influence man [so] that her more spiritual and unselfish nature shall gradually be infused into him."[18] Aguilar explained that Eve was Adam's "equal in . . . responsibility towards God and in the care of His creatures; [but] endowed . . . DIFFERENTLY . . . to soothe, bless persuade to right, and help."[19] According to Aguilar, Eve's sin was not in eating from the Tree of Knowledge of Good and Evil, but in neglecting to ask God for the strength to resist temptation. If she had asked God's help, Aguilar wrote, God would have responded to her prayer and Eve would not have succumbed to her inherent weakness. No matter "how weak, faulty, and abased" a woman feels herself to be, Aguilar assured her readers that "nothing can throw a barrier between (her) yearning heart and the healing compassion of her God."[20]

In Sarah's story, Aguilar expanded the Jewish regard for *shalom bayit* (peace at home) to assert that Jewish women prefer domesticity to public life.[21] Aguilar's British audience no doubt appreciated her portrayal of Sarah as an aristocrat, a "gentle woman" for whom the journey from Ur to Haran must have been "a trial." It is "woman's . . . nature to cling to home," she informed her readers.[22] Repeating a tradition from Jewish folklore, Aguilar assured her readers that Sarah taught religion to her servants and neighbors in Haran and that the many "souls" who left Haran with Sarah and Abraham were people whom they had converted.[23] Genesis calls Sarah beautiful, but Aguilar gave her "quiet, retiring dignity."[24] The "beautiful confidence and true affection," which Aguilar said existed between Abraham and Sarah, marked their equality. Josephus's treatment of Sarah emphasized her submissiveness and chastity; in Aguilar's hands, Sarah is a strong, spiritual woman devoted to domestic life. Rabbinic writings on ways to achieve *shalom bayit* emphasized a husband's obligation to satisfy his wife's sexual desires;[25] Aguilar never mentioned sexuality and instead portrayed domesticity as the basis for women's spiritual and psychological satisfactions. A preference for a life bounded by domesticity was central to the Victorian middle-class ideal of womanhood. A domestic focus separated middle-class women from poorer women who participated in the public world of work, and from aristocratic women whose servants freed them from a hands-on concern with domestic responsibilities.

Rhetoric lauding the spiritual pleasures of motherhood was central to literature about true womanhood, and Aguilar urged her readers to be emotionally demonstrative mothers. Youth "CANNOT love . . . unless love, . . . FELT (and) DISPLAYED in confidence and caressing kindness, marks the parental conduct," she wrote.[26] Repeatedly, she remarked that the Bible applauded "natural affections" and discouraged coldness. It is easy to forgive when we don't care, she asserted; it is more important to our spiritual lives to fully love.[27]

In contrast to Josephus, who constructed matriarch's stories so that they enhanced Jewish men, Aguilar looked at the stories of biblical men to enhance women. She interpreted Isaac's personality to prove that Sarah was a loving and devoted mother. Very little is written about Isaac in the Bible. He is born, his life is threatened, he remains at home while a servant travels east to find him a wife, and he is deceived by his son in old age. From this threadbare narrative, Aguilar concluded that his "meek, yielding, affectionate (nature) almost as a woman's disinclined to enterprise—satisfied with his heritage—all prove the influence which his mother had possessed."[28] From Sarah's story, Aguilar also deduced the spiritual lesson that one must not lose faith in God no matter how long it takes for God to fulfill divine promises.

According to Aguilar, God demonstrated concern for maternal feelings by not asking Sarah to sacrifice Isaac.[29] Contrary to the common Christian focus on Sarah's relationship with Hagar and the conclusion that Sarah was mean-spirited, Aguilar expanded on Josephus's interpretation of the tale and wrote that it was impossible for Sarah not to have loved Ishmael, and that it was only her concern for the welfare of the boys, given the inheritance squabble that would, inevitably, arise between them, that prompted her to evict Hagar and Ishmael. Aguilar urged her readers to "think of [Sarah] . . . and our minds will become ennobled and our hearts enlarged."[30]

Aguilar's Rebekah epitomizes steadiness, gentleness, unselfishness, and "proper self-esteem." She told Jewish women that they could "exalt . . . the cause of Israel" by emulating Rebekah's "kindly cordiality" in their relations with non-Jews.[31] In an era of increasing Jewish immigration, Aguilar told Jewish women that Rebekah's life should show them that they ought not "LOOK ABROAD for opportunities [because] . . . we [will] find them without leaving . . . home." Most important for Aguilar, when Rebekah asked God for help, God answered her. "Women . . . [do not need] the mediation of men to bear up our petitions to the throne of grace. . . . We need not Christianity either to . . . direct us how to pray."[32]

Drawing again on folklore, Aguilar wrote that when Rebekah first saw Isaac walking in his fields at dusk, Isaac, who had a pensive mind, was deep in solemn, holy thought.[33] That scene occasioned Aguilar's remark that at evening the "soul of the departed comes back to the spirit of the bereaved . . . confirm[ing] our immortality."[34] Isaac's presumed thoughts prompted Aguilar to assure mourners that they will "meet again those whom [they] love" in Heaven. But, she added, it is the "invisible soul" that we really love, not the "mortal habitation of that soul." She assumed the immateriality of the soul and told women that their love for people, not only for God, had a spiritual foundation.

Aguilar's portrayal of Leah continued her overall theme of the spiritual nature of Israel's women. Aguilar broke with the traditional translation of the Hebrew *rakot* as "weak" and the conclusion that Leah's eyes were weak. She insisted that *rakot* also means "soft and delicate." For Aguilar, Leah's soft and delicate eyes were her "only good feature." Knowing that her audience would infer that eyes are windows to the soul, she described Leah's soft and delicate eyes, which, in Victorian terms, meant an especially spiritual disposition.[35] When God gave Leah three sons because she was not loved, Aguilar explained, God proved divine concern for women's innermost feelings. Leah must have had some "vague yet true notions" of God before she met Jacob because early in the story Leah thanked God for her children. Thus, Leah, the unloved wife, was proved by Aguilar to have been happier than her favored sister, who said to her husband "give me children else I die!" To Aguilar, Leah's message was that women can find happiness in their relationship with God and need not depend on men for joy.

Compared to Leah, Aguilar found Rachel uninteresting. Rachel must have had many endearing qualities, she wrote, although the Bible only mentions her beauty. To Aguilar, beauty was not "sufficient to retain" love, and Rachel must have had a loving spirit because Jacob stayed devoted to her for many years.

The spiritual qualities of Sarah, Rebekah, and Leah were those that Victorian Jewish women were supposed to develop. But it was while discussing Jochebed, Moses' mother, that Aguilar gave detailed advice about the spiritual significance of Jewish motherhood. Jochebed's story led directly into Aguilar's discussion of the ways the Pentateuch's laws regarding women displayed respect and concern for their spiritual, emotional, and physical welfare.

Just as she found evidence for Sarah's personality in Isaac's story, so Aguilar found in the "peculiar, much forgiving character of [Moses] the molding of (Jochebed's) hand."[36] Through prayer, Jochebed found "grace and strength" to trust in God, overcame the Egyptian threats to kill male newborns, and saved her son. Aguilar explained that even in "free and happy England" Jewish women are still in "bondage" and must overcome Christians who warn Jews to be baptized in order to escape oppression. Jewish mothers should be like Jochebed and influence their "sons" to be faithful to God.[37]

Aguilar defended the Pentateuch's laws regarding women by asserting that "every . . . nation who [acknowledges] the Bible owe[s] the elevation . . . dignity . . . [and] holiness of woman" to Judaism. "God . . . proclaimed [motherhood] sacred."[38] Wives, daughters, widows, and maid-servants too are cared for by divine law, she explained. The Hebrew Bible, she asserted, limited polygamy and portrayed monogamy based on love as the ideal, allowed women to choose their husbands, allowed fathers to annul the vows of impetuous and immature daughters, allowed daughters to inherit from their father's estate, and prohibited mistreatment of widows and female servants. Moreover, the laws requiring both male and female obedience regarding forbidden food, rejoicing at festivals, and morality, indicate that women too were depended on to "uphold and make manifest the glory of their God."[39]

Women of Israel was reissued twenty-seven times, twenty-two times in New York and five times in Aguilar's native London. American Jewish women read Aguilar's work avidly and named literary clubs and libraries after her.[40] Some women writers even copied her literary style. Aguilar's books were reviewed by leading American Jewish men, one of whom said that she proved the "truth of her assumptions from biblical evidence," and that anyone who read the Bible could see that it taught "perfect spiritual equality between man and woman."[41]

Aguilar's literary ability made her didactic arguments for fidelity to Judaism enjoyable for a growing American Jewish reading public comprised of men and women with little or no formal education in Judaism. Her presentation of good Jewish-Protestant relationships, especially in the introduction to her book *The Jewish Faith,* and her optimism over increasing Jewish equality in predominantly Christian societies matched the hopes and, in some cases, the experiences of English and American Jews. For American Jews who confronted attempts to Christianize America, Aguilar's books offered hope and guidance for improving Jewish-Christian relations.[42] Finally, by centering her books in the experience of women, she encouraged her female Jewish audience to teach and defend Judaism.

As the nineteenth-century's cult of true womanhood captured the imagination of America's rising bourgeoisie, her work became more important to American Jewish women who found themselves measured by that Victorian cultural standard.

Rebekah Gumpert Hyneman (1812–75) of Philadelphia, Pennsylvania, was one of the first American literary woman to be obviously influenced by Aguilar. Hyneman's poetry was first published in the 1840s in *The Occident and American Jewish Advocate*, an antebellum journal based in Philadelphia and distributed throughout the United States. Hyneman's poetry also was published in the *American Israelite*, a newspaper founded in mid-century and published in Cincinnati by Isaac M. Wise, the leader of Reform Judaism. Her poetry series "Female Scriptural Characters" constructed imaginative inner worlds for the matriarchs and other leading biblical women.[43] Hyneman's short poem "Sarah," published in 1855, depicted Sarah as a queen with a "royal robe" and a crown. Hyneman portrayed Rebekah as an ideal nineteenth-century woman: she was virginal, modest, faithful, humble, loving, and a ministering angel who brought peace and joy to Isaac's home. Although Jewish folklore asserts that Sarah is the only woman to whom God spoke directly, Hyneman said that God spoke also to Rebekah[44] and inferred that Rebekah should be considered a prophet. Folklore limited Rebekah's prophecy to knowledge about the number of children she would bear.[45] Hyneman suggested that Rebekah could foresee all of future Jewish history. By enlarging Rebekah's prophetic abilities, Hyneman invited her women readers to consider the idea that they too may be important in the future history of the Jews.[46] Hyneman's "Rebekah" refuted evangelists' assertions that Judaism's patriarchy excluded women.

Turn-of-the-century American Jewish women continued to create and claim a special spirituality. Like earlier Jewish women, they used the matriarchal tales to express their ideas and to lend their work biblical authority. In 1896, a poem called "At Haran's Well" appeared in a new glossy magazine called the *American Jewess*. In the poem, six pages of verse retold Genesis, chapter 24, in which Rebekah becomes Isaac's wife. The author, Ida Elizabeth Skinner, reflected the growing empiricism and naturalism in late nineteenth-century American literature. Taking Rebekah's spirituality for granted, Skinner embellished the details of Rebekah's biblical setting. She described a hot, dusty Syrian desert, with "bleaching bones of animals and human skeletons," which emphasized the importance of Rebekah's offer to water Eliezer's camels. Skinner's Rebekah was a virgin with "darkly brilliant eyes . . . olive skin . . . [a] wavy mass of hair but half-concealed—Beneath a head-dress of spotless white, . . . a . . . pure . . . and serene (spirit)." Skinner inserted the covenant between Abraham and God into her narrative and repeated Aguilar's account that Rebekah's gifts from Eliezer were an earring and bracelets, rather than a nose ring and arm bands. She too assured her readers that Rebekah was an aristocrat, an idea made familiar to American Jewish readers by Aguilar, Hyneman, and Jewish folklore.[47]

Beginning after the Civil War and increasingly after World War I, a new construction of female sexuality supplanted the spiritual self-denial deemed pleasurable by American Victorian women since the antebellum era.[48] The collapse of Victorian culture in England and America after World War I coincided with the rise to prominence of first- and second-generation East European Jews who entered England and America during the last two decades of the nineteenth and the first two decades of the twentieth centuries. East European immigrants resisted the cultural style of more established Jews who had adopted Aguilar's Jewish true womanhood.[49] When Victorian culture died, Aguilar was forgotten.[50]

Although late twentieth-century Jewish women often ground their spirituality in female physicality rather than in Victorian self-denial, they continue, like Aguilar and the sixteenth-century writers of supplicatory prayers, to use the matriarchs for an authoritative and legitimizing frame. Their original spiritual writings articulate changes and continuities in Jewish and female self-understandings. For example, Ellen Umansky and Savina Teubal, two Jewish feminist writers working today have expanded on Sarah's character. Teubal's recent book compares literatures and archaeology of the ancient Near East and argues that Sarah was not a princess but a priestess.[51] Umansky's midrash on Sarah's response to the binding of Isaac legitimates her own commitment to construct a Jewish feminist theology.[52]

By drawing on sacred literature, today as in the past, Jewish women claim legitimacy for their own spirituality. Historically, insights framed in sacred terms and phrases have identified contemporary Jewish women with ancient founders of Jewish existence. By blurring the distinction between the ancient and the contemporary, radical change is undercut, tradition is carried forward, and a sense of eternal truth is brought to women's own original writings.[53]

The existence of Jewish women's own distinctive interpretations of matriarchal narratives implies that Jewish women may have been freer to express innovative and unusual ideas because they were not indoctrinated in Judaism through the mastery of authoritative texts, as was the case with Jewish men. Because Jewish women, like Aguilar, were able to find their own personal meanings in biblical narratives, they were free to creatively resolve some of the tensions between Christian, secular, and Jewish worldviews. When women expressed their personal spirituality in writing, their ideas often circulated among the general community, which sometimes accepted them. Their work offered Jews greater subtlety and depth in developing individual understandings of Judaism. Jewish women's biblical interpretations point out one way Jewish spiritual life has adapted to modern society.

The record of Jewish women's spirituality also enlarges our understanding of how Judaism functioned in the lives of non-elite Jews. By eliding the distance between their contemporary world and the biblical world, Jewish women read themselves into authoritative texts. The conflicts in meaning between the ancient and contemporary worlds were mitigated by their own lives. In a sense, Jewish women themselves became mythic characters, and their identity as such requires their active commitment to a religious life. The social construction of their religious identities required that they themselves embody a resolution to conflicts in meaning and order posed by Jewish immersion in Christian society and in secular culture. The matriarchal theme in Jewish women's spirituality maintained Jewish women's collective identity while creating a "hybrid" in an inventive process.[54] Jewish women shaped, expressed, and conveyed their own spirituality while, at the same time, reaffirming a distinctly Jewish meaning system. Sometimes, as we have seen in the case of Grace Aguilar, Jewish women wrote expressions of their own spirituality, which they hoped would influence, on social and political levels, an uncertain Jewish future. Over centuries of change, theirs has been an effective tactic for establishing the spiritual legitimacy of Jewish women on both the social and religious stages.

NOTES

1. Ellen M. Umansky and Dianne Ashton, eds., *Four Centuries of Jewish Women's Spirituality: A Sourcebook* (Boston: Beacon Press, 1992).

2. On the cultural impact of nineteenth-century Christian revival movements see Marion Bell, *Crusade in the City: Revivalism in Nineteenth-Century Philadelphia* (Lewisburg, Pa.: Bucknell University Press, 1977); Barbara Welter, *Dimity Convictions: The Rise of American Women in the Nineteenth Century* (Athens: Ohio University Press, 1976); George L. Berlin, *Defending the Faith* (Albany: State University of New York Press, 1989).

3. Louise Mannheimer, *Proceedings of the Jewish Women's Congress* (Philadelphia: Jewish Publication Society, 1894). This manner of Bible study is a variant of a traditional Jewish method of exegesis, the midrash.

4. See especially: Ann Douglas, *The Feminization of American Culture* (New York: Avon, 1977); Colleen McDannell, *The Christian Home in Victorian America* (Bloomington: Indiana University Press, 1987); Barbara Welter, "The Feminization of American Religion," in *Dimity Convictions*, pp. 83–102.

5. Lynda Nead, *Myths of Sexuality* (Oxford: Basil Blackwell, 1988), pp. 12–47.

6. Aguilar remarked that her work was correcting work by "Mrs. Ellis, Sandford, and Hamilton" (*The Women of Israel* [London: George Routledge and Sons, 1845], p. 10), who collectively wrote ten advice books for women that linked Christian piety to national patriotism and good manners.

7. Aguilar wrote, "Eve walked . . . secure in her innocence. . . . the young animals gamboling about her, calling forth her caresses and her smile, the little birds springing from tree to tree in joyous greeting. . . . so may our fancy imagine her" (*Women of Israel*, p. 24).

8. Aguilar dedicated her book *Home Influence* (London: George Routledge and Sons, 1840) to a Mrs. Herbert Townshend Bowen, whom she described as an "earnest Protestant" and a friend.

9. Aguilar, *Women of Israel*, p. 10. Aguilar wrote, "(Authors Sandford, Ellis, and Hamilton) . . . believe that to Christianity alone they owe their present station in the world, their influence, their equality with man, their spiritual provision in this life, and hopes of immortality in the next. . . . We cannot pass such assertion unanswered, lest . . . daughters of Israel may believe it." See also Linda Gordon Kuzmack, *Woman's Cause: The Jewish Woman's Movement in England and the United States, 1881–1933* (Columbus: Ohio State University Press, 1990), pp. 15–17.

10. Betsy Halpern-Amaru, "Portraits of Biblical Women in Josephus' Antiquities," *Journal of Jewish Studies* 39, no. 2 (1988): 148.

11. Louis Ginzberg, *Legends of the Jews* (Philadelphia: Jewish Publi-

cation Society, 1961). For rabbinic views of men and women, see also Judith R. Baskin, "Silent Partners," in this volume.

12. Philip Weinberger, "The Social and Religious Thought of Grace Aguilar" (Ph.D. diss., New York University, 1970), p. 26.

13. David Aaron de Sola, M. J. Raphall, and I. J. Levi, *The Sacred Scriptures, Hebrew and English* (London: n.p., 1844).

14. Chava Weissler, "Tkhines: Yiddish Supplicatory Prayers," in Umansky and Ashton, eds., *Jewish Women's Spirituality*, and "Images of the Matriarchs in Yiddish Supplicatory Prayers," *Bulletin of the Center for the Study of World Religions* (Harvard University), 14, no. 1 (1988): 44–51.

15. Yosef Yerushalmi, *Zakhor* (New York: Schocken Books, 1989), pp. 27–53. A similar point is made by Emil Fackenheim in *Jewish Return into History: Reflections in the Age of Auschwitz and a New Jerusalem* (New York: Schocken Books, 1978).

16. Aguilar, *Women of Israel*, pp. 13–14, 522–24.

17. Todd Endelman, *Radical Assimilation in English Jewish History 1656–1945* (Bloomington: Indiana University Press, 1990).

18. Aguilar, *Women of Israel*, p. 20.

19. Ibid., p. 22.

20. Ibid., p. 13.

21. David Feldman, *Marital Relations, Birth Control, and Abortion in Jewish Law* (New York: Schocken Books, 1974), p. 43.

22. Aguilar, *Women of Israel*, p. 45. Sarah's aristocracy was established in rabbinic midrash discussing her changed name from Sarai (my Lady or my princess) to Sarah (lady or princess) (Gen. 17:15; Aguilar, *Women of Israel*, p. 59).

23. Aguilar, *Women of Israel*, p. 203; Ginzberg, *Legends of the Jews*, vol. 1, p. 203, and vol. 5, notes 42–44.

24. Aguilar, *Women of Israel*, p. 57; Gen. 12:11.

25. Feldman, *Marital Relations*, pp. 8–97; Monford Harris, "Touch, Sight and Hearing in Jewish Sexuality," *Judaism* 33, no. 3 (1984): 346–52.

26. Aguilar, *Women of Israel*, p. 244.

27. Ibid., p. 61.

28. Ibid., pp. 65–66.

29. Ibid., p. 71.

30. Ibid., pp. 67, 74; Ginzberg, *Legends of the Jews*, vol. 1, p. 264, and vol. 5, note 211; Josephus, *Antiquities*, 1:12.3.

31. Aguilar, *Women of Israel*, p. 87.

32. Ibid., p. 85.

33. Ibid., p. 297.

34. Ibid., p. 82.

35. Ibid., p. 108. Cf. Ginzberg, *Legends of the Jews*, vol. 1, p. 359:

Leah's eyes grew weak as a result of her incessant weeping caused by rumors about her future husband's bad character.

36. Aguilar, *Women of Israel,* p. 139.

37. Ibid., p. 140.

38. Ibid., p. 153.

39. Ibid., pp. 176–77.

40. Naomi Cohen, *Encounter with Emancipation* (Philadelphia: Jewish Publication Society, 1984), p. 334.

41. S. Solis, "Remarks on Miss Aguilar's *Women of Israel,*" *Occident and American Jewish Advocate* 4 (1846): 81.

42. Jon Butler, *Awash in a Sea of Faith: Christianizing the American People* (Cambridge: Harvard University Press, 1990), pp. 225–57.

43. Rebekah Gumpert Hyneman, "Female Scriptural Characters," *Occident and American Jewish Advocate,* no. 4 (1846): I. "Sarah," p. 168[186–87]; no. 4 (1846): II. "Rebekah," p. 246[241]; no. 6 (1846): III. "Leah" and "Rachel," pp. 286–88; no. 7 (1846): IV. "Miriam," p. 330; no. 9 (1846): V. "Ruth" and "Naomi," p. 429[431]; no. 12 (1846): VI. "Esther," p. 585[587].

44. Hyneman, "Rebekah" (1846) 241.

45. Ibid.; Ginsberg, *Legends of the Jews,* vol. 1, 78.

46. Rebekah Gumpert Hyneman, "Sarah," *American Israelite* 1, no. 28 (1855): 222; (1846): 241; Jacob R. Marcus, *The American Jewish Woman: A Documentary History* (New York: Ktav, 1981), pp. 183–85.

47. Ida Elizabeth Skinner, "At Haran's Well," *American Jewess* 2, no. 10 (1896): 580–55.

48. Sheila Jeffreys, *The Spinster and Her Enemies* (London: Pandora, 1888); Lee Chambers-Schiller, *Liberty: A Better Husband: Single Women in America: The Generations of 1780–1840* (New Haven: Yale University Press, 1984).

49. Kuzmack, *Woman's Cause,* p. 10; Susan Glenn, *Daughters of the Shtetl: Life and Labor in the Immigrant Generation* (Ithaca: Cornell University Press, 1990), pp. 176–77; Elizabeth Ewen, *Immigrant Women in the Land of Dollars: Life and Culture on the Lower East Side, 1890–1925* (New York: New Feminist Press, 1985), pp. 96–97, 138–39.

50. Aguilar's novel about Jews in Spain, *The Vale of Cedars,* was translated into Yiddish in 1888 and into Hebrew in 1893, both in Russia. Her treatise on motherhood, *A Mother's Recompense,* was translated into German in 1859 and 1893, both in Leipzig.

51. Savina Teubal, *Sarah the Priestess: The First Matriarch of Genesis* (Athens, Ohio: Swallow Press, 1984).

52. Ellen Umansky, "Creating a Jewish Feminist Theology: Possibilities and Problems," *Anima* 10, no. 2 (1988): 133–34. Note Ginzberg, *Leg-*

ends of the Jew, vol. 1, pp. 286–87, regarding a midrash that Sarah's death was caused by her grief at learning that Abraham had gone to sacrifice Isaac (vol. 5, note 256).

53. Michael Meyer notes that this tactic was also used by the Jewish Reform movement and differentiates reform from revolutionary movements in general (*Response to Modernity* [New York: Oxford University Press, 1988], p. 3).

54. James Clifford, *The Predicament of Culture* (Cambridge: Harvard University Press, 1988), pp. 11–14.

· 5 ·

Testimony, Narrative, and Nightmare: The Experiences of Jewish Women in the Holocaust

MYRNA GOLDENBERG

Through numerous sources—recently uncovered archive files, recovered diaries and journals, oral histories, testimonies, autobiographies, biographies, and autobiographical novels—Holocaust victims and survivors have told and are telling their stories. The twelve years that comprise the Holocaust, from 1933 to 1945, left a legacy of millions of victims, each with an individual story of Nazi cruelty. These sources yield the details that tend to be lost in encyclopedic general histories of the era.

From thousands of volumes of books and hundreds of hours of audio and video tapes, we know that the Nazi imagination was fueled by a fusion of unrestrained racism, patriarchy, and misogyny. Although some scholars and survivors have claimed that it is divisive to differentiate victims by gender, Hitler's frequently repeated statement "The Nazi Revolution will be an entirely male event" betrays his goal of male Aryan supremacy.[1] It is especially important, then, that recently a small number of scholars have devoted their energies to studying gender differences in the behavior of Holocaust victims.[2]

In 1934, Hitler enunciated the link between feminism and Jews, first by denouncing the New Woman as the "invention of Jewish intellectuals" and then by exhorting German women to reject the unnatural "overlapping of the spheres of activity of the sexes as embodied in "Jewish intellectualism."[3] In spite of their (apparent) threat to the German ideal of womanhood in the eyes of the Nazis, Jewish women were virtually anonymous and invisible in their suffering and death during the Holocaust. But their life-stories, as told by witnesses or perpetrators or by themselves, allow us to observe the strength and courage of Jewish women who were victims of Nazism but who also were, at the same time, active agents of their own survival. In this chapter I am especially interested in women's own accounts of their Holocaust experiences.

A reading of testimony, personal narrative, or survivor memoirs leads us to conclude that Jewish women *used* their normal skills and activities as coping strategies in the abnormal world of the concentration camp. Women who had been raised to perform routine household and family chores used those experiences in a concentration camp setting where, if they did not fall victim to the ubiquitous random brutality and murder, these same skills—the so-called female skills—helped them survive. Moreover, Jewish women's narratives reflect an awareness of the value of nurturing skills and the ability to connect as characteristics that were part of the routine socialization process for European women. Women and girls found that this socialization, which also included sewing and food preparation techniques, provided avenues for survival that were not usually available to men and boys. Males had far less experience in settings in which "female skills" were meaningful, or, in fact, customary. The "cliché of feminine passivity" does not, therefore, hold true for female Holocaust victims who were able to transfer familiar domestic values to a setting designed to accomplish mechanized mass murder and who, as actively as possible under the circumstances, managed to survive and to help each other to survive.[4]

Treatment of Women

Very recently uncovered testimony prepared as trial evidence in 1945 and 1946, and never used, provides new and valuable information about women's lives in concentration camps and about the severity of treatment suffered by Jewish women. Deliberate cruelty and violence in all forms dominate this material.[5]

Several sources comment on the severity of treatment reserved solely for Jewish women. In her testimony, a former Ravensbrueck prisoner recalls, "Jewish women were thrown out of the dispensary. . . . The cries and the moaning of the tortured was terrible. The Jewish women had a specially hard time of it."[6] Until the recent focus on gender, literary analyses have been peculiarly insensitive to the extent of Nazi misogyny.

Physical and emotional stamina characterize much of women's testimony. Among the survivors of Dachau were four women from Rhodes who provided an astonishing record of their imprisonment, deportation, and survival. They begin their testimony, published as an article, "The Odyssey of the Women from Rhodes," with the Nazi deportation of the Jews.[7] The women explain that on July 20, 1944, all the Jewish males were arrested. Within hours, the women and children were also arrested. All seventeen hundred[8] men and women were locked up without food or water and soon afterward shipped out to Athens. Ordered to keep their "heads lowered . . . and on no account allowed to look up [because] anybody who dared to do so would be executed on the spot," these Jews were "locked in the coal storage room[s] of the ship[s]" for ten days. In Piraeus, just south of Athens, the women were "forced to strip in front of the SS men" and a "body search was conducted." One survivor recalls that SS beat men with sticks and pulled women by the hair. Reluctant women were "pulled by the breasts."[9] In the notorious Athenian prison, the men and women were separated and locked into barracks again. The Nazis (identified throughout this testimony as SS) beat the Jews incessantly with clubs and leather belts and, these four women explained, whipped even the women and children in the face. Younger women were taunted to be "nice" to the SS in return for favors.

The deportees were fed by the Red Cross in Athens, where they were imprisoned for another three days before boarding cattle cars— seventy or eighty to a car—for Auschwitz. After a fifteen-day trip, on August 17, they were once again separated by sex and "selected." Again, the women were forced to undress in front of the SS, and "completely naked . . . were led into a different room, where female barbers shaved their entire body." They were "disinfected with a rag soaked in kerosene, which heavily irritated the freshly shaved skin." Finally, each was issued a "ragged dress without any regard paid to length or size." Beaten by gypsy prisoners if they asked to exchange their dresses for better fitting garments, they soon understood that the one rag they wore was their dress, underwear, towel, and handkerchief. Testimony from another survivor reveals that after they were shaved, the women from Rhodes found SS men holding bellows and "shouting at us to bend over and pushed the nose of the bellows into our anuses and vaginas to disinfect us."[10]

During the two and one half months at Auschwitz, the women from Rhodes endured daily roll call in a kneeling position for hours. Their daily ration of food consisted of a liter of soup for five women and some so-called coffee. They believed that chemicals had been added to the soup to prevent menstruation. More likely, lack of nourishment led to amenorrhea. These four women describe some of the more common ailments, such as "swellings and patches" all over their bodies and "actual holes in their mouths and deep cracks on the tongues." They note that many women died of starvation and dysentery and further that they were shaved and disinfected one more time because they were "full of lice." In November, they were prepared to be moved west, to Germany, by standing "barefoot and without coats in snow and ice" in below zero temperature. "In this way," the four survivors tell us, the SS doctor in charge of their "pilgrimage" was able to select the strongest women: "If they turned pale and passed out they were put on the transfer list." For the next few months, they were shipped from one labor camp to another, often doing outside work that necessitated fourteen-hour stretches of marches (from eight to eighteen kilometers to and from the work sites) and hard labor, often clearing rubble. In one camp, they slept in filthy, vacated dog kennels. "Nevertheless," they report, "the women managed to stay more or less clean and free of lice by trading their bread for soap from the men. This is why the men looked bedraggled and full of lice," according to the women. Old habits of responsibility for hygiene were stronger than the satiation of hunger.

The threat of advancing American troops shortened their incarceration in a "really terrible camp" where they "received absolutely nothing to eat through the entire work-filled day." As the Germans retreated west, they set the vacated camps afire to eliminate any evidence of the brutalities that occurred there. These women's "odyssey" concludes with the description of a harrowing train transport in open freight cars. Halted next to a munitions dump, they were "bombed and shot at several times," suffered many casualties, and, during one night, fled the train because the SS set it on fire, "both to prevent it from falling into the hands of the approaching troops, and to exterminate the deportees." From the meadows and woods where they hid, they "heard the noise of an explosion: the munitions train had blown up." They saw the "brilliantly lit sky above Landsberg, which was on fire because of the air raids." In the chaos that followed, the road and tracks were strewn with dead bodies. Attempting to escape, many women deportees walked directly into German fire or were crushed by the train, which was "set in motion again. The "few surviving women reached Dachau on 28 April, 1945," one day before American troops liberated the camp.[11]

One can hardly overestimate the importance of the testimony of these four women survivors. Describing the experience of one specific group, their narrative includes most of the issues and experiences raised separately, in one place or another, in all women survivor narratives: sadistic violence, separation of family, fear of rape, sexual abuse, amenorrhea and fear of sterility, nakedness, humiliation, vile filth, incredible deprivations, starvation, forced labor, and resistance. Their "odyssey" is typical of individual survivor testimony—largely understated reports or summaries of unimaginable cruelties. While each oral history or testimony discloses a unique nightmarish experience, the accumulated documents present a clear outline of the deportation and concentration camp experience.

Women's identity as caregivers and homemakers and their prior experience in the domestic sphere ironically enhanced their likelihood of acclimatizing themselves to the hellish environment into which they were thrown. Men, on the other hand, whether they had been laborers or scholars, were deprived of their work by Nazi deportation policies and practices. That Jewish men had dominated Jewish women through their positions in the workforce, the synagogue study groups, the shops, and the professions contributed to their perceptions of victimization in concentration camps. Denied their usual duties and thrust into faceless, humiliating slave labor, they had fewer skills, habits, and experiences with which to sustain themselves than women did. Moreover, the nature of childrearing and housekeeping, which was the major preoccupation of the vast majority of Jewish women in the thirties and early forties, demanded more flexibility and resiliency than did men's usual activities. For mothers, infants' and children's needs take primacy, and the chores of food and holiday preparations were tucked in and around the more essential needs of children and the adult men of the household. To be sure, women learned patience and self-control in their role as caretakers. Thus, it is not surprising to read one survivor's reaction to the observation that "most men had to learn behaviors that women already knew." She wrote that men, "unable to control themselves, . . . display such a lack of moral fibre that one cannot but be sorry for them . . . their behavior here is merely a natural continuation of their past."[12]

Sybil Milton investigated the treatment of German and German-Jewish women who were persecuted for "religious, racial, or political reasons," distinguishing between the verbal abuse Jewish women received in the thirties and the physical violence they suffered from 1939 to 1945. She cites Nazi documents recognizing their own underestimation of the strength of the empowerment women give one another. She quotes a 1939 letter from the first director of Ravensbrueck that reveals the need to revise the plans for the camp so that the spirit of their women prisoners could be broken:

> We will soon move into the new women's camp at Ravensbrueck, where I have established the fact that detention cells have neither been built nor planned. Women have been placed in solitary confinement by Gestapo orders in the Lichtenburg camp. It is impossible to maintain order if the defiance and stubbornness of these hysterical females cannot be broken by strict confinement, since no more severe punishment can be used in a women's camp. Denial of food does not suffice for discipline and order in a women's camp.[13]

The implication here is that women resisted the hardships and degradation of the camps and forced the Nazis to rethink policy in the women's camps.

Further evidence of women's resiliency during the Holocaust comes from literary accounts of life in hiding or in concentration camps. Written years, sometimes decades, after the Holocaust, these autobiographical accounts are thoughtful—often well-written and artistic—reflections of experiences that have no literary antecedents. They have the curious advantage of distance and detachment mixed with unforgettable vignettes of pain and loss. Usually devoid of bitterness, they focus on details that still hurt, scenes that remain, as more than one survivor has said, on the "insides of my eyelids." They are public expressions of private nightmares; a survivor's attempts to reclaim her right to normal society.

They also disclose the unanticipated effects of gender that, for decades, were ignored or denied, or, at the very least, went unnoticed. A preponderance of these works reinforce the hypothesis that Jewish women who survived believed they owe much of their survival to their socialization as caregivers. In the broadest sense, these narratives indicate that gender accounted for differences in "adjustment" to the concentration camp experience and ultimately in survival. That is, the women who were not the targets of random or premeditated capricious murder often credit their survival to their prewar experiences. Essentially, women, accustomed to maintaining the family, transferred their behavior to the concentration camp where, in the absence of normal and natural family structures, they created and strove to maintain surrogate families. In other words, many female survivors believe that their training and experiences as traditional housekeepers and family care-givers contributed to their survival.

Most survivor narratives begin in the mid- or late thirties with a sketch of predeportation times but with the specter of the Nazis looming in the background. The Nazis take over and strip the Jews of their rights as citizens or residents, confiscate their goods, establish ghettos run by puppet governing bodies (Jewish Councils of Elders), limit the ghetto residents to a starvation diet, and organize mass murders and later deportations to labor, concentration, or extermination camps. The narratives describe evacuation of the camps in the face of the advancing armies, liberation, and emigration or the promise of emigration. Less frequently, the survivor-writers begin their narratives in the concentration camps and recall their days of freedom.

Female survivor-writers focus on the affection and security the family shared before the Nazi victory. In fact, precious family photographs taken before the Nazi era are often included in the narratives. The women survivor-writers also discuss violence, filthy, vicious guards (particularly female guards), lice, typhus, and dysentery. What distinguishes their works from those by men and from depositions and evidentiary testimony are the deep, unhealed wounds left by their experiences of nakedness, degradation, hunger and starvation, and sexuality (and occasionally childbirth). Almost all these works implicitly or explicitly focus on sisterhood as the sustaining balm of their Holocaust years.

Two authors in particular describe their arrival at Auschwitz in cinematic detail. Sara Nomberg-Przytyk relates the effect of unexpected violence and degradation. After days on a crowded, filthy transport with little or no food, water, or sleep, a vulnerable new arrival was "so surprised that she would not even shield her face [from repeated blows] and would look around innocently and ask: 'Why are you hitting me? I am a human being.'" Standing naked for inspection by the SS, women *zugani* (new arrivals) were herded before barbers, accompanied by blows and kicks, "in silence with tears streaming down [their] cheeks," as they were required to spread their legs and be shaved. Without their hair and clothes, feeling thoroughly humiliated and victimized, they were initiated into the hell-hole of the world. She later relates that she imagined "thousands of fingers . . . pointing" at her, saying, "Here is a victim you can hit; you can pour your anger out on her and she will not protest, not even if you perform unusual acts of torture on her. If she can't take it, that's even better."[14]

Livia Bitton Jackson, fifteen years old when she was deported to Auschwitz, is slapped and slashed by the whip of an SS guard before she begins to understand that she has to undress in front of all the deportees and the guards. Her humiliation is heightened by her age and the natural shyness of adolescent girls:

> I stare directly ahead as I take off my clothes. I am afraid. By not looking at anyone I hope no one will see me . . . I hesitate before removing my bra. My breasts are two growing buds, taut and sensitive. I can't have anyone see them. I decide to leave my bra on.
>
> Just then a shot rings out. The charge is ear-shattering. Some women begin to scream. Others weep. I quickly take my bra off.

Shorn of clothing and hair, Jackson's nakedness is ironically protective: "A burden was lifted. The burden of individuality. Of associations. Of identity. Of the recent past." She and thousands of other girls and women have "become members of an exclusive club. Inmates of Auschwitz."[15]

Thoughts related to sexuality (humiliation through nakedness, amenorrhea, fear of rape, fear of sterility, pregnancy, and childbirth) were important focal points in women's minds and conversations.

Isabella Leitner opens her book with three paragraphs that set the stage for her imprisonment in Auschwitz. Writing in 1945, in New York, she is incredulous that only one year earlier she had been deported to Auschwitz. Among the details that identify her as a female narrator is the statement that she had not "menstruated for a long time." Thus, in one understated, almost casual line, she introduces the possibility of planned sterility and eventual annihilation of her people. She reinforces the Nazi attempt to reverse nature in a ghoulish chapter on the birth of a baby in the Auschwitz barracks.[16]

Gerda Klein is haunted by a recurring dream—"the thought of a baby, warm, new, clean as freedom itself. How wonderful it would be to have my own baby!" But amenorrhea and the fear of forced sterilization fill her with "unspeakable horror" that does not seem to affect her barrackmates. She feels alone in her despair and decides, "I must have a baby of my own. I felt that I would endure anything so long as that hope was not extinguished."[17]

In virtually all the witness literature by women, we read about women caring for other women, women who "adopt" a surrogate sister or aunt or mother, women who worked at keeping one another alive. Leitner says simply, "If you are sisterless, you do not have the pressure, the absolute responsibility to end the day alive." The expectation to stay alive because others expect you to was, for her, an "awsome" burden: "Does staying alive not only for yourself, but also because someone else expects you to, double the life force?"[18] Frances Penney writes that the women in her barrack "had to drag the debilitated Roza [a sister prisoner brutally beaten by the SS] down to the courtyard, for roll call. Since she was unable to stand on her feet, we supported her and propped her up, so that her weakness would not be noticed by the German Commandant."[19]

Penney's story is not unique or even unusual. Nomberg-Przytyk tells of similar incidents—of bonding among Jews and political prisoners and of daily risks they took to manipulate the camp bureaucracy to help a friend. Autobiographical stories by women physicians and nurses assigned to camp "infirmaries" (actually, barracks to isolate sick prisoners in the process of dying) are replete with scenes of women stealing food into the infirmary to help a friend or relative improve.[20]

Hunger was the single common deprivation of all Jewish concentration camp prisoners, but witness literature reveals that there were differences in the way males and females responded to the lack of food. Men apparently fantasized about splendid meals while women, in addition to imagining plentiful meals, traded recipes and spoke about the ways they "stretched" food to feed their families. Thus, men wrote only as deprived consumers and women, more often than not, as creative cooks.[21]

In *All but My Life*, Gerda Klein talks about the chaos in the labor camps toward the end of the war. Prisoners were marched west, toward Auschwitz, locked in barns and empty barracks during the nights. Conditions were disgusting and "food was meager. Hungry and without anything to do, the girls began to speak of food, exchanging recipes for the richest pastries."[22] "After the war" talk in Ilona Karmel's autobiographical novel *Estate of Memory* centered on food—feasts of "cakes, bowls of broth or fruit"—and fashion and vacations.[23]

Judith Isaacson and her bunkmates exchanged recipes on the Sabbath, at their menorah-less Hanukkah celebration, and on their transports from Auschwitz to labor camps: "Mostly we sang or exchanged recipes. I recall a lengthy discussion about *retes*, the incredible flaky Hungarian strudel. Marcsa liked it filled with peppered fried cabbage, but the rest of us preferred it sweet, with apples, sour cherries, or creamed cottage cheese." Just before liberation, as slaves in a munitions factory, she and the other girls tried to distract one another from their misery: "We were so hungry that [for amusement we used] to tell each other what kind of soups and meats and vegetables and cakes our mothers used to make. Nobody of us knows exactly how to make, but we found out and explained very seriously."[24] Gerda Haas and her Theresienstadt friend and bunkmate tried to forget their hunger by "describing to each other our favorite foods, right down to their remembered smells. We'd rub our stomachs while imaginary feasts rose before us . . . and we'd laugh at our cleverness: Wasn't it indeed gastronomic masturbation, this futile exercise?"[25]

Conclusion

The lives and deaths of Jewish women during the Holocaust are, in fact, the most striking embodiment of women's potential for violence, for nurturing, and for indifference. There are stories of cruelties—incredible cruelties and unimaginable barbarities that exceed fictional accounts of atrocities and sadism, but there are also many stories of caring and sisterhood. The women [re]construct themselves in documents and narratives as strong nurturers capable of outliving and outperforming men in the most difficult of circumstances. The experiences of Jewish women during the Holocaust must therefore be examined not only as a valuable part of the historical record of extraordinary and heinous human indifference, a "metaphysical evil,"[26] or the cataclysmic event of the twentieth century, but also as equally extraordinary examples of human love and selflessness,[27] as memories that valorize the "female" experience of nurturing and connectedness. Like Ashton's Grace Aguilar and Schely-Newman's Jula as well as other women in this volume, women who directly endured the horrors of the Holocaust represented their experience in their own words, and in their own image.

NOTES

I wish to thank Robert Kesting, U.S. National Archives, for his guidance and assistance with the archives documents; and Sybil Milton, U.S. Holocaust Memorial Museum, for her thoughtful criticism and strong encouragement. Their keen devotion to historical accuracy strengthened my conclusions even as it stimulated my imagination.

1. Claudia Koonz, *Mothers in the Fatherland: Women, the Family, and Nazi Politics* (New York: St. Martin's Press, 1987), p. 56.

2. See, for example, Sybil Milton, "Women and the Holocaust: The Case of German and German-Jewish Women," in Renate Bridenthal, Atina Grossman, and Marion Kaplan, eds., *When Biology Became Destiny: Women in Weimar and Nazi Germany* (New York: Monthly Review Press, 1984), pp. 297–307; Joan Ringelheim, "Women and the Holocaust: A Reconsideration of the Matriarch," in Judith R. Baskin, ed., *Jewish Women in Historical Perspective* (Detroit: Wayne State University Press, 1991), pp. 243–64; Marlene Heinemann, *Gender and Destiny: Women Writers of the Holocaust* (Westport, Conn: Greenwood Press, 1986).

3. J. Noakes and G. Pridham, eds., *Nazism, 1919–1945: A History in Documents and Eyewitness Accounts* (New York: Schocken Books, 1983).

4. Wolfgang Benz and Barbara Distel, "Editorial," *Dachau Review* 1 (1988): 2. However, this does not mean that the women who survived the Nazis were generally responsible for their own survival. It is well documented that survival was random and exceptional. See Leni Yahil, *The Holocaust: The Fate of European Jewry, 1932–1945* (New York: Oxford Uni-

versity Press, 1990), pp. 561–62; see also Milton, "Women and the Holocaust," pp. 311–16.

5. A short excerpt from a lengthy and graphic testimony, taken at the close of the war, summarizes the Nazis' treatment of the Jewish prisoners in Ravensbrueck: "At noon in winter, lining up for work. The old and sick women, most of them Jewesses between 70 and 80 years of age, remain in the block as long as possible. The protective custody commander arrives, accompanied by SS men and dogs which attack the old women, tear the clothes from their bodies and bite their breasts, legs, faces. At the time, many died of the consequences" (Boxes 522 and 523, War Crimes Case File Number 000-50-11 [Records of the Deputy Judge Advocate, 7708th War Crimes Group, United States Forces European Theater, Cases Not Tried, 1945–1947]; Records of the U.S. Army Commands, 1942, Record Group 338, National Archives, Suitland, Md. (hereafter cited as Ravensbrueck).

6. Lore Rolling Perl, Ravensbrueck, Box 523, National Archives.

7. Rhodes, under Italian control from 1912 until September 1943, when it succumbed to German rule, is the most southeastern island of the Aegean, very close to Turkey. The Jews of Rhodes, descended from the Jews of Spain who had been expelled in 1492, comprised a homogeneous Ladino-speaking community for over four and one half centuries.

8. Yahil (*The Holocaust*, p. 420) sets this figure at 2,000.

9. Martin Gilbert, *The Holocaust* (New York: Henry Holt, 1985), pp. 706–8.

10. Ibid., p. 724.

11. Sara Bentor, Anne Cohen, Giovanna Hasson, and Laura Hasson, "The Odyssey of the Women from Rhodes," *Dachau Review* 1 (1988): 234–40.

12. Quoted in Koonz, *Mothers in the Fatherland*, pp. 380–81.

13. Milton, "Women and the Holocaust," pp. 297–307.

14. Sara Nomberg-Przytyk, *Auschwitz: True Tales from a Grotesque Land* (Chapel Hill: University of North Carolina Press, 1985), pp. 13–16.

15. Livia E. Bitton Jackson, *Elli: Coming of Age in the Holocaust* (New York: Times Books, 1980), pp. 59–61.

16. Isabella Leitner, *Fragments of Isabella: A Memoir of Auschwitz* (New York: Laurel, 1978), pp. 44–45.

17. Gerda Klein, *All but My Life* (New York: Hill and Wang, 1957), p. 156.

18. Leitner, *Fragments of Isabella*, pp. 14, 40–44.

19. Frances Penney, *I Was There* (New York: Shengold, 1988), p. 103.

20. Nomberg-Przytyk, *Auschwitz*, pp. 79–82. See also Olga Lengyel, "Accursed Births," *Five Chimneys* (London: Granada, 1972), pp. 110–13.

21. Myrna Goldenberg, "Different Horrors, Same Hell: Women Re-

membering the Holocaust," in Roger Gottlieb, ed., *Thinking the Unthinkable: Meanings of the Holocaust* (New York: Paulist Press, 1990), pp. 150–66.

22. Klein, *All but My Life*, p. 195.

23. Ilona Karmel, *An Estate of Memory* (New York: Feminist Press, 1969), p. 300.

24. Judith Isaacson, *Seed of Sarah: Memoirs of a Survivor* (Urbana: University of Illinois Press, 1990), pp. 111, 152.

25. Gerda Haas, *These I Do Remember: Fragments from the Holocaust* (Freeport, Maine: Cumberland Press, 1982), pp. 43–44.

26. Joan Ringelheim, "Thoughts about Women and the Holocaust," in Gottlieb, *Thinking the Unthinkable,* pp. 141–49.

27. Goldenberg, "Different Horrors."

· IV ·
RITUAL
VOICES

· 6 ·

A *Drink from Miriam's Cup*: Invention of Tradition *among* Jewish Women

PENINA ADELMAN

Until a strong line of love confirmation, and example stretches from mother to daughter, from woman to woman across the generations, women will still be wandering in the wilderness.
—Adrienne Rich, *Of Woman Born*

As Jewish women dip deeper and deeper into the tradition that has been handed down to them, first by collective study and then by enactment, they find it more natural to generate their own "traditions." Although creating new traditions often causes them to be at odds with the strict preservers of normative Judaism, it enables them to be an integral part of an equally "traditional" Judaism, one that encompasses "a process of interpretation, attributing meaning in the present though making reference to the past."[1]

In redefining "traditions," anthropologists and folklorists provide a useful tool to the students of Jewish feminism and feminist spirituality. They ask questions such as: Does "tradition" imply only "old" or can it also be "new"? Does "tradition" demarcate a corpus of items that can be listed as one might list an inventory of a particular culture or does "tradition" signify a process by which cultures are transmitted?

In Linnekin and Handler's study of the creation of tradition among French-speaking Quebeçois and among Hawaiian nationalists, they conclude that the "authentic" feeling of a tradition is ascribed and not innate. This new notion of authenticity paves the way for any number of new activities: rituals, pottery-making, and storytelling, which may not have stood the test of time but which, nonetheless, are called "traditional" by those who perform them.[2] This redefinition of "tradition" embraces the cultural expressions of those groups outside the mainstream culture and places these expressions on a spectrum of "traditional" activities in which all people may be full participants.

The redefinition of "tradition," as Linnekin and Handler see it, is particularly applicable to Judaism, where the very fabric of Jewish culture is woven from a distinctive warp and weft. The warp in Judaism, the background upon which everything else is woven, is known as the Written Law, the words Moses received on Mount Sinai directly from God, which he then delivered to the Jewish people. Also known as the Five Books of Moses, these words have remained constant, preserved on the parchment scroll of the Torah. What is ever-changing is the Oral Law or the Talmud and all the commentaries on the Torah right up until the present day. The Oral Law contains the interpretation of tradition by those privileged to be privy to that tradition; that is, those who were able to spend hours each day studying the Torah and its commentaries—the men. Therefore, at the heart of Judaism is the dynamic tension of a tradition that has a constant, unchanging background (the Torah [Five Books of Moses]) across which the threads of interpretation are unceasingly being woven.

Ironically, only certain members of the community have been able to participate fully in that tradition. For Jewish women to experience themselves as enfranchised members of the tradition, they have had to invent "new" traditions that have resulted from their own interpretations of the tradition. They have had to break free of the old, static notion of tradition as a list of items (studying Torah, praying three times a day, being counted in a prayer minyan) and to embrace instead the notion that they are, in fact, part of a strand of Jewish tradition that has existed since the time of Moses. They are engaged in the process of interpreting and re-enacting the texts of Jewish tradition. In so doing, they are involved in an endeavor that is both ancient and new. There is a verse that is sung at the end of the Torah service on Shabbat: "Hadesh yameinu k'kedem" (Renew our days as of old.) Within Judaism, one who participates in the ongoing interpretation of tradition is renewed as the tradition, it-self, is also renewed.

David Hartman, an Orthodox rabbi and scholar in Jerusalem, supports the notion of Judaism as a tradition that is eternally in process. He holds that for a Jew who is "competent" in negotiating the exceedingly complex and intricate road of the Oral and Written Torah, the possibilities for interpretation are almost endless. What ultimately limits the interpretation is the community's willingness to affirm it.[3]

Today, Jewish women challenge this idea of competency by lay-ing equal claim to the "tradition" even without necessarily being well versed in text study. Literacy in the Oral and Written Torah has never been a requirement for Jewish women who, nonetheless, have always been competent in interpreting the impact of God and Torah on their lives.[4] Further, they have expressed their connection to God in myr-iad ways.[5]

Unfortunately, so few of these expressions have been document-ed. Contemporary women in Jewish tradition who are finally able to read the sacred texts discover that the experience of Jewish women has been sadly invisible. Only by reconstructing a context in which new oral traditions can flourish—namely, women meeting together regularly in prayer groups, ritual groups, study groups—are Jewish women finally able to experience themselves as part of an unbroken chain of tradition. This chain goes back through all the generations of women who preceded them, and it is all that is needed to give Jewish women the authority to "invent" their own traditions. One woman from a study group has explained her sense of connected-ness to the past through the image of a well: "I have always felt that I am sitting at a well and that it's deep and there is a way of dipping into it and other people have dipped into it before. . . . That well is, I would say, the collective experience of Jewish women."[6] As they meet in groups devoted to developing a stronger sense of their own spirituality, Jewish women are creating the very communities they need in which to test their interpretations of the "tradition."

In addition to the concept of "tradition" undergoing significant changes in the fields of anthropology and folklore, the notion of who are the *bearers* of tradition has also expanded. As Hanson has stat-ed in his research on the Maori, scholars who have studied this peo-ple "have been active participants in the invention of tradition that

Maoritanga (the movement of Maori ethnic pride) presents to the world."[7] Likewise, in the evolution of new rituals and symbolic forms within the community of Jewish women, scholars of these phenomena have been in large part responsible for the dissemination of information that has enabled such activities to take place.[8]

Feminist theology has much to offer to this discussion of tradition. Despite her resistance to the dominance of the patriarchy at the root of Judaism, Plaskow recognizes that "the same sources that are regarded with suspicion can also be used to reconstruct Jewish women's history."[9] She understands the need for both warp and weft in a thriving tradition. She also sees the creation of new rituals and symbolic forms by women as an essential way to make women's experience part of Jewish tradition.

Indeed, the work of Linnekin and Handler, Hanson, and Plaskow demonstrates that previous notions of "tradition" have excluded people whose relationship to their tradition has been considered peripheral or even inconsequential by those who have set the standards for that tradition. These standard-setters have included a whole spectrum of individuals from anthropologists to tribal elders. Feminist scholars as well as folklorists have cried out for a consideration of all people as potential tradition-makers.[10]

In this chapter, I will focus on the evolution of a new ritual called *Kos Miriam,* the Cup of Miriam, by the women who invented it. The process by which this ritual came about is as full of meaning as the ritual itself. By focusing on the process, one witnesses an intricate weaving back and forth between the varied strands of an ancient warp and contemporary fibers to produce a new symbolic form. The Cup of Miriam demonstrates how the invention of this tradition by a group of Jewish women became this group's ticket of entry into the heart of the very tradition from which they had previously felt excluded.

Origins of Kos Miriam

The new ritual, Kos Miriam, developed in the context of the ancient women's ritual of Rosh Hodesh, the New Moon, which has undergone a revival in the last twenty years. According to legend, Rosh Hodesh was a holiday given as a reward to Jewish women for

· 112 ·

refusing to contribute to the making of the Golden Calf.[11] Originating in ancient Near Eastern cults of the moon, the holiday was incorporated into synagogue worship by the rabbis of the first centuries of the Common Era who feared it would draw people away from the relatively new Jewish fold. As the New Moon was observed in the synagogue, it lost its distinctive connection to women.

However, in the early 1970s, with the resurgence of feminism in the United States, some Jewish women rediscovered the holiday and its origins as a sacred time for women.[12] Simultaneously in cities across the United States and in Israel, groups of Jewish women began marking the New Moon again. Some groups studied inspirational texts together in Hebrew and in English. Other groups prayed and meditated together or danced, sang, and told stories based on the themes of the particular month they were celebrating. Despite the diverse ways of observing Rosh Hodesh, all groups share a sense of the New Moon, the beginning of each month, as a sacred time for women. Moreover, there is an assumption that the unique feminine character of this holiday existed *before* the dawn of Judaism.

Those women who observe Rosh Hodesh monthly have had an opportunity to engage in myth-making and ritual-making.[13] Using the Jewish year-cycle as their "text," they have delved into each month and unearthed meaning for their lives, individually and collectively. In this time set aside for women only, they have been able to explore the Jewish tradition, to share the experience of their tradition *as women*. Studying the stories of biblical women, saying prayers together, sharing anecdotes from their own lives and the lives of their mothers and grandmothers have brought them insights into the significance of Jewish tradition for women. With this has emerged much pain, sadness, and turmoil, along with an urge to create rituals and myths, or midrashim (new interpretations), which will integrate the new insights gained from meeting together as women with the legacy of their religious and cultural heritage.

Matia Angelou-Osmond, my informant, is a member of the Boston Rosh Hodesh group of which I was a participant-observer from 1981 to 1987. She has been a Jewish educator for many years and brings a teacher's sensitivity to her ability to transmit new rituals successfully. She first told me of Kos Miriam, a new ritual that emerged from a Rosh Hodesh celebration in 1989. I was struck by two points: (1) the group had provided the catalyst for an activity that could take place outside the group with men participating; and (2) this activity had a physical object as its focus. Moreover, this particular symbolic form seemed to have come into being in such a natural and spontaneous way that, according to Angelou-Osmond, "it was as if Kos Miriam already existed and was just waiting to be discovered."

Kos Miriam refers to a vessel containing the waters of Miriam's Well, a legendary well said to have been created on the second day of Creation. From that time on, the Well has been passed on to those who were in desperate need of water in the desert and whose merits caused them to deserve such a divine gift. Miriam received the Well on behalf of the Children of Israel who were wandering in the desert after their escape from Egypt. According to the legend, she was able to call forth the water with her beautiful voice. When she died, the waters of her Well dried up. They reappeared many centuries later to the Kabbalists of Safed in Israel and to the Hasidim of Eastern Europe.[14]

The process of creating Kos Miriam had begun when I heard the legend of Miriam's Well told by a member of a Philadelphia Rosh Hodesh group in 1979. That story, part of the well-accepted body of traditional Jewish lore, furnished me with a powerful metaphor for the experience of Jewish women as sustaining the Jewish People during times of adversity, a metaphor upon which I based my book on the Rosh Hodesh revival. Once my book was published, the rituals and stories in it entered the public domain. Jewish women began to have a dialogue with the book, *Miriam's Well,* much as Jewish men have engaged in dialogues with Jewish texts since the time of Moses. The women in the Boston Rosh Hodesh group made the leap into action from the text I had written, meditating on the image of Miriam's Well and creating the ritual of drinking from the Cup of Miriam in their own homes.[15] Thus, the constant interplay between written word, spoken word, and ritual act generates ever-evolving forms of the ritual.[16]

The Ritual of Kos Miriam

What follows is the text of the ritual as chronicled by Matia Angelou-Osmond of the Boston Rosh Hodesh group.

Introduction

G-d gave us many gifts when we left Egypt. We were fed with manna every morning to satiate our hunger. Clouds of glory protected us and led our way through the desert. With awe and fear at Mt. Sinai we accepted G-d's gift of Torah which continues to influence our lives today. Manna is associated with Moses and clouds of glory with Aaron. One other special gift was given for the sake of the Poet-Prophetess Miriam. Because of her righteousness, we were given a wandering well of sparkling pure water which travelled with us on our journey through the desert. This well was filled with *mayim hayyim*, living waters, miracle-working waters through which G-d gave spiritual nourishment, healing, and redemption. The well became known as "Miriam's Well," and it is said that when Miriam died, the well dried up.

Today we're trying to rediscover Miriam's Well and its pure sparkling waters. We fill this goblet with spring water as a symbol of *mayim hayyim*, G-d's living waters. May we drink deeply from Miriam's Well and feel G-d's ever-present spiritual sustenance, G-d's continual strength and healing, working in our lives. May we be blessed to find Miriam's Well whenever we need it. May its living waters sustain each of us as we continue our search.

Lift Cup Full of Spring Water or Sparkling Water

LEADER: *Zot Kos Miriam, Kos Mayim Hayyim. Hazak, Hazak V'Nithazek.* This is the Cup of Miriam, the Cup of Living Waters. Strength, Strength, and may we be Strengthened.

ALL: Strength, Strength, and may we be Strengthened.

N'varek et Eyn haHayyim sh'natnah lanu Mayim Hayyim. Let us bless the Source of Life that gives us living waters.

Barukh Atta Adonai, Eloheinu Hei haOlamim, sh'hakol n'hiyeh b'd'varo. Blessed are you G-d, Life-Source of the Universe, by Whose word everything is created.

All Drink.[17]

Symbolic Aspects of Kos Miriam

Miriam as Redeemer

How did the symbol of Miriam's Well engender such creativity in the Boston Rosh Hodesh group? For the same reasons that the story of the Well resonates deep within the souls of Jewish women, it sparked the creation of Kos Miriam, the Cup of Miriam. The first reason is that the Well recalls a female ancestor, Miriam, whose role in the Exodus, the central historical event of the Jews, has often been underemphasized or even ignored.[18] Jewish women seek female models within the tradition whose quick wits and strong voices aid in the redemption of their people. Miriam's prophetic powers were evident when she was a young girl. She revealed to her parents what she had seen in a dream—that Moses, her brother, would become a great leader and that everything must be done to save his life. She found a way to do this, by handing him over to Pharoah's daughter.[19]

Miriam's voice had supernatural powers, for, like the lyre of Orpheus, it evoked a response in the natural world. Miriam had only to sing and water sprang forth from the dry ground. Jewish women find inspiration in the healing qualities of Miriam's voice when they feel oppressed by Orthodox Jewish law, which states that a woman's singing voice should not be heard in public, that a man who hears it will fall into temptation.[20]

Despite Orthodoxy's emphasis on the negative qualities of the female voice, in the writing of the prophet Micah, Miriam assumes a status equal to that of Moses and Aaron.

> "Hear what the Lord says: . . ."
> O my people, what have I done to you?
> In what have I wearied you?
> Answer me!
> For I brought you up from the land of Egypt,
> and redeemed you from the house of bondage;
> and I sent before you Moses,
> Aaron, and Miriam.[21]

In Micah's vision, the Lord holds Moses, Aaron, and Miriam to be of equal importance, while honoring their different roles.[22] Moses speaks directly to God and receives wisdom (the Ten Commandments and the entire Torah) from God. However, he is unable to convey this to the people waiting at the base of Mt. Sinai. We know this from the biblical passages concerning Moses' inability to speak without stuttering or faltering and from his constant questioning of God's judgment in choosing him to be the leader of the Jewish People.[23] Aaron is the conduit of communication between Moses and the people. He is able to make the words of Moses clear and audible. Miriam takes the tradition received from Moses, from God, and transforms the words into poetry and song so that the people understand them on a level deeper than mere literal comprehension. The three siblings represent three strands of tradition: Moses—the original receiver of tradition directly from God; Aaron—the one who conveys the tradition to the people exactly as he has heard it from Moses; Miriam—the inventor of tradition who takes the ancient tradition and effects the changes necessary to make it accessible to those receiving it.[24]

This interpretation of the passage in Micah demonstrates the connection between the "inventor" of tradition and the "redeemer" of the Jewish People. Miriam's Well, itself, seems to possess the qualities of renewing and reinvigorating ancient traditions that enable the redemption of the Jewish People to occur. The folklore about Miriam focuses on the themes of birth, water, salvation, creativity, innovation, risk-taking, and celebration. Kos Miriam likewise encompasses these themes by allowing each individual, each family, to "drink" from Miriam's Well, bringing the experience of redemption and renewal into the present.

The Well

Because of its ever-changing character, the well has great symbolic potential. Miriam's Well seems to reflect the history of the Jewish People, drying up in times of crisis and bubbling forth when called upon in times of renewal. The relationship between Torah, the sustaining story, and water, the sustaining substance, is expressed in commentaries on the Torah and the rest of the Hebrew Bible.[25] The Torah fed the people's spirit, but the waters of Miriam's Well enabled them to survive physically in the desert. Without water to drink, they could not have lived long enough in the desert to receive the Torah at Sinai.

In addition, Miriam's Well symbolizes survival in the contemporary world. Spiritual and physical thirst seem to have merged today in a world where concern about the fundamental availability of pure water and questions of how to live simply and ethically in relation to each other and to the earth prevail in the larger community.

Kos Miriam is a response to those questions and concerns. By sanctifying an object that is portable and small enough for a child to hold, Jewish women have made the Well more accessible to more people. Every home can have a Cup of Miriam. They have also taken a bold step by making a physical object represent an ethereal well named for a woman.

The Cup

Although the Boston Rosh Hodesh group was aware of the existence of Kos Eliyahu, Elijah's Cup, used during the Passover seder, no member of the group consciously set out to make a parallel cup for Miriam. Rather, the wealth of Jewish symbols and the Jewish attitude toward learning the meanings of these symbols lent itself to experimenting with new combinations in different contexts. How does Elijah's Cup shed light on the meaning of Miriam's Cup?

The prophet Elijah is the subject of many folktales, much superstition, many customs. The rabbis saw him as a redeemer. The folk portray him in their tales as a divine messenger who visits the earth in order to right wrongs in society. At Passover time, Elijah is believed to ensure that even the poorest family can make a seder. He also comes to the aid of Jewish communities being persecuted for their beliefs and being accused of human sacrifice especially during Passover. Jews fill the Cup of Elijah on the seder night as a way of offering hospitality to the prophet whose arrival presages that of the Messiah.[26]

As the fifth cup of wine at the seder table, Kos Eliyahu symbolizes another important aspect of Elijah: his ability to settle disputes. The rabbis disagreed on whether there should be four or five cups at the seder table. Since the belief was that all disputes would be resolved when Elijah came, they named the fifth cup after him.[27]

Just as Elijah's Cup signifies something extra, that which lies outside the expected number, so does Miriam's Cup represent something that seems to exist outside normative Jewish tradition while being solidly connected to it. Both cups lie on that threshold of tradition between what was handed down from Mt. Sinai and what is created anew in each generation to accommodate its needs to the tradition. The Passover Haggadah says, "In every generation, one must see oneself as if s/he has come forth from Egypt." This statement embodies the strong current in Jewish tradition that demands constant change and revisioning in order to keep Judaism alive.

Another explanation in the Talmud for the fifth cup is that the observance of Passover, like other Jewish holidays, is seen as a way of guarding against evil spirits. Thus, the sick and vulnerable are encouraged to drink an extra cup of wine at the seder.[28] As the waters of Miriam's Well offered sustenance to the Jewish People, the water from her Cup makes this strength available now. A drink from Miriam's Cup proclaims the existence of the prophetess is ongoing, just as a drink from Elijah's Cup professes his imminent arrival.

The Water

The cup is the vessel for the water (*mayim hayyim*), which has transformative properties. In all the legends of Miriam's Well, drinking the water or bathing in it is what gives people strength, healing, and inspiration. The women who developed the rituals for Kos Miriam did so because they needed a sign, a reminder of Miriam's presence, just as the circumcision of a Jewish boy is an *ot b'rit* (sign of the covenant) and blessing the cup of wine before the Sabbath meal is *zikaron l'ma'aseh v'reshit* (a remembrance of the Creation). Remembering Miriam by drinking water from her well enables the participants in the ritual to feel filled with the waters of Creation, with the waters of a well whose depths are connected with creativity, generativity, and the life force.

Plaskow affirms this when she demonstrates how Jewish women are discovering a multitude of ways to image God, "as fountain, source, wellspring. . . . [These] remind us that God loves and befriends us as one who brings forth all being and sustains it in existence."[29]

The water of Kos Miriam is such a powerful Jewish symbol in part because the notion of fresh, pure water reverberates with meaning in the world outside of Judaism as well. We are learning how much the survival of the earth and its varied species depend on maintaining the purity of clean water and on transforming the water that is already polluted into "living waters."

Conscious of the plight of the earth, the women of the Boston Rosh Hodesh group found the ancient Jewish symbol of Miriam's Well to be appropriate for creating a new symbolic form with accompanying rituals. The work that went into making the ritual of Kos Miriam is also the work of *tikkun olam* (literally, mending the universe). The women who celebrate Rosh Hodesh every month are well aware of God's promise to their ancestors who received the holiday as a reward for their faith and who, in the world to come, will be renewed as the light of the moon is constantly renewed. They experience all the activities they engage in during the holiday to be presentiments of redemption. Miriam and her male counterpart, Elijah, embody this in their lives and actions.

Kos Miriam as Performance

Judaism contains the seeds for countless "new" traditions to be invented. This is most clear in the Haggadah when it says, "The more one tells of the Exodus from Egypt, the more is that person to be praised." The longer one sits and studies the Haggadah around the seder table, the more one is celebrating the holiday the way it was meant to be—as a communal study session.

More than this, when one gains a new insight through study and performs it rather than merely restating it, one participates in a time-honored Jewish tradition. As Heilman contends in his firsthand account of men's study circles in Jerusalem, "The book or written word may thus be considered as a kind of script for a play. . . . For the Jews, the Torah can transform its people only insofar as they repeat its words, chant in its cadences, think along its syntactic lines, and thus make them their own."[30] Jewish women began hearing the texts on Miriam together in a Rosh Hodesh context, one which is conducive to group study and reflection by women. The Boston Rosh Hodesh group spontaneously enacted these texts and Kos Miriam was born.[31] However, the ritual was not born in a vacuum; rather, it illustrates a major principle on which all Jewish ritual is based, one that helps to establish it firmly on the most recent part of the spectrum of Jewish tradition.

Laura Geller, a creator of new rituals, has isolated this element, which is essential to Jewish ritual: it must contain a part of the story of the Jewish People. For a new ritual to work, she maintains, it must include elements of the Creation, the Exodus, or the Redemption stories.[32]

Miriam's Well came into being on the second day of Creation. The prophetess played a key role in the Exodus when she acted to save her brother, Moses, from drowning. The Well itself is redemptive as all the legends about it seem to emphasize. Thus, the ritual of Kos Miriam contains all three parts of the story of the Jewish People. This completeness explains why it feels so authentic to those who developed it as well as to those who participate in it.

Jewish women "studied" the text of Miriam's Well together and enacted it as a script.[33] Furthermore, the process of developing the ritual of Kos Miriam has been healing and affirming for the participants. In providing the catalyst for the invention of a new ritual, the Boston Rosh Hodesh group has made a strong statement about their new roles as women in an ancient tradition that has consistently been opposed to women as creators of ritual and liturgy. What Geertz said of the Balinese cockfight applies here: "it is a Balinese reading of Balinese experience, a story they tell themselves about themselves."[34]

What story are these women telling?

1. Women's experience has largely been ignored in Judaism, in the realms of text interpretation, liturgy, and ritual-making.

2. Jewish women do not need a rabbi or the official stamp of approval of the Jewish establishment in order to create new rituals and liturgy.

3. Women are able to invent new religious forms most easily within a group.

4. When women trust their instincts and each other, they can find ways of invoking the ancestors. This brings them the strength that is needed spiritually, emotionally, intellectually, and physically to contribute to the survival of the Jewish People.

5. Jewish women have reached a new level of feminist consciousness where they feel it is time to bring the results of their "study" in women-only groups to the larger community that includes men as well.

The story Jewish women are telling is that they are feeling empowered to invent new traditions and to assume a fully active role in the tradition-making process. What has enabled this change to occur among Jewish women?

Jewish women have assumed the challenge as they did in Egypt long ago when the men were utterly demoralized and weakened by Pharoah's oppressive regime. At that time, the women encouraged the men to have children with them, no matter what the conditions. In the present day, Jewish women have rediscovered Miriam's Well, a symbol of the hard times in Egypt, and have transformed it into a vessel small enough to hold in one's own hands. The Boston Rosh Hodesh group has made Miriam's Well live again in the Cup of Miriam, which, like the portable ark in the desert, may be carried everywhere, brimming full of the living waters that sustain the Jewish People to this day.

NOTES

An expanded version of this chapter appears in the *Journal of Feminist Studies in Religion* 10, no. 2 (Fall 1994): 151–66.

1. Richard Handler and Jocelyn Linnekin, "Tradition, Genuine or Spurious," *Journal of American Folklore* 97, no. 385 (1984): 287.

2. Ibid.

3. David Hartman, *A Living Covenant: The Innovative Spirit in Traditional Judaism* (New York: Free Press, 1985), p. 8.

4. For a discussion of the exemption of women from the study of Torah, see Saul Berman, "The Status of Women in Halakhic Judaism," in Elizabeth Koltun, ed., *The Jewish Woman* (New York: Schocken Books, 1976), pp. 118–22. See also Rachel Biale, *Women in Jewish Law* (New York: Schocken Books, 1984), pp. 29–41.

5. See Susan Sered, "The Domestication of Religion: The Spiritual Guardianship of Elderly Jewish Women," *Man* (n.s.) 23 (1989): 506–21. See also Ellen Umansky and Dianne Ashton, eds., *Four Centuries of Jewish Womens' Spirituality* (Boston: Beacon Press, 1992), for an excellent survey of the variety of Jewish womens' spiritual expression through the ages.

6. This is part of an interview with Aviva Cohen-Kiener, principal of Midrasha Hebrew High School in West Hartford, Connecticut, recorded in Suri Levow Krieger, "The Effect of Creative Ritual, Myth, and Symbolism on Group Dynamics in the *Rosh Hodesh* Celebration" (Ph.D. diss., Temple University, 1981), p. 176. A fuller version of this excerpt is in Penina V. Adelman, "The Golden Calf Jumps over the New Moon: Mythmaking among Jewish Women," *Anima* 16, no. 1 (Fall 1989): 31–39.

7. Allan Handon, "The Making of the Maori: Culture Invention and Its Logic," *American Anthropologist* 91 (1989): 895.

8. See E. M. Broner, *A Weave of Women* (New York: Bantam Books, 1978); Claire R. Satlof, "History, Fiction, and the Tradition: Creating a Jewish Feminist Poetic," in Susannah Heschel, ed., *On Being a Jewish Feminist* (New York: Schocken Books, 1983); and Arlene Agus, "This Month Is for You," in Koltun, *Jewish Woman*.

9. Judith Plaskow, *Standing Again at Sinai* (San Francisco: Harper and Row, 1990), p. 15.

10. See Sered, "Domestication of Religion"; Barbara Myerhoff, "'Life Not Death in Venice': Its Second Life," in Victor Turner and Edward Bruner, eds., *The Anthropology of Experience* (Urbana: University of Illinois Press,

1986), pp. 261–86; and Barbara A. Babcock, "Modeled Selves: Helen Cordero's 'Little People,'" in ibid., pp. 316–43. Babcock's work focuses on the Pueblo potter Helen Cordero, who started a "new tradition" of storyteller doll modeled after her grandfather, a foremost storyteller. Cordero feels that her work is so popular because she makes her figures "in the old way, the right way."

11. See Penina Adelman, *Miriam's Well: Rituals for Jewish Women around the Year* (New York: Biblio Press, 1990), pp. 32–33, for a more complete version of the legend.

12. Agus, "This Month Is for You."

13. For a more detailed history of the holiday of Rosh Hodesh (the New Moon), see Adelman, *Miriam's Well*, pp. 1–9, 19.

14. See Adelman, "Golden Calf."

15. See Adelman, *Miriam's Well*, for a more detailed version of the legend of Miriam's Well, with sources.

16. The blessing created by Stephanie Loo Ritari, the originator of the ritual, is said in Hebrew. For a detailed account of the development of Kos Miriam, see Matia Angelou-Osmond, "Kos Miriam: The Development of a Women's Ritual" *Neshama* (Summer 1990): 1–2.

17. After much debate within the group about who "owned" the ritual, the members decided to copyright it together and to permit its use by people outside the group. The ritual may be used, but not sold, by notifying *Kol Isha* in writing. Please include the following copyright notice on all copies: © 1991 *Kol Isha*, P.O. Box 132, Wayland, MA 01778.

18. See Satloff, "History, Fiction, and the Tradition: Creating a Jewish Feminist Poetic," in Susannah Heschel, ed., *On Being a Jewish Feminist* (New York: Schocken Books, 1983), pp. 186–206, who remarks on the importance of this interplay for the creation of Jewish womens' rituals.

19. Most Haggadoth disregard Miriam's part in the saving of Jewish boys from Pharoah's fatal decree and in the singing of the song of celebration (Exodus 15) on the other side of the Sea of Reeds.

20. See Adelman, *Miriam's Well*, pp. 69–71, 130–31, for more legends of Miriam.

21. See Carol Gilligan, *In a Different Voice* (Cambridge: Harvard University Press, 1982); Mary Belenky et al., *Women's Ways of Knowing: The Development of Self, Voice, and Mind* (New York: Basic Books, 1986); and Tillie Olsen, *Silences* (New York: Dell Publishing, 1978), for ways in which the voice of woman is an analog for woman's status in the world (i.e., *invisible = silence; powerful/inspiring fear and terror = a scream; nurturing = a voice that is soothing and beautiful*).

22. Mic. 6:1, 3–4.

23. Ex. 4:10–17.

24. I am grateful to Rabbi Alan Ullman for making the passage in Micah known to me and for coming up with the interpretation of the three strands of tradition.

25. See *Song of Songs Rabbah* 1:2 for older commentary; and see also Norman Cohen, "Miriam's Song: A Modern Midrashic Reading," *Judaism* (Spring 1984): 179–90, and Adelman, *Miriam's Well,* pp. 31–32.

26. For a full history of Elijah, see *Encyclopaedia Judaica,* 1972, s.v. "Elijah."

27. Eliyahu Kitov, *The Book of Our Heritage,* vol . 2 (New York: Feldbein Publishers, 1978), p. 275.

28. Ruth Gruber Fredman, *The Passover Seder* (New York: New American Library, 1983), pp. 108–9.

29. Plaskow, *Standing Again at Sinai,* p. 165.

30. Samuel Heilman, *The People of the Book* (Chicago: University of Chicago Press, 1987), p. 161.

31. This is akin to the process mentioned in Satloff, "History, Fiction, and the Tradition," p. 193.

32. I learned of Rabbi Laura Geller's unpublished teachings on ritual from several conversations with Rabbi Ruth Sohn of Boston University Hillel who has studied with her.

33. I use "study" in the sense in which it is frequently understood during a Rosh Hodesh celebration. Suri Levow and Andrea Cohen-Kiener, members of the first Philadelphia Rosh Hodesh group that formed in the late 1970s, informed me at that time that everything women did during a Rosh Hodesh gathering—singing, praying, meditating, dancing, storytelling—amounted to "studying" the text of that particular month.

34. Clifford Geertz, *The Interpretation of Culture* (New York: Basic Books, 1973), p. 448.

The Bar Mitzvah Balabusta: Mother's Role in the Family's Rite of Passage

JUDITH DAVIS

Family Context

"How did you choose the date [for the bar mitzvah]?" I asked the family sitting before me. An innocuous question to ease into the interview. Puzzled looks all around. It was hard to remember such a detail so far back. Then suddenly Michah, the bar mitzvah boy-to-be, piped up with a smile: "It was because of Bubby's (grandmother's) feet!
"Bubby's feet?" I asked. "Yeah, she lives in Florida and has bad feet. So we had to make my *bar mitzvah* in May instead of in February when my birthday really is, so it wouldn't snow and Bubby could wear open shoes."

Despite the widespread performance and increasing popularity of the contemporary American bar mitzvah, exceedingly little serious secular study has been devoted to this uniquely tenacious ritual.[1] Perhaps this lack of scholarly attention reflects the negative stereotypes of glitz and chopped liver center pieces, or the sense that this is, after all, a religious event "best left" to rabbis and Jewish educators. Or perhaps it reflects an intense ambivalence about this ritual that so dramatically and confusingly mixes the sacred and the profane and, on the face of it, engenders great skepticism.[2] But for whatever the reasons, most of what we generally think about bar mitzvah (aside from our own personal experiences with it) comes from stand-up comics and coffee table gift books. To the extent that this continues to be the case, we continue to ignore, I believe, a rich source of data about contemporary North American Jewry and in particular the evolving Jewish family.

As a student of family therapy (and recent bar mitzvah mother), I became interested in studying the phenomenon at a time (1980–81) when the family therapy field was first experimenting with the use of therapeutic ritual to help client families "stuck" in behavior inappropriate to their life stage. My particular interest was less with families labeled dysfunctional and more with those considered healthy (defined only as nonclinical). What was it about ritual that was therapeutic? What, I wondered, could be learned about naturally occurring cultural rituals that could be useful in helping healthy families stay healthy and not need to go to therapists (who would prescribe therapeutic rituals)?

The research on bar mitzvah families that grew out of these questions resulted in detailed ethnographic portraits that revealed the way in which families idiosyncratically use the ritual process to negotiate developmental change. It is reported in full elsewhere.[3] This essay presents only a brief synopsis of the study's basic findings and then goes on to explore the role of the bar mitzvah mother, the role least well understood and most often ridiculed.[4]

From the psychological literature on healthy family functioning and the anthropological literature on ritual, the theoretical linkages between developmental health and life cycle ritual were clear: The family's ongoing task of providing its members with balanced opportunities for both autonomy and connectedness is enabled by ritual's classic capacity to facilitate change and stability simultaneously. In order to stay healthy over time, the family must provide its members with appropriate opportunities for change and continuity. Ritual's magic is precisely its paradoxical ability to promote change in the context of continuity and to maintain the status quo while *celebrating* change. It is no wonder, then, that ritual is considered humankind's original form of therapy. The end product of both is the same: change in the context of stability.

But how did this process actually work with the bar mitzvah? To begin the research, I studied four families over a six-month period during which they planned, participated in, and reflected on the bar mitzvah of their first child. I deliberately restricted the study to bar and did not include bat mitzvah for two reasons: one, because I was looking for intergenerational patterns and it was obviously less likely that I'd find families where mothers (let alone grandmothers) had had bat mitzvahs, and two, because I felt that to include bat mitzvah as if there had been no gender differences in the religious and cultural histories of the two phenomena would not only be adding an unnecessary complication to the research but would ultimately be insulting.[5] I deliberately restricted the study to the first child, because it is this child, it is said, who takes the family over its "growing edge."[6] I further limited the observation to families specifically not in therapy—one, because I wanted to avoid, as much as possible, putting more stress on families already in a very stressful situation, and two, because I wanted to observe the process unhindered by professional intervention.

My attempt was to focus not simply on the condensed public performance in the synagogue and the banquet hall but also on the protracted private process surrounding it, the process taking place all through the year encompassing the event, the period described by Ed Friedman, a family therapist and rabbi of many years, as "hinges of time,"[7] time when the system is most open to change. Throughout the six months during which I conducted interviews, participated in family events, and attended the bar mitzvahs (researcher-as-guest), I was constantly exploring "the circular connections between who the families were, what they were doing, and what it all meant to them."[8]

In this study, the families were extraordinarily different from one another. One was a divorced Conservative family in which father had remarried—a woman who was not Jewish, who was feeling very much "the *goy*" (non-Jew), and who, at the beginning of the observation period, became pregnant with her first child; the second was a financially comfortable Reform family in which this was the first bar mitzvah in three generations. The third was a single-parent immigrant family in which the child's *brit* (circumcision) had been held in Russia—in secret; and the fourth was a Hasidic family with four generations of rabbis on both sides. I hypothesized that no matter what their differences, all of the families would have to make certain decisions (for example, when to have the ceremony, where to have it, whom to invite, where to house them, what to feed them, what kind of party to have, what kind of music to play, who to include in the service, etc.), that in each family different points of decision would be important or difficult, and that these important or difficult logistical decisions would be symbolically or metaphorically linked to the emotional work the family was doing at the time. I further hypothesized that by managing these logistical, concrete tasks of preparation the family would, in fact, be working to manage the emotional tasks associated with moving from being a family with a child to being a family with—not an adult but an adolescent, someone "getting ready" to be an adult.

These emotional tasks involve readjusting the boundaries between the generations, not only in the nuclear family, but in the extended family as well. According to the developmental literature,[9] families with a first adolescent are facing a number of very specific tasks. Among others these include (1) allowing for the child's increased autonomy, (2) mourning for the loss that autonomy implies, and (3) allowing for the evolution of the parents' relationship, not only with each other, but with their own parents who are generally aging and increasingly requiring a different way of relating.

Thus the detail of the date quoted above. With grandmother's health failing, father's role as caretaking son was expanding. Within this family, even the seemingly mundane decision about when to have the bar mitzvah highlights and reinforces this transitional reality. In addition, it implicitly models values about intergenerational responsibility meant to be transmitted to future generations.

In the second family, an early source of anxiety related to the fact that the two sets of in-laws had met only once in the couple's fifteen years of marriage. That meeting occurred at the couple's wedding, and it had been extremely tense. Now, three months before the event, it seemed that the next meeting would take place at their son's bar mitzvah. Responding to the stress of this impending reunion, Father, who had always been extremely clear, if not rigid, about generational boundaries, acted in a completely uncharacteristic manner. He flew to Chicago and successfully convinced his parents to visit his in-laws in Florida during their upcoming vacation there. That visit took place, and the two sets of grandparents, much to everyone's surprise, actually enjoyed themselves, sharing old stories and baby pictures.

The entire family was relieved, and in addition, several corresponding changes seemed to emerge between Mother and her parents. For the first time in the fifteen years since she had been married, Sandy visited her parents alone—without her husband or her children. She went to see for herself if, in fact, her parents needed additional help in their home. They were both aging quickly and her mother's arthritis was threatening to become incapacitating. Sandy was beginning to worry that perhaps they would not be able to attend the bar mitzvah. She found her parents in better shape than she had imagined, and described her unusual visit with them as "very nice. I didn't go out to the pool or visit friends. I just stayed with them and it was 'quality time.'"

On the pragmatic level, Sandy was performing a task associated with the bar mitzvah. At a deeper level, Sandy (and her parents) were preparing for the caretaking reversals that the parents' increasing age and deteriorating health would soon be necessitating. During the preparation period, both Mark and Sandy changed significantly in relation to their parents. It was, then, no accident, I think, that both sat with their son on the *bimah* (synagogue stage) *during the entire ceremony*. While at first I understood this unusual seating arrangement as a missed opportunity to enact the child's growing independence, it later became clear that what they were doing up there was vicariously sharing their son's ceremony. Never having had a bar or bat mitzvah of their own, they were using this occasion not only to celebrate their son's development but also to mark their own development as well.

Through my research I found that the ceremony in the synagogue is the "tip of the iceberg" regarding what is happening at the level of family process. During the months of preparation before the ceremony, the family is implicitly attempting to create a "sacred space," a space in which it and the child can be nurtured and cushioned through their transitions.[10] Without a doubt, it seems to me, the ordeal of bar mitzvah, this "trial by recitation," is not simply the child's initiation[11] "but a rite of passage for the entire system." Families dealing with the physiological and psychological emergence of an adolescent are in what change theorists describe as a "sweatbox,"[12] a period where old patterns no longer suffice and new patterns have not yet emerged. In this interregnum, preparing for a bar mitzvah adds a second layer of stress on top of the inherent, developmental stress. But by dealing with this second level of stress, I believe, the family is in fact dealing with its primary stress.

From the perspective of family systems, I concluded that the bar mitzvah is "a natural coping mechanism" for contemporary North American Jewish families facing the normative crises of adolescent transition. It is a coping mechanism in that it potentiates internal resources for achieving change and maintaining continuity simultaneously. Just as the child, beginning the first of his teenage years with this affirming public event,[13] gains strength for the struggles ahead, so too does the family as a whole benefit. Through their private performance (in which they demonstrate unprecedented maturity and competence, and in which they negotiate change in relation to the child, to themselves, and to their extended families), the parents discover and reinforce new strengths. Through the public performance, in which they are literally surrounded by the good will and support of family and friends in the trancelike state of "communitas,"[14] they discover and reinforce resources both in themselves and in their extended systems.

From this perspective, the ritual provides a format in which the child is given a way to show his "readiness"[15] to be treated differently, the parents are given a way both to help him demonstrate this readiness and to mourn the loss it implies, and the rest of the extended family is given a way to support the child and his parents in their new relationship to each other.

Mother's Role

It just underlines how important family is to me. I felt real good about myself in terms of all the warmth flowing from family and friends. *I felt responsible for having created the space in which that warmth could have happened.* I'm happy it happened for Seth. I don't know what he may feel, but I think it was important that all of these people showed up for him and if I should die tomorrow, I think it will now be important to him to keep up with the family. (emphasis added)

Three months after her son's bar mitzvah, Stacy, who had been, for years, "regrettably distant" from her extended Southern family "with its amazing Jewish spirit and warmth," reflects on the event. With all of her aunts and uncles attending, the bar mitzvah had affirmed connections between her ancestors and her only child that were deeply important to her.

This quote opening the section on Mother's role in the bar mitzvah process speaks with rare insight about that role. If it is true that little thought is given to the relationship between bar mitzvah and family life-cycle transition, how much more so is it the case that the meaning of mother's participation in her son's rite of passage goes undocumented and unexplored. One has only to stop and think for a moment of the derogatory images of the hysterical party planner searching for the right colored table cloth, or the sequined dinner dance hostess ushering her guests to mock lobster hors d'oeuvres to realize with what disdain the bar mitzvah boy's mother is held in the popular imagination. Even with my respect for the systemic power of the ritual process and with what I'd considered a reasonable degree of gender sensitivity, it had not occurred to me to look explicitly at the meaning of mother's role. It was only in retrospect and only in response to the disproportionately enormous amount of effort that all of the mothers in my study demonstrated (and their accompanying sense that they still had not done enough) that I began to look seriously at what these women were doing and what meaning could be made of it in terms of women's development.

Given the premise that the bar mitzvah process is a ritual of developmental transition, not for the child alone, but for the entire family, how does it function to facilitate mother's growing maturity and power? Looking simply at the public ceremony, where mother traditionally has no formal part and appears, on the surface, consigned to the role of spectator, one might wonder.[16]

A look behind and below the scene, however, reveals a very different picture. At some level, a first child's bar mitzvah is as much a developmental milestone for mother as it is for her child. For her, the "ritual ordeal" comes not in the form of a public performance but rather in the form of a private one—one that begins months before the first guest arrives. What mother is being tested on (by herself as well as by others) is her capacity as *balabusta,* competent homemaker, in the best, most sacred sense of the word.[17] It is she who, with varying degrees of collaboration and assistance from her husband or other relatives, is implicitly expected to manage the logistics of the event, an event that, in most families, is larger, more complicated, more costly, more emotionally ladened than any in the nuclear family's experience.

When you think about it, it is, after all, the first occasion in which the parents—as adults—are bringing together all of their and their children's friends, family, neighbors, colleagues, to be met, not with the different faces usually reserved for each of these different relationships, but with one face. They are presenting themselves publicly in relation to their religious tradition, their child's development, and their family's evolution all at the same time and to everyone most important to them. That the conflicting pulls are often extreme should come as no surprise. Friedman likens the weekend-long gathering of large numbers of people from all parts of the family's life to the "original Encounter Marathon."[18] It is here, in this context, that Mother's ability as preparer of food, provider of comfort, and protector of harmony is measured. It is here in her capacity to organize a communal celebration of her child's coming of age that she herself, at some level, comes of age. Behind the scenes, mother is manager of the whole gestalt. She is in charge of the pragmatic details, and attention to these details not only ensures management of the event but at a deeper level serves both to contain the emotional stress inherent in the family's aging and to demonstrate her individual maturation as well.

I return now to Stacy. That Seth's bar mitzvah should have turned out as well as it had was by no means a foregone conclusion. Planning it with her recently remarried former husband, who was soon to be a new father, had been difficult, to say the least. It took deliberate cooperation on the part of all three adults, and exceptional determination on Stacy's part, to prevent the tensions from becoming overwhelming, from defiling the sacred space.

When I first met this family, just three months before the event, tension was mounting. The invitations had not yet been written, let alone printed and sent out. The problem was in the wording. From whom was the invitation coming? Stacy felt strongly that her ex-husband's new wife's name should not be included in the invitation. "After all," she said, "Seth is my child, not hers. She didn't diaper him or take care of him when he was sick." Stepmother, as one might imagine, was equally adamant; she was "paying for part of this shindig" and certainly, as custody was shared equally between the two households, she was "definitely helping to raise this *bar mitzvah* boy." Poor Father (not to mention Son) was caught between these two very strong women and their equally legitimate claims.

It was Stacy, in charge of the invitations, who came up with the compromise. And it was fascinating. Seth's middle name, it turned out, was her maiden name, which she had never relinquished, and his last name was Father's surname. By using the child's full name and saying, "The family of Seth Lerner Steinberg fondly invites you," both Mother's name and Father's name were included, and Stepmother's name was neither included nor excluded. Father and Mother were united so that the child did not have to choose between them. Through this logistical detail, Mother was protecting emotional connections and the family was developing and practicing ways of negotiating change. Through this invitation, they were, as well, instructing their guests about their commitment to compromise and harmony.

Another example from this same family speaks further to the meaning of preparation details. This was a family whose financial resources were very limited. All of the logistical decisions were influenced by cost. Only one decision was not; it was in which hotel to house the out-of-town guests. For Stacy, it had to be the one with "the best hospitality suite," because this is where the three extended families would meet together for dinner on Friday night before services, would relax and socialize after the ceremony and before the party Saturday night, and would have brunch together on Sunday before leaving the area. It had to be a place, then, that could comfortably accommodate the families together—so that, as Stacy explained, "the child would not be pulled apart." The effort worked. Not only was it a joyous and gracious event, one in which Seth did not have to choose between families, but it was one in which Stacy was able to reconnect with her extended family whose tradition of gracious hospitality was a long and important value. This reconnection with a larger family would prove very important for this woman whose involvement with her nuclear family would necessarily be diminishing. Her child's growing maturity was necessitating not only decreased involvement with him but also with her ex-husband.

In the other research families as well—no matter how different from Stacy's—it was the mother who was implicitly expected to orchestrate the event and attend to the emotional implications of that orchestration. No matter how otherwise occupied (they all had professional positions) and no matter to what extent her husband or, in one case, her mother helped, the unspoken expectation was remarkably clear: the task of coordination was mother's; the task of managing (both pragmatically and symbolically) the family's celebration of its development was hers. And even though (or perhaps because) this requirement (to be a *balabusta,* to manage the "household") was not explicit, there was something sacred about it. Everyone expected it. It was as "ordered and rule governed"[19] as any ritual. To the extent to which Mother's attention to details served to contain the family's anxiety (about both the event and the loss of their child), served to mediate conflict, and served to create a sense of order and safety, she fulfilled the requirement.

While it is tempting here to enter into the politics (both secular and religious) of gender-defined role expectations, I will resist.[20] The purpose of this essay is not to critique the context in which the contemporary North American bar mitzvah is experienced but to acknowledge the role the mother currently plays in that experience, to explore the developmental implications of that role, and to value the skills she is necessarily honing and demonstrating in order to accomplish that role.

So far I have been focusing on the way Mother's management of details facilitates the family's development. I want to look now at the way in which it facilitates her own "individual" development. Beyond the obvious fact that as a member, she benefits by all that benefits the family, and beyond the fact that taking on and passing the test enhances her self-concept and her standing in the community, I believe that the effort has a more fundamental meaning in terms of women's emotional development. Again, this meaning can be seen from the perspective of the details.

Take, for instance, the area of food preparation. Without exception, all of the mothers in the study were in charge of this detail.[21] Whether they were cooking the entire banquet themselves or "simply" augmenting the caterer's efforts, all of the mothers worried about the quality and quantity of the food. Before the event, no matter what they were planning to provide, it was somehow not going to be enough. Afterward, no matter how successful the meal(s) had been, each wished she had done yet one more thing. Obviously, the concern about food was not a concern about nutrition. As Maurie Sacks[22] asserts in her study of women preparing *shalach mones* (Purim foods to share with others), the details of preparation contain an "embedded love message," a message that implicitly binds mother, family, and community. The research she quotes on immigrant tamale makers[23] has direct implications here: "women who engage in lengthy and complicated food preparations bind individuals in the group, 'metaphorically conveying to the recipient . . . that the women who prepare [the food are] willing to engage in such complicated tasks for the sake of interpersonal bonds.'"

In the context of the bar mitzvah, this idea of interpersonal bonding is of course central, but here, specifically, it is central to the analysis of mother's effort. The bar mitzvah is, at its core, a ritual of bonding the child to his family and its tradition (while paradoxically enabling and celebrating his differentiation from it). Beyond this, the bonding effect reverberates reflexively throughout the larger system and is central to mother's development as an emotionally mature woman.

To the extent that feminist psychology is beginning to understand women's emotional development in terms of our capacity to connect, the developmental value of being a bar mitzvah mother takes on meaning beyond that of passing a ritual test. As the Stone Center's "Self in Relation" theory suggests, "continued self development for women occurs, not through a progressive series of separations, but through the experience of evolving empathetic relationships. . . . (The developing woman's) sense of continuity with past relational ties serves as a foundation for increasing self-differentiation."[24]

With this view in mind, Stacy's poignant efforts to make her son's bar mitzvah a harmonious occasion through which she (and he) reengaged her family, and Sandy's unusual visit with her arthritic mother and her subsequent use of the ceremony as her vicarious bat mitzvah, take on additional importance. If developmental growth is about connecting and differentiating, the bar mitzvah is a perfect vehicle as well as metaphor. For the child, it is an episode of individuation in the context of connection. As the celebrant, he is symbolically declaring his teenagehood, his separation from his parents—but through a ceremony that binds him to them fundamentally. For the mother, it is an inverse drama. For her, it is an episode all about connections, but in the context of differentiating. Everything she does, from deciding on the guest list to getting her son to write his thank-you notes, is about connections; but everything she's doing, she is doing as an adult, in charge of the event. For most (traditionally aged) first-time bar mitzvah mothers, the last major life-cycle ceremony of this magnitude and importance was her own wedding, and there, at most, she shared management of the event with her mother. On *this* occasion, mother is a guest and daughter is fully in charge. The event reflects *her* values, *her* standards, *her* accomplishments, *her* growth.

It also reflects a kind of ability most associated with women that is often overlooked and taken for granted. That she can manage so logistically and emotionally complex a task speaks to what Mary Catherine Bateson describes as women's "capacity for sustained attention to diversity and interdependence." It is a capacity that, she suggests, might allow them "a different clarity of vision, one that is sensitive to ecological complexity."[25]

According to Bateson, this ability, developed over the millennia, needs to be named and valued. To the extent that it continues to be ignored and invisible, we contribute to women's ongoing sense of inferiority. By "evoking" and "defining as worthy of memory" women's managerial ability, we contribute to women's increased sense of self.[26] As Bateson puts it, "When one has matured surrounded by implicit disparagement, the undiscovered self is an exceptional resource."[27]

Likewise, to the extent that we continue to overlook the systemic implications of the bar mitzvah and continue to image the bar mitzvah mother as stereotypically hysterical, overbearing, and controlling, we contribute to a view that fundamentally underestimates the value of rites of passage and not only devalues mother's role in these rites but, indeed, supports a long psychological tradition of blaming her for most of what goes wrong (with them).

In this chapter, I offer a new perspective on the bar mitzvah and mother's role as its manager. I name the importance of what mothers do and the necessary skill that role requires. In a social context (both secular and religious) in which "women do not name reality but are named as part of a reality that is male constructed,"[28] we must necessarily create new names for what we do.[29] It is important to be part of the "larger narrative being constructed, deconstructed, and reconstructed" about ordinary women's lives.[30] To the extent that we are successful in this task, we create Bateson's opportunities for discovering "exceptional resources."

NOTES

Portions of this chapter appeared in "Mazel Tov: The *Bar Mitzvah* as a Multigenerational Ritual of Change and Continuity," in E. I. Black, J.

Roberts, and R. Whiting, eds., *Rituals in Families and Family Therapy* (New York: Norton, 1988), pp. 199–208; in "Learning about Women through (of All Things) a Study of *Bar Mitzvah:* Toward a Dialogical Research Paradigm" (paper presented at the Association for Jewish Studies Meeting, December 1988); in "Bar Mitzvah: A Family Systems Analysis" (paper presented at the Canada-Israel Conference on Social Scientific Approaches to the Study of Judaism, Concordia University, Montreal, Canada, May 1989); and in "Learning about Women through a Study of *Bar Mitzvah:* Some Thoughts about Feminist Fieldwork," *Jewish Folklore and Ethnology Review* 12, nos. 1, 2 (1990): 27–28.

All names, locations, and other identifying characteristics of families in the research have been changed.

1. With the exception of Stuart Schoenfeld's work, most sociologists dismiss the bar mitzvah as a nostalgic, if not regressive, remnant of an earlier age, anthropologists ignore it entirely, and psychologists see it simply as Oedipal drama. See the following works by Schoenfeld: "Changing Patterns of North American *Bar Mitzvah:* Towards a History and Sociological Analysis" (paper presented at the Canadian Sociology and Anthropology Association meetings, 1984, Waterloo, Ont.), "Theoretical Approaches to the Study of *Bar* and *Bat Mitzvah,*" *Proceedings of the Ninth World Congress of Jewish Studies, Division D* 11 (1986): 119–28; "Folk Judaism, Elite Judaism, and the Role of *Bar Mitzvah* in the Development of the Synagogue and Jewish School in America," *Contemporary Jewry* 9, no. 1 (1987): 67–85; "Ritual Performance, Curriculum Design, and Jewish Identity: Towards a Perspective on Contemporary Innovations in *Bar/Bat Mitzvah* Education" (paper presented at the Research Conference of the Coalition for Alternatives in Jewish Education, June 1987, Los Angeles, Calif., and at the Association for Jewish Studies, Dec. 1987, Boston, Mass.); "Integration into the Group and Sacred Uniqueness: An Analysis of Adult *Bat Mitzvah,*" in W. P. Zenner, ed., *Persistence and Flexibility: Anthropological Studies of American Jewish Identities and Institutions* (Albany: State University of New York Press, 1988), pp. 117–35; with L. Davids, "Practical and Symbolic Social Cohesion in the *Bar Mitzvah* Practices of an Orthodox Congregation" (manuscript, 1988).

2. Most skepticism is aimed at the perceived hypocrisy regarding (1) religious commitment ("The family is not observant. What a farce to have the child proclaim his commitment to a tradition his parents have abandoned. We all know he's going to quit Hebrew school as soon as the *bar mitzvah* is over"); and (2) adult responsibility ("How can anyone seriously proclaim that that baby-faced little boy barely visible behind the lectern is 'a man'? No, he's only a richer 7th grader").

3. J. Davis, "Mazel Tov: A Systems Exploration of *Bar Mitzvah* as a Multigenerational Ritual of Change and Continuity" (Ph.D. diss., University of Massachusetts, 1987); and "Mazel Tov: *Bar Mitzvah* as a Multigenerational Ritual of Change and Continuity," in E. Imber-Black, J. Roberts, and R. A. Whiting, eds., *Ritual in Families and Family Therapy* (New York: Norton, 1988), pp. 177–208.

4. This second view does not take mother out of the family context but rather emphasizes her position in relation to her family of origin rather than her nuclear family. It is a form of "double vision" that allows exploration in terms of both family and "individual development."

5. With the increasing popularity of bat mitzvahs and the growing "feminization of religion," feminist scholars (and others) are now beginning to look seriously at this ritual and beginning to explore its potential. See Cynthia Saltzman, "The Contemporary *Bar* and *Bat Mitzvah* in Theory and Practice" (paper delivered at the American Anthropological Association Meetings, Washington, D.C., 1989); and Stuart Schoenfeld, "Ritual and Role Transition: Adult *Bat Mitzvah* as a Successful Rite of Passage" (manuscript, 1989).

Increasingly, women are beginning to design bat mitzvah ceremonies that do not simply mirror bar mitzvahs but deliberately incorporate elements that specifically nurture and celebrate the sensibilities and competencies of emerging young women. In any case, the bat mitzvah speaks dramatically to Carol Gilligan's research as described by Prose, in which she contends that between the ages of eleven and fifteen or sixteen, the young woman's "moment of resistance," her "clarity of vision goes underground" and she "starts not knowing what [she] had known. . . . The morally articulate preadolescent is transformed into an apologetic, hesitant teen-ager" (F. Prose, "Confident at 11, Confused at 16," *New York Times Magazine*, Jan. 1990, pp. 22–25, 37–39, 45–46, reporting on Gilligan, *Making Connections: The Relational Worlds of Adolescent Girls at Emma Willard School* [Cambridge: Harvard University Press, 1990]).

6. N. Golan, *Passing through Transitions: A Guide for Practitioners* (New York: Free Press, 1981).

7. E. H. Friedman, "Systems and Ceremonies: A Family View of Rites of Passage," in E. A. Carter and M. McGoldrick, eds., *The Family Life Cycle: A Framework for Therapy* (New York: Gardner Press, 1980), pp. 429–60.

8. K. Tomm, "Circular Interviewing: A Multifaceted Clinical Tool," in D. Campbell and R. Draper, eds., *Applications of Systematic Family Therapy: The Milan Method* (Orlando: Grune and Stratton, 1985), pp. 33–45.

9. For example, Carter and McGoldrick, *Family Life Cycle*; E. Culler, "Change in the Context of Stability: The Design of Therapeutic Rituals for

Families" (Ph.D. diss., University of Massachusetts, 1987); F. Walsh, ed., *Normal Family Process* (New York: Guilford Press, 1982).

10. Needless to say, we all have examples of bar mitzvah "horror stories" in which this preparatory space was *not* kept sacred. There is no question that in troubled families, the bar mitzvah process can be used to maintain and intensify destructive patterns as much as it can be used for constructive growth. What I am describing is the positive potential inherent in the process.

11. J. A. Arlow, "A Psychoanalytic Study of a Religious Initiation Rite: *Bar Mitzvah,*" in R. S. Eissler, A. Freud, H. Hartmann, and E. Kris, eds., *Psychoanalytic Study of the Child,* vol. 6 (New York: International Universities Press, 1951), pp. 364–74.

12. L. Hoffman, *Foundations of Family Therapy: A Conceptual Framework for Systems Change* (New York: Basic Books, 1981).

13. This is in contrast to the well-known negative rites of passage more usually associated with the teenage years (e.g., misuse of alcohol, drugs and sex, rebelliousness, endangering behaviors). Much literature on adolescent development laments the loss of positive ritual markers for these transitional years. See, for example: D. Elkind, *The Hurried Child: Growing Up Too Fast, Too Soon* (Reading, Mass.: Addison-Wesley, 1981); A. Stevens, "Attenuation of the Mother-Child Bond and Male Initiation into Adult Life," *Journal of Adolescence* 4 (1981): 131–48; W. Quinn, A. Newfield, and H. Protinsky, "Rites of Passage in Families with Adolescents," *Family Process* 24 (1985): 101–11.

14. V. W. Turner, *The Ritual Process: Structure and Anti-Structure* (Chicago: Aldine, 1969).

15. A. van Gennep, *Les Rites de Passage,* trans. M. B. Uizdeom and G. L. Caffee (1909; Chicago: University of Chicago Press, 1960).

16. Although not too much more explicit, Father's role is definitely much clearer, certainly more public, and dramatically less ridiculed. Within the patriarchal tradition, Father is implicitly the representative elder whose ranks his son is joining. He is the role model with whom the boy is bonding. It is he who implicitly passes on the secrets of the tribe and it is he who publicly recites the "prayer of riddance" declaring that his son is now responsible for his own (religious) actions. Symbolically, father embodies the sense of loss, the sense of the changing of the generational guards. "Just yesterday" it was the father standing in the place where his son now stands, and "overnight" the boy has become the father. In all of the research families, grandfather's shadow (living or dead) was palpable as father and son stood together on the *bimah*. Symbolically also, son's bar mitzvah is a statement about father's achievement in the secular world of work. No matter how much mother's salary contributes to the family income, it is still

generally assumed that the amplitude of the event is a result of father's economic success.

17. *Balabusta* is a Yiddish word meaning "woman who manages the household and/or the family business efficiently and effectively." (In the past, the Jewish wife was often expected to manage the secular affairs of the household as her husband was otherwise occupied with study.)

To the extent that in traditional Judaism the family and home are considered sacred, mother's competence in this domain is highly valued. Furthermore, to the extent that family and home are considered sacred, the dichotomy between religious and secular analysis that I was forcing on the research was, understandably, problematic. Although I was attempting to look at the developmental (i.e., secular) implications of the bar mitzvah rather than its religious implications, the two are, of course, intertwined. To the extent that the religious/cultural aspects of any family's identity are part of it's "story," they cannot be "separated out" for the purpose of research. How much more so is this the case when the research focuses not only on families that are Jewish but also on families engaged in a bar mitzvah. It is, after all, a religious ceremony, not just a thirteenth birthday party. An unpublished paper by Rabbi H. Kushner, "Imagining the Synagogue: These Are the Generations of Abraham and Terah" (1989), has been useful in bridging this artificial dichotomy between family life and religious life: "To the extent that the *bar mitzvah* is about family," he says, "it is holy." It is "an experience in which one generation hands itself over to the next. . . . This reverence before the generations past and future may be the root experience of the holy. We meet God in the faces of our parents and our children. . . . All of us, no matter how unimaginative, prosaic, or irreligious, encounter the sacred in the faces of our parents and the faces of our children, for in them we behold our own birth and death" (p. 1).

18. E. H. Friedman, "*Bar Mitzvah* When Parents Are No Longer Partners," *Journal of Reform Judaism* 28 (1981): 53–66. For the traditional immigrant family in the early part of the century, the "event" consisted of a small kiddish for congregants and family in the synagogue. "Some shnopps and a little herring" constituted the feast, and mother's role was minimal.

19. J. Laird, "Women and Stories: Restorying Women's Self Constructions," in M. McGoldrick, C. M. Anderson, and F. Walsh, eds., *Women in Families: A Framework for Family Therapy* (New York: Norton, 1989), pp. 427–50.

20. The debate among Jewish feminists about the relative value of private versus public performance is beyond the purview of my research and this essay. I believe both sides have legitimate worldviews and deserve respectful appreciation.

21. The only exception seems to be in families where father has some

special (culturally unusual) relationship to food preparation (e.g., he is a professional chef, or a caterer, or has been for years, for whatever reasons, the acknowledged "cook in the family"). Although here I explore a positive meaning of mother's role in preparing the feast, I do not ignore the by now well-known problematic meanings of the expectation that women cook. Letty Cottin Pogrebin, in her beautifully written memoir *Deborah, Golda, and Me: Being Female and Jewish in America* (New York: Crown, 1991), explores this complex relationship of women to food and families. Within a context where Jewish wives have always prepared the ritual feasts over which their husbands presided, she speaks poignantly: "It took me years to see that my father's virtuosity depended on my mother's labor and that the seders I remember with such heartwarming intensity were sanctified by her creation even more than his" (p. 18).

22. M. Sacks, "Computing Community at Purim," *Journal of American Folklore* 102 (July–Sept. 1989): 275–91.

23. L. K. Brown and K. Mussel, eds. *Ethnic and Regional Foodways in the United States: The Performance of Group Identity* (Knoxville: University of Tennessee Press, 1985), p. 21.

24. R. Klein, "Commentary on Values and College Women's Development," *Journal of College Student Psychotherapy* 1 (Fall 1986): 25–29, 30.

25. M. C. Bateson, *Composing a Life* (New York: Atlantic Monthly Press, 1989), p. 166.

26. B. Stagoll, "From Vanguard to Old Guard: Can Family Therapy Reclaim Its Relevance?" *Family Therapy Networker* 14, no. 3 (1990): 75–77.

27. Bateson, *Composing a Life*, p. 2.

28. J. Plaskow, *Standing Again at Sinai: Judaism from a Feminist Perspective* (San Francisco: Harper and Row, 1990), p. 2.

29. At a time in our history when new "bat mitzvah options" are opening for women (e.g., girls have bat mitzvahs almost as automatically as their brothers have bar mitzvahs; women can have adult bat mitzvahs, indeed, they can be rabbis and cantors and bar/bat mitzvah tutors), it is still important to rename the "old option," that of being the bar mitzvah boy's mother, and to "restory" it with the dignity it deserves.

30. J. Laird, "Women and Stories," p. 428.

· 8 ·

Experiencing Hasidism: Newly Orthodox Women's Perspectives on Sexuality and Domesticity

DEBRA RENEE KAUFMAN

The data in this chapter reflect some of the ways in which Hasidic women who have voluntarily entered the world of Jewish Orthodoxy simultaneously accommodate and recast ritual,[1] particularly in the areas of sexuality and family. In Hebrew, women who have "returned"[2] to Orthodoxy are called *ba'alot teshuvah*. Of the 150 women I interviewed[3] across five major urban areas in the United States in the mid-1980s, 85 women[4] identified themselves as either from the Lubavitcher or Bostoner Hasidim.[5] Unlike most other Hasidic sects, these two groups believe in and have active outreach programs.

Contemporary Hasidism is based on a Jewish pietistic movement founded in eighteenth-century Poland by Israel ben Eliezer (known by Hasidim as the *Besht,* or the Master of the Good Name). Hasidism broke with the elitist tradition of scholarship common to Orthodox rabbinical academies of that time by making Judaism more accessible to poor Jews. It stressed prayer, joy, and religious devotion in all aspects of daily life, and disseminated variations on kabbalistic and mystical thought, particularly regarding the coming of the Messiah.[6] Many of the Hasidic women I studied believe that the Hasidic tradition stresses functions that honor feminine imagery and female roles and that it is through their everyday activities as Orthodox wives and mothers that the Messiah will come.[7]

Perhaps the most distinguishing feature of Hasidim, however, is their attachment and obedience to a single authority, the man known as their rebbe, who represents their specific sect's rabbinic dynasty. Bonnie Morris argues that Hasidic women differ from other Orthodox women in that they, like men, have as their central authority only one person, the rebbe. For Morris, the control of one man over his followers has opened, rather than limited, the opportunities for Hasidic women.

In the eighteenth century, writes Morris, women played an important role in disseminating Hasidic teachings. Moreover, the often literate wives and daughters of rabbis frequently served as role models for other women. Morris notes that some women were even "designated as prophetesses, received male seekers, wrote manuscripts or led discourses on the nature of the Hasidic path."[8] Despite the obvious criticism that such women represent the exceptions rather than the rule in Hasidic communities, female activism, expressed through proselytizing and maintaining the household as breadwinners for scholarly husbands, was, and often still is, quite common. Today, as in the past, especially among the Bostoner and Lubavitcher sects, women are active participants in the outreach campaigns of their respective communities. However, Hasidic women, like their other Orthodox sisters, depend on men for spiritual leadership and theological scholarship in the public corporate community that calls itself Orthodox.

Some Background

In the larger study of which these women were a part, 71 percent identified with the counterculture of the 1960s and 1970s (70). A little over 92 percent (65) of those women were Hasidic.[9] Implicit in the complaints of countercultural youth, and among the *ba'alot teshuvah* as well, was a discontent with the pluralistic relativisim of modern living. Steven Tipton believes that this kind of relativism forces us to migrate through discrepant worlds, so that "the cognitive and normative definitions of modern culture become abstracted and emptied of specific content in order to be flexible." In this way, he argues, no activity has any intrinsic value and each person is set at the center of his/her own "universe of calculated consequences."[10] For all the women in this study, the return to Orthodox Judaism constitutes a conscious rejection of secular culture and the relativism of modern living to which Tipton alludes. Most *ba'alot teshuvah* describe themselves as searching for moral guidelines, absolute truths, and above all a sense of community to counter the individualistic bent of modern culture.

Although there had been neo-Orthodox revivals before the counterculture, the "hippies'" attraction to such movements recast and popularized them. The *ba'al teshuvah* (contemporary Orthodox revival) movement in America originated in this period of "hippie" religious sentiment. Writing about the history of the contemporary revival of Orthodox Judaism, Danzger notes that the late sixties and early seventies brought a new population of believers to Jewish Orthodoxy.[11] Danzger believes that "hippies" were initially attracted to Jewish Orthodoxy because they found an affinity between their countercultural interests and their distorted understanding of Hasidism; there was its mystical philosophy, its gurulike rebbe,[12] its emotional expression of religiosity and its communal-like organization. Danzger also notes that, paralleling Eastern religions, Hasidism placed a "far heavier emphasis on ritual than was found in established American religions."[13] Reform and Conservative Judaism, the more progressive branches of Judaism, were identified with mainstream American values. Therefore, the more assimilated wings of Judaism were not suited for those youth who wanted a spontaneous and ecstatic religious experience.[14]

As they told their stories of return, women reported a common experience: their lives had been spiritually empty and without purpose before their return. The meaninglessness of modern living became a euphemism for specific issues, most commonly expressed in their perception of a cultural ambivalence and confusion toward women, toward women's sexuality, and toward family and gender roles. In contrast, Jewish Orthodoxy places family and the home above the individual. It has strict codes of behavior for both men and women. The religious world substitutes for aggression, pride, self-indulgence and an individualistic orientation (often equated in the secular world with masculinity), humility, self-restraint, and a collective orientation.

Before their "return" to Orthodoxy, the *ba'alot teshuvah* claim that they could find no "valid," "legitimate," or "moral" precepts upon which they could conduct their interpersonal relations. The norms guiding their personal lives, especially around issues of sexuality, were common features in their stories of return. For most of these women, sexuality as a means of gaining intimacy and closeness with others had become depersonalized. And indeed the late sixties and early seventies saw rapid social change in both technology and ideology surrounding sexuality, reproduction, and family. These women described familial life as no longer a place of retreat, with defined rules of behavior, but rather as yet another domain where individuals may or may not be successful in working through the order and meaning of their lives. The return to Jewish Orthodoxy among these women was as much a return to a revalued domesticity and personal life as to religion.

From Discontent to Orthodoxy

In my research, I found that despite some demographic differences, content analyses of the interview material reveal certain persistent themes. For example, almost all the women interviewed expressed some concern about the loss of boundaries in marital, familial, and sexual relations prior to their return to Jewish Orthodoxy. They spoke freely about their poor heterosexual relationships and especially of their relationships to men unwilling to make lasting commitments. To make their points when discussing the "decline" of the family, they often referred to the high divorce rate and seemingly high rate of adultery.

Almost to a woman, the *ba'alot teshuvah* in this study believe in clear and persistent differences between the sexes. Like Schely-Newman's storyteller and Sered's elderly Mideastern women (in this volume), these *ba'alot teshuvah* affirm gender differentiation and celebrate traditional feminine qualities, particularly those associated with mothering. They assert an unambiguous "profamily" stance. Deeper probing revealed other strengths associated with family and marriage, particularly among the Hasidic women. Using the kabbalistic meaning for "indwelling or presence of God," many of the Hasidic women used the word "Shekhina" to refer to the feminine in *Hasidut* (Hasidic philosophy). "Marriage," notes one woman, "is the union of God and the *Shekhina.*" Unlike some classical Christian sources that demean marriage and sexuality (for instance, marriage as a concession to the frailty of the flesh), the Hasidic women celebrate the "sacred," if not mysterious, quality of marriage and indeed of their own physicality.

In particular, the Hasidic women were very sure of their place in the family. While not necessarily excluding their husbands from family decision making, the women expressed strong feelings of control. "What I say is law," emphasized one woman. She continues: "I don't mean that my husband has nothing to say about how we spend money or raise the children, but he defers to me on most of these issues." Another woman spoke of her strong motivation to be sure that her daughters have a good secular education. "My husband agrees with me," she notes, "when I say that Dvorah [her daughter] should be afforded every opportunity to go to medical school. She is very good in science, like I was. This, of course, after she has had a good religious education. You know, there are Orthodox women doctors. There is nothing in Orthodoxy that prevents women from receiving advanced training or education."

The specialness of woman and the importance of her sphere of activity was stressed throughout the interviews and often was juxtaposed against a rather rigid concept of what was described as feminism. Feminism, for the majority of the Hasidic women in this study, is defined as the women's liberation movement focused on dismissing differences between men and women and on the world of work, where equal pay is the most important issue. In general, women felt they had gained through their Orthodoxy, and especially through their roles in the family, a new dignity, a dignity they felt most contemporary feminists disregarded and devalued. Ironically, however, they often used feminist rhetoric and emphasis when describing their current lives. This is especially evident in their discussion of the family purity laws. These laws demand a two-week sexual separation between husband and wife during the wife's menstrual cycle. To end the period of *niddah* (sexual separation), the *ba'alot teshuvah,* like other observant Orthodox women, immerse themselves in a *mikvah*[15] on the seventh day after they have completed menstruating.

Almost all women in the study noted the positive functions of the family purity laws. At the top of the list were claims of increased sexual satisfaction within the marriage. Although newly married women were more likely to complain about sexual separation, those married over longer periods of time and with more children found the laws quite positive over the adult life cycle. One Hasidic woman notes, "When we were first married I found it hard to consider sexual separation as a positive thing. In fact, during my menstrual cycle I felt I wanted to be held and loved more than at other times of the month. But I must admit over the years it truly serves as a renewal. . . . it is really like being a bride again . . . well almost."

Even among the newly married, many claimed that forced separation heightened desire. Hasidic women, more than others in the study, were the most likely to fully discuss their experiences with the family purity laws. They often referred to the autonomy and control they experienced when practicing such laws. Almost parodying Virginia Wolfe, one woman notes, "It allows me a bed of my own." Others referred to the increased time for themselves. "I can curl up with a good book during *niddah* and not feel in the least bit guilty." Others spoke of a sense of control. "I can say no with no pretence [*sic*] of a headache if I wish." The women almost unanimously characterized the laws as positive for their marriages.

Specific data on the frequency of sexual intercourse and sexual satisfaction and experimentation were not forthcoming. Modesty rules inhibit truly open discourse about such details. However, perhaps because they are *ba'alot teshuvah* and not *frum* (Orthodox) from birth, as they often refer to other Orthodox women, *ba'alot teshuvah* may be more forthcoming than other Orthodox women about their sexual lives. While it is neither clear nor very probable that all of these women are sexually satisfied, in control of their sexuality, or personally happy with marriage and/or sexuality, it is quite clear that they believe that the laws of *niddah* function positively for them.

The experiences that grow from these practices reflect more than feelings of control. The symbolic framework emerging from their language, imagery, and experiences moves beyond the self and the dyad to the community at large. For instance, no woman doubted the importance of the *mikvah* to the community. As one Hasidic woman states, "There is no doubt about it. . . . if a choice has to be made a community has to build a mikvah before it can build a *shul* (synagogue) or even acquire a *Sefer Torah* (Five Books of Moses)."

However, it is to yet another community that these women feel connected. "I feel connected to history and to other women," says one woman who has practiced the family purity laws since her marriage twelve years ago. Feeling a sense of history one woman muses, "The Jews at Masada used the mikvah." "Each time I use the *mikvah* I feel I come back to the center of Judaism and to my own core," a Hasidic woman married fifteen years proclaims. What became clear after several years of interviewing was that for these women the core of Judaism emanates from activities and obligations shared with other women—even, and perhaps most particularly, when speaking of the religious ritual surrounding their sexuality.

Rather than viewing their sexuality as merely physical/personal and/or individual, many of these *ba'alot teshuvah* place their physicality and sexuality in a timeless, spiritual context. Regarding the two-week sexual separation during menstruation, one Hasidic woman notes that "one half of the time I belong to my husband the other half to God." These women view their sexuality in what Penelope Washbourn would define as a "graceful" rather than "demonic" experience.[16] Their physiology is integrated into a wider social and symbolic framework, not reduced merely to its biological aspects. They place the family purity practices in the context of purification rites for the temple (when sexual sanctions applied to all members of the community) and hold to that "graceful" context in all of their interpretations.

One particularly articulate *ba'alat teshuvah,* who had come so far in her own studies that she taught seminars for other Hasidic women on the family purity laws, notes that "during niddah, the woman falls between categories of life and death." Calling on nonlegal but traditional sources of explanation, she argues, "When it is asked why women and not men are still subject to purity rituals I look to traditional explanations—you can find one that suggests women are closer to God because of their ability to create life. . . . still another views the woman's body as a sacred temple. I like to think of a woman's cycle as part of all the sacred time rhythms in Judaism—the Shabbat, holidays."

According to these Hasidic *ba'alot teshuvah,* a woman's cultural status in Orthodox Judaism is not devalued symbolically, explicitly, or socioculturally. These women affirm that the family purity laws are a unique engendering force, a sensuous, transformative power, symbolic not only of life but also of life's continuity.

Conclusions

The worldview expressed by many of the Hasidic *ba'alot teshuvah* in this study embraces a code in which the purpose of life is more than domination and acquisition; rather, it is the elevation of things to a sacred quality here on earth. As one woman phrased it, "A dwelling place for God below." In particular, the Hasidic women claim that they play an active role in the creation of the sacred on earth, in the transformation of the physical into the spiritual.[17] This argument does not differ from many of those made by some radical feminists who describe the reclaiming of Christianity on feminine and female terms.[18]

The concerns that these *ba'alot teshuvah* have about an impersonal world devoid of an emphasis on female, feminine, and family brings them, in some sense, almost full circle back to the countercultural roots and protest from which many of them started. By their own admission, their searches were often prompted by a sense of meaninglessness in their interpersonal relations. Caught in the dilemma of twentieth-century individualism, where personalism is reduced not only to the private arena of life but to a context where each person is set at the center of his/her own "universe of calculated consequences,"[19] these women reconstruct their personal lives by reconnecting, through the practices of Orthodox Judaism, the self, body, and family to the public Orthodox community of timeless truths.

According to formal traditional Jewish law, women are forbidden to participate in either the creation or the interpretation of those laws that govern their lives; nor can they represent the public corporate community that calls itself Hasidic in prayer or study. Yet despite this dictate, the data suggest that newly Orthodox Hasidic women experience Hasidism in ways far less restrictive than formal patriarchal law prescribes. Indeed, the values, modes of communication, personalism, and language of nurturance that emerge in these women's interviews need not be explained as based on women's unique sensibilities or differences (as most of them would claim) but rather as a product of the shared actions and meanings they derive from the activities and relationships involved in their many homosocial activities.

These Hasidic women represent an energetic community, strong in a commitment and belief that the female, and those symbols and activities identified with her, are vital and highly valued in the community at large. These women are not incorrect in their assessments that they represent the guardians of the tradition. Moreover, in their everyday lives as mothers and wives they maintain the vital distinctions between the profane and the sacred for the community as a whole (from maintaining the many dietary laws to purification in the *mikvah*).

Like women cited in Michelle Rosaldo's overview of women in anthropological studies,[20] the *ba'alot teshuvah* seem to use the very symbols and social customs that set them apart to establish female solidarity and worth and to refashion male-made symbols. The extra-domestic ties these women share with one another seem to be important sources of power and self-esteem. In such a highly sex-segregated world, these Hasidic women appear free to develop their own systems of meaning. In so doing they also make it possible to make claims upon the community, not only as individuals, but as a community of women. Separatist living may serve as a way for these women to have some control over what they define as theirs in the Hasidic community. While I do not wish to conflate all women's experiences into one simple and unvaried theme, if we open our investigations of Hasidic women beyond the activities and perspectives of men, we can glimpse yet another view of the Hasidic social order.

However, we cannot neglect the context in which these women negotiate their religious and gender identities. While Hasidism may provide these women with a woman-centered identity and communal recognition of the importance of female-linked practices and symbols, if gender identity is negotiated within the boundaries of patriarchal, social, and religious authority, it runs the risk of reinforcing essentialist formulations about women as patriarchally defined. It simultaneously reinforces patriarchal politics by further empowering those already empowered to define and refine Orthodoxy.[21]

In all likelihood, time will alter many of these women's experiences with Hasidism, especially those experiences that tie their private and religious lives so closely. If the expression of their spirituality is so closely connected to the lives they lead as wives and mothers, what might happen when those roles are completed or substantially diminished as they move along the life cycle from young wives to widows? Their choices have been made at a particular point in time and at a particular time in the life cycle. While their female collective consciousness may now mesh well with the overall definitions of themselves within the sex-segregated world of Orthodoxy, what will happen when a disjuncture arises between what is culturally given and what is subjectively experienced? The close connections the *ba'alot teshuvah* make between their domestic and religious lives may continue to affect the way they collectively interpret the symbols and rituals of the Orthodox community. (See Sered in this volume for observations about elderly Orthodox women.)

As women live longer and spend more time without children and without husbands, as most demographic projections suggest,[22] will the issues concerning their spirituality in the public religious community, as opposed to the private sphere of home, become more important to them? Will the virulent attacks against the women, including Orthodox women, who attempted to pray at the Western Wall in Israel (without violating Jewish law),[23] for instance, become problematic for women when they find more time for public rituals and spirituality? Will the aggressive stance taken against the Palestinians and the vigorous defense of Israeli settlements in the West Bank lead any of these women to question their belief that a "feminine ethos," as they collectively define it, is at the heart of Orthodoxy? The answers to these and other questions await longitudinal research.

In this chapter I have touched briefly on some of the ways in which Hasidic women experience Jewish Orthodoxy. Paralleling current theoretical thinking among social scientists interested in "new ethnography" and postmodernism,[24] I have stayed close to the "text" the Hasidic women in my study have provided. Rather than presenting them as passive representatives of a fixed and oppressive past, I have tried to capture the ways in which they expand upon meaning and symbol in response to Jewish Orthodox practice and ritual. Such agency, however, is always limited by patriarchal boundaries that are, paradoxically, often reinforced by women's activism.

NOTES

An earlier version of this chapter appeared in *Rachel's Daughters* (New Brunswick: Rutgers University Press, 1991), © 1991 by Debra Renee Kaufman. Used by permission of Rutgers University Press.

1. Sometime in their adult lives, these women consciously chose to live a Hasidic life. Some were never Orthodox, and some are more traditional than their parents, or may have lapsed in their Orthodox beliefs and practices for some period of time. Generally, most had lived outside traditional Orthodox beliefs and practices. In addition to identifying with a Hasidic community, they had to be strictly observant of the Sabbath and all the dietary laws in order to be included in this study.

2. The term *teshuvah* can be translated from the Hebrew to mean either "return" or "repent." Orthodox Jews believe that all Jews who are not currently Orthodox are considered to be in the process of "returning" or "repenting." The term in English is a misnomer in that most of these women had never been Orthodox.

3. The interviews began with a number of predefined topics but were unstructured and in-depth, focusing on the history of women's return to Orthodoxy, their current familial and communal life-style, and their views about gender roles and feminism.

4. For the majority of Hasidic women, the range of return was between the ages of eighteen and twenty-five. At the time of interviewing, most had been *ba'alot teshuvah* for an average of five years. Most came from middle-class backgrounds and currently occupy a middle-class socioeconomic status. Although they are all committed to childbearing and childrearing, close to one-third of them work outside of the home. Of those who work, the majority are in female-dominated occupations or, if in male-dominated ones, in female-dominated subspecialties. Irrespective of work status, household help and childcare of some sort is common.

5. Schneur Zalman (1745–1813) was the founder of Chabad Hasidism, which became known as Lubavitch Hasidism when its leaders moved to the Belorussian town of Lubavitch, two years after Zalman's death. Susan Handelman notes that his writings were a "unique synthesis of Rabbinical Judaism, Kabbalah, Rationalism, and applied Mysticism" ("The Crown of Her Husband: The Image of the Feminine in Chassidic Philosophy" [manuscript, Department of English, University of Maryland, College Park, 1984], p. 3). Following in his father's footsteps, the Bostoner rebbe, Rabbi Levi Yitzhak Horowitz, tailored Hasidism to the United States and located his group in Boston (although one need not live in Boston to be a follower of the Bostoner rebbe).

6. S. Sharot, *Messianism, Mysticism, and Magic* (Chapel Hill: University of North Carolina Press, 1982); B. Morris, "Women of Valor: Female Religious Activism and Identity in the Lubavitcher Community of Brooklyn, 1955–1987" (Ph.D. diss., State University of New York at Binghamton, 1990); and Liz Harris, *Holy Days: The World of a Hasidic Family* (New York: Summit Books, 1985).

7. Adopting and sometimes transforming ideas from the kabbalist and mystic Isaac ben Solomon Luria, the Hasidim embraced the idea that many divine sparks had fallen into the sphere of evil. Therefore, Hasidism is a monistic system where absolute evil has no independent existence. See Gershom Scholem, *Modern Trends in Jewish Mysticism* (New York: Schocken Books, 1961); Sharot, *Messianism;* Handelman, "Crown of Her Husband." The key task, then, of the Hasid is to uncover or penetrate the appearance of evil in order to see and have contact with the real. This places a great emphasis on contact with and transformation of the material world. It is women's greater association with the physical and material world (and women's life-sustaining functions) that these women use to support their claims that the female and feminine imagery are central to Orthodoxy.

8. Morris, "Women of Valor," p. 11.

9. Interviews with leading rabbis, lay community leaders, and known *ba'alot teshuvah* in each of five major urban cities helped locate both the Lubavitcher and Bostoner Hasidim. Once within these settings, the referral method or snowball technique of sampling (see James Coleman, *The Adolescent Society* [Glencoe, Ill.: Free Press, 1971]) was employed, thereby identifying smaller interactive groups of *ba'alot teshuvah* in each community. Interviewing ended when no new names were generated. No claims are made that the women under study were randomly drawn as a sample of a defined universe, nor can the interviewed be considered statistically representative of those who return to Orthodoxy or Hasidism, or of Orthodoxy itself.

10. S. Tipton, *Getting Saved from the Sixties* (Berkeley: University of California Press, 1982), p. 24.

11. M. H. Danzger, *Returning to Tradition: The Contemporary Revival of Orthodox Judaism* (New Haven: Yale University Press, 1989).

12. What distinguishes Hasidim from other Orthodox Jews is their devotion to their rebbe. The rebbe is considered a moral instructor and spiritual leader.

13. Danzger, *Returning to Tradition,* p. 81.

14. Robert Bellah explains that at this same period of time most mainline Protestant denominations reflected the culture's dominant ethos in being virtually devoid of anything like "ecstatic experiences" (Bellah, "New Religious Consciousness and the Crisis in Modernity," in C. Glock and R. Bellah, eds., *The New Religious Consciousness* [Berkeley: University of California Press, 1976], p. 340).

15. The *mikvah* is a collection of a special pool of water constructed according to rigid legal specifications. Until a woman has immersed herself in the *mikvah* after menstruation, she cannot resume a physical relationship with her husband.

16. P. Washbourn, "Becoming Woman: Menstruation as a Spiritual Experience," in C. Christ and J. Plaskow, eds., *Womanspirit Rising* (New York: Harper and Row, 1979), p. 228–45.

17. For further elaboration, see these works by Debra Kaufman: "Women Who Return to Orthodox Judaism: A Feminist Analysis," *Journal of Marriage and the Family* 47 (1985): 543–55; "Feminism Reconstructed: Feminist Theories and Women Who Return to Orthodox Judaism," *Midwest Sociologists for Women in Society* 5 (1985): 45–55; "Patriarchal Women: A Case Study of Newly Orthodox Jewish Women," *Symbolic Interaction* 12 (1989): 299–314; *Rachel's Daughters* (New Brunswick: Rutgers University Press, 1991).

18. See also Christ and Plaskow, *Womanspirit Rising.*

19. Tipton, *Getting Saved,* p. 24.

20. M. Rosaldo, "Women, Culture, and Society: A Theoretical Overview," in Michelle Zimbalist Rosaldo and Louise Lamphere, eds., *Women, Culture, and Society* (Stanford: Stanford University Press, 1974), pp. 17–42. See also Rosaldo, "The Use and Abuse of Anthropology: Reflections on Feminism and Cross-Cultural Understanding," *Signs* 5, no. 3 (1980): 389–417.

21. Moreover, by conflating the political with the cultural world of Jewish Orthodoxy, these newly Orthodox Jewish women ideologically support an authoritarian trend in U.S. politics, despite the fact that for the most part Orthodox Jewish leaders do not assert a self-conscious domestic political agenda.

22. J. Giele, *Women and the Future* (New York: Free Press, 1982); and H. Lopata, *Women as Widows: Support Systems* (New York: Elsevier, 1989).

23. See, for instance, the article by Rabbi Susan Grossman and R. Susan Aranoff, "Women under Siege at the Western Wall," *Women's League Outlook* (Spring 1990): 7–10.

24. See, for example, F. Mascia-Lees, P. Sharpe, and C. Cohen, "The Making and Unmaking of the Female Body in Postmodern Theory and Culture: A Study of Subjection and Agency" (manuscript, 1989).

· V ·

FOLK
VOICES

· 9 ·

Role Changes of
Tunisian Women in Israel

ESTHER SCHELY-NEWMAN

The Tunisian Jews who immigrated to Israel in the late 1940s and early 1950s left a country and a culture. They underwent a transformation from a traditional religious-patriarchal society, with a clear definition of gender roles, to a modern society with a Western secular orientation and ambiguous gender roles. The purpose of this essay is to explore one woman's responses to these changes as manifested in a traditionally female mode of expression, the folktale.

Having studied Tunisian women's narratives over a period of time, I have found that women continue to transmit their traditional values while adjusting to a changing reality. The tension between old values and new social contexts will be explored here through the analysis of one folktale told twice by the same narrator with a twenty-five-year interval between the tellings. Although the narrator acknowledges changes in the cultural surrounding, she clings tenaciously to deeply held values of her culture of origin.

The Narrator

Jula, the narrator of "The Woman Who Saved Her Husband," was born in 1917 in Tunisia and emigrated to Israel in 1949, accompanied by her husband and children. She and her family still live in Tsomet, a small agricultural community (moshav) in the Negev desert, founded by them and other Tunisian immigrants in 1949.[1] In Tunisia Jula lived in an extended family, and her life could be compared to that of other women of her age in Tsomet. She did not grow up with her biological parents but was given at the age of three to the care of her mother's childless sister. Like other women in the community Jula had a French elementary education from the Alliance Israelite Universelle schools in Tunisia. Before her marriage, she worked for few a years helping in the family store and then sewed embroidered trousseaux for rich Jewish or Moslem brides. After Jula married in 1940, she lived with her in-laws and later moved back to the house of her adoptive parents, a residence pattern typical of other Tunisian women.

Tsomet women remember with nostalgia mornings in Tunisia spent with other women in the household and visiting female relatives in the afternoons and on Saturday. They describe how women shared their work, their concerns, and their stories, and how during long winter nights family members would listen to the family storyteller. As a child in Tunisia Jula heard stories in these family settings. By contrast, in Israel, people in Tsomet live in houses occupied only by the nuclear family; most women of Jula's age have grandchildren, only some of whom live in Tsomet. Today's children have interests other than listening to stories: they read books, play computer games, and mostly watch television. Women complain about the lack of narrative occasions and lament that they enjoy only infrequent storytelling events, generally around gatherings of relatives for family celebrations. Nevertheless, women find opportunities to continue to tell their traditional tales.[2] Like most women in Tsomet, Jula is an occasional storyteller; her audience is the immediate family and close friends.[3] Stories told to her as a child form the core of her repertoire today.

Mimi, Jula's oldest daughter who was born in 1942, started collecting tales when she was in high school. These tales, told by Tsomet people in Judeo-Arabic and French, were written down in Hebrew and sent to the Israeli Folklore Archives (IFA). As Jula's younger daughter, I also collected stories from family and friends, and eventually made the narratives of Tsomet settlers the subject of my doctoral dissertation at the University of Chicago. Tsomet people enjoy narrating and welcome the opportunity to have their stories tape-recorded and their pictures taken. Recording stories I heard many times as a child allowed me to compare old and new versions, as I was able to document tales that had been recorded in earlier periods.

Among the stories collected for the second time was "The Woman Who Saved Her Husband." I found this story of particular interest because it was narrated by the same woman in a similar context: to a daughter collecting folktales. I can therefore assume that the differences between the versions cannot be attributed to factors such as narrative traditions belonging to different narrators or to a significant change in the context in which the stories were told. Faulty memory and limited occasions for hearing and narrating the tale may account for some changes; nevertheless, the changes between the two versions of this tale are not unique to Jula's repertoire. I have collected narratives with similar changes from other women as well. I believe the tale clearly indicates issues of general concern to women of the same background with similar life experiences.

The Woman Who Saved Her Husband—First Version

This version of the tale was narrated in 1959 to Mimi, who wrote the story in Hebrew and sent it to IFA to be published in a collection of Tunisian folktales (synopsis):

Once there was a beautiful woman whose husband loved her dearly and could not part from her side. One time, however, his business required that he travel and he took his wife's picture with him for comfort. Arriving at his destination and alone in his room at night he felt lonely and lit a candle to look at his wife's picture, unaware that it was the night that the queen went to her bath and that the king had ordered that no light should be in use in deference to the queen's modesty. The next day he was brought before the king and accused of disobedience. After explaining his situation the king demanded to see the picture and immediately was smitten with the wife's beauty. The husband was put in jail and one of the ministers was sent to bring the wife to the king.

The wife was suspect of the messenger's sincerity despite presents and an invitation from her husband to join him. She pretended to agree and lured the messenger to her husband's room with a promise of a fine dinner. In route, she dropped him into a dry well and forced him to work for his food. After a while the king sent another messenger and he too was imprisoned. The king became suspicious of the situation and went himself to see the woman. Like his messengers he was so dazzled by the beauty of the woman that he fell into the well. In exchange for food the king sent an order to release the husband to her and to compensate him for his business loss.

The wife dressed as a man and traveled to the town where her husband was jailed. She freed him and returned home in secret, to release the king and his servants. The husband returned home and the couple lived happily ever after.[4]

This folktale is a woman's tale, defined both by its content and the context in which it is performed. The narrated events (the story) deal with the family unit, a concern of women. The structure of such tales is often based on the "Lack → Lack Liquidated" formula.[5] The tale begins when the heroine loses or lacks something of great importance; frequently it is a husband or children who disappear. This "lack" is liquidated when the heroine retrieves her loss and the family unit is restored. The role of women is defined by their gender: they are (or are expected to be) good wives and mothers. The context of narration—the narrating event—is also female dominated: this story and similar ones are told by women primarily to female audiences in the home, in typical exchanges of information and stories that occur during women's visits and collective work efforts.[6]

The plot of the tale and its basic premises support traditional North African views of a woman's place and role, and the narrative elements (motifs) typify many tales from the area. The public sphere is the male domain and the woman's role is defined by her family and house. The heroine is a wife waiting for her husband's message or his return home. She is to be found in the confinement of her home or when the whole city is turned into a private domain. The sight of a woman, even if only in a picture, causes the plot's entanglement. Men, on the other hand, travel freely in the world and encounter other people openly.

The Woman Who Saved Her Husband—Second Version

On May 12, 1984, I recorded a conversation with Jula. The taped conversation, in Judeo-Arabic and French, includes childhood memories and miraculous healings, a legend about Elijah the prophet, and two folktales that have appeared in the printed collection of Tunisian tales. One of these is "The Woman Who Saved Her Husband." A synopsis of the "new" tale reveals variations from the 1959 version.

Once there was a beautiful woman whose husband loved her dearly and could not part from her side. One time, however, his business required that he travel and he took his wife's picture with him for comfort. He became successful in the town of his destination and the local merchants complained to the king who summoned him for interrogation. While showing his documents, the picture of the wife was revealed. The king demanded to see the picture and immediately was smitten with the wife's beauty. The husband was put in jail and one of the ministers was sent to bring the wife to the king.

The wife was suspect of the messenger's sincerity despite presents and an invitation from her husband to join him. She pretended to agree and lured the messenger to her husband's room with a promise of a fine dinner. In route she dropped him into a dry well. Then came the second messenger, who also was locked up. The king himself finally arrived and the wife, who saw the lust in his eyes, tricked him into the well with his messengers. The king gave her an official release for her husband in exchange for food and she went to the town where her husband was jailed and released him. The united couple returned home and lived happily ever after.[7]

Jula was unaware that she had changed the tale. When asked, she assured me that this was the "true" story and that she always told it that way. Nevertheless, when one compares the earlier and later versions three main changes are evident:

1. The episode about the taboo on seeing the queen is omitted in the second version.

2. The encounter between the king and the husband, during which the picture of the wife is seen, has been altered.

3. In order to rescue her husband the woman does not dress up as a man or hide her actions in the later version.

What is the significance of these changes? Do they indicate changes in attitude toward women's role, suggesting that the narrator rejects the traditional notion of woman's place? Is it appropriate to consider the second version as an oikotype, a tale adapted to different ways of life and beliefs?[8] Or, perhaps, do the changes represent only a modernization of context, making the tale more acceptable to a contemporary Israeli audience. I will demonstrate that Jula reconstructs this tale, on both surface *and* deeper conceptual levels, in her efforts to assimilate the different gender relations to which she had been exposed in her new life in Israel.[9]

Women's Role

The transformations in Jula's tale can be better understood when we compare the traditional role of Jewish women in North Africa with contemporary women's lives in Israel. Jewish tradition emphasizes the role of women as wives and mothers. The Mishnah (code of Jewish law) states that women will die at childbirth if they do not adhere to three mitzvoth (commandments): (1) lighting Sabbath candles, (2) burning a portion of the dough when baking bread (*challah*), and (3) observing the laws of menstruation (*niddah*).[10] These clearly are marked as women's commandments—no man can ever die at childbirth—and they create a framework for female activity. On an everyday basis, these commandments stress the home as the center of women's activity.

An analysis of beliefs and behavioral patterns of Tsomet women indicates that although they are not versed in Jewish religious arguments they do define their womanhood in terms of procreation (*niddah*), food preparation (*challah*), and preserving the Sabbath. Not only do they see women's principal roles as mothers and wives, and the kitchen as a female domain, but they also express a conceptual connection between the three mitzvoth. For example, women see a direct relationship between the health of children and the mother's adherence to laws of food preparation. A story is told about a woman in Tsomet who had a sick child, and when she vowed to avoid cooking on the Sabbath, her son recovered.[11] Another story is told about a pregnant woman in Tunisia whose Sabbath bread did not rise properly; she was so upset that she miscarried the child right there at the public baking oven.[12] Jewishness and womanhood for the older women in Tsomet mean home, husband, and children.

Jewish and Moslem traditions complement each other concerning the role of women. Studies of women in North Africa treat the role and place of women in the traditional Islamic world.[13] The data indicate a division of space between men and women: the public space is exclusively male, while the private space is shared by both genders but is controlled by women. While the Jewish tradition does not require a strict separation between genders or the veiling of women, the influence of Islamic culture is strong among North African Jews who lived side by side with Arabs for hundreds of years.[14] It is not surprising therefore to find in both cultures numerous folkloristic expressions about the home as woman's place. Many Jewish as well as Moslem proverbs and riddles identify the woman as the house, household items, property, or edibles.[15] By metaphorical persuasion, then, women are relegated to the private domain, the locus of food preparation and procreation.[16]

North African folktales generally also express these traditional views: women are beautiful and irresistible, and men frequently fall in love with them at first sight. Thus, being outside the private sphere, exposed to men, results in severe repercussions for women. Even if the woman does not leave the house but inadvertently is seen through a window or from a roof top, or if her beauty is merely mentioned in public, it may lead to tragic developments because men cannot resist challenging women's chastity. Crossing the boundary (whether actual or not) of the private sphere for women is a serious transgression of the North African moral code.

Jula and other women of her generation encountered a very different world from their Judeo-Moslem one upon emigration from Tunisia. The people who settled Tsomet emigrated mostly as individuals or young couples and were housed on small farms that were designated for nuclear families. Extended families were not always allowed to settle in moshavim because the older parents were seen as a burden on the developing farms. Furthermore, families did not always emigrate as one unit because some members preferred to remain in Tunisia, to emigrate to France, or to join their Israeli relatives some years later. Additionally, not all members of the same family were willing to radically change their urban life-style and to become farmers in the new country.

The traditional structure of family has changed and women no longer have the support of co-residing extended families. Women rely on friends, neighbors, and their husbands in times of need. There also were changes in the division of labor: women participated in the building of the community and worked in the fields side by side with men. Economic necessities and new opportunities for employment allowed women to join the work force and to search for employment outside the home or family farm. Thus, a new type of partnership between husband and wife was created that challenged traditional marital relationships and perceptions of women's proper role and place.[17]

In addition to these changes the North African immigrants were introduced to different values from other, especially European cultures. They met women in official positions and saw women soldiers participating in traditional male domains. Finally, the increased level of education available to women exposed older Tsomet women to new female role models. In 1950 only one woman had received a high school diploma; in Tsomet in 1990 several college graduates, teachers, nurses, and a variety of semiskilled workers could be counted among the resident women. Through the example of the younger generation, the older women experience changes in gender relations and division of labor within their own community and households.

Discussion

The reality depicted in the first version of the tale, where women do not appear in public and should not be seen by men (other than their husbands), is no longer the case in Israel. Jula and other narrators understand this, and therefore the taboo of seeing the queen on her way to the bath can no longer provide a realistic background for Jula's story. In the second version Jula changes this scene to a business encounter between the king and the husband. She equates the unlimited power of past kings with the authority of bureaucrats. Jula now has this encounter take place in a typical modern setting where individual material success may be a reason for jealousy and competition. The division of private and public space no longer exists in Jula's world, and the need for disguise and secrecy in the rescue has also become obsolete. In the second version Jula acknowledges this change by omitting any mention of the woman wearing men's clothing: the wife obtains the release of the husband, and the couple returns home together. These substitutions reflect the narrator's modernization of reality on the descriptive surface level and may be equal to changes of names or places to familiarize a story to the audience. An analagous example would be the substitution of a car for a camel or a plane for a magic carpet as means of transportation.

These same changes in the tale, however, lend themselves to a deeper theoretical interpretation utilizing the concept of "honor and shame." Although the importance of the "honor and shame" complex as a central unifying value in all Mediterranean societies is in dispute, it is assumed to be salient in many cases.[18] As explained by

Gilmore, "Honor is everywhere 'closely associated with sex.' Its basic currency and measurement is the 'shame' of women, by which Mediterraneanists mean female sexual chastity."[19] From this point of view, the interaction between the king and the merchant husband in the story acquires additional meaning. The king's order to darken the houses when his queen goes to her bath in effect makes the streets into a private domain for the queen's sole use. By disobeying the order, in having his room lit, the husband enters the queen's private space, infringes on her chastity, and thereby challenges the king's "honor." It is only appropriate for the king to punish the man in the same manner, by attempting to invade, literally, the merchant's "property," his wife in her own house.

The alternate scene in Jula's second version—the merchant presenting his papers according to the king's demand and the wife's picture accidentally disclosed—represents not only a modern way of life but a different relationship between men and women. Women's chastity is no longer the sole yardstick of men's honor, as a wife now is only one of many concerns of her husband. This change is metaphorically depicted in the treatment of the wife's picture: in the first version the husband cherishes the picture, lighting a candle to look at it when lonesome, whereas in the second version the picture lies between other documents and is easily discovered in an ordinary marketplace transaction.

Note that the main plot of "The Woman Who Saved Her Husband" was not altered. As indicated by Noy, changes that create a new context occur mainly in the beginning and the end of tales.[20] The nucleus of the tale remains intact: the clever woman outsmarts the king and saves her husband. In both versions the woman is vulnerable and thought to be easy prey for men but turns out to be active, resourceful, and wise. It is important to point out, however, that her initiative is displayed within the boundaries of the traditional role of a faithful wife, ready to commit herself to the dangers of the male public world in order to save her husband. The type of dangers the woman is subject to in the public domain are the same in both versions because men are conceptualized as unable to resist women's sexuality in Judeo-Moslem culture.[21] The message remains clear: women should be careful in the presence of nonfamiliar men and in their interaction with them.

Adjustments to the new reality notwithstanding, Jula shows no indication of altering her perception of an ideal women's behavior, and her stories illustrate this attitude. Even in other tales where the woman is strong and initiates her own actions, her goal nevertheless is to return to her traditional role. In the Mediterranean Judeo-Moslem tradition women can fulfill themselves only by being wives and mothers; they marry to achieve social status and visibility.[22]

Subsequently, in folktales, the only acceptable reason for a woman to leave the safety of the private sphere is to rescue a lost husband or children. It is for these reasons alone that a woman would cross the otherwise rigid boundary between the private and public spheres. All activities, adventures, and initiatives are but a means to be able to return to the role of wife and mother. A woman without her husband is lacking an important element of her identity and social status. Without a husband she must wear men's clothes, not only because of the dangers she faces in the public sphere, but also because without her manly complement woman is not complete.[23] It is only when she regains her loss and her status of "wife" that she can once again wear women's dress. In the second version of the story, the clothing or "packaging" of the woman in public loses some significance, but the wife's purpose remains the same: to rescue her husband and thereby to become once again whole. In folktales, the rescue of the husband and the return to the status of "woman" completes the structural formula of the "Lack → Lack Liquidated" theme.

Although the perception of ideal womanhood did not change in the eyes of the older Tunisian immigrants in Israel, other changes did occur that generally have bearing on women's narratives. Performance is not only a dynamic process built on collaboration between narrator and audience but also a social interaction based on complementary responsibilities of the participants and the existence of formal or stylistic patterns. Therefore, social realities have an effect on narrative traditions.[24] For example, some differences between the versions may be attributed to the setting, the immediate context of narration: the first version was told to the elder daughter, then an unmarried high-school student, while the second was told to the younger daughter when she was married and lived and worked away from home. The division of domains between genders is perhaps not easily transmitted to a mature career woman, and therefore Jula altered the story. However, the changes discussed here are unique neither to Jula nor to this particular context of narration: similar adjustments to contemporary life are found in other tales collected from Tunisian Israeli women in recent years.

Furthermore, changes in the division of labor between genders afford women life experiences that hitherto were exclusively male. Women currently encounter men who are not their husbands or close relatives in a variety of social and business settings, and the opportunities for cross-gender interactions are greater than in Tunisia. Women also have access to a larger audience and are not restricted to all-female and child audiences: they can express their concerns and point of view to men as well as to women; these liberties are reflected in their storytelling.

My data from Tsomet support Webber's contention that Tunisian women traditionally narrate fictive tales that are metaphorical representations of the world. Men, on the other hand, tell stories based on their experience in the public sphere, a genre considered to be "true" stories. Modernity, both in Tunisia and in Israel, produces changes; to wit, women are gaining access to real-life stories.[25] In the case of Tsomet, many group interactions now take place where men and women share narratives of different genres. As a general rule men do not visit women or vice versa, but if a woman comes to visit a neighbor on a Saturday afternoon, the husband may stay with the women and join the conversation. Such group conversations frequently include storytelling of personal experiences and fictive narratives. Women use stories to construct their world and formulate their attitudes toward others. Through storytelling they communicate to the next generations their ideal female image. Notwithstanding the significant changes in women's behavior from generation to generation, the message remains the same: the *real* place of the woman, if not literally in the house, is in the domestic sphere, and her duties are to be a faithful wife who helps her husband in need.

Conclusion

The variations observed in "The Woman Who Saved Her Husband" as told in 1959 and 1984 by Jula in Tsomet, Israel, are similar to those in tales collected from other Tunisian women in recent years. The narrator and women of her generation recognize changes in modern life and tend to adapt their tales to the new reality; but these changes are not only surface-level adjustments. The disguise in men's clothing or the taboo on seeing the queen on her way to the bath may not be relevant or acceptable reality in Israel today; the substitution of these motives indicates a change in attitudes of women vis-à-vis men. Women in recently collected tales are stronger, more outspoken, more active in the public sphere, and more likely to take the initiative than those in tales collected in earlier years in Israel and in Tunisia. Perhaps this is to be expected given an Israeli reality where women go to school, serve in the Israeli Defense Forces, participate in the work force, and have opportunities in the public sphere.

At the same time that Jula and women of her generation recognize the effects of modern life, they still define womanhood primarily in terms of house and motherhood, as expressed in this particular tale. Ironically, the public exposure, the freedom of women, increases their vulnerability and the tale appropriately warns younger women of the dangers in the public sphere. In Israel today, men's honor may not be measured solely by women's chastity, but women like Jula still see sexual behavior as the measure for their own honor.

NOTES

1. Narratives of founders of Tsomet have been studied as representing personal and communal identity. Names of people and places have been changed. See Esther Schely-Newman, "Self and Community in Historical Narratives: Tunisian Immigrants in an Israeli Moshav" (Ph.D. diss., University of Chicago, 1991).

2. My data include 149 folktales and 62 legends collected from Tunisian immigrants. Of those totals 115 of the folktales and 27 of the legends were narrated by women (see below on genre/gender distinctions), mostly from the older generation. Additionally, 74 of the folktales were about women. The narrator discussed here, Jula, contributed 43 folktales and 6 legends. Narratives were collected in 1977, 1984–85, and 1987–91.

3. There are a few individuals in Tsomet who are considered "storytellers," and they would be asked to narrate when people got together. For example, I was visiting the community center where older women gather and asked them about folktales; they pointed at one woman and urged her to narrate.

4. Israel Folklore Archives, University of Haifa (hereafter IFA), #1247, tale #68, published in Dov Noy, ed., *Jewish Folktales from Tunisia* (Hebrew)

(Jerusalem: Jewish Agency, 1966); translated into French and published as *Contes populaires racontes par des Juifs de Tunisie* (Jerusalem: Jewish Agency, 1968).

5. Cf. Alan Dundes, "Structural Typology in North American Folktales," in Alan Dundes, ed., *The Study of Folklore* (Englewood Cliffs, N.J.: Prentice-Hall, 1965), pp. 206–15.

6. See also Margaret R. Yokom, "Woman to Woman: Fieldwork and the Private Sphere," in Rosan Jordan and Susan Kalcik, eds., *Women's Folklore, Women's Culture* (Philadelphia: University of Pennsylvania Press, 1985), pp. 45–53.

7. IFA #15688.

8. Dov Noy, "The Jewish Versions of the 'Animal Language' Folktale (AT 670): A Typological Structural Study," in Joseph Heinemann and Dov Noy, *Studies in Aggadah and Folk Literature* (Jerusalem: Magnes Press, 1971), pp. 171–208.

9. See Lauri Honko, "Four Forms of Adaptation of Tradition," *Studia Fennica* 26 (1981): 19–33; Eli Yassif, "The Tale of the Man Who Did Not Swear: From Jewish Oikotype to Israeli Oikotype" (in Hebrew), *Jerusalem Studies in Jewish Folklore* 8 (1985): 7–32.

10. Tractate Shabbat, 2:6.

11. See discussion of women's perception of self in Esther Schely-Newman, "The Peg of Your Tent: Narratives of North African Israeli Women," in Harvey E. Goldberg, ed., *Sephardic and Middle Eastern Jews in Modern Times: Historical and Anthropological Studies* (Bloomington: Indiana University Press, forthcoming).

12. The narrative is treated in Schely-Newman, "Peg of Your Tent," and in Esther Newman, "The Three Sins of Jewish Women" (paper presented at the 1989 Annual Meeting of the American Folklore Society, Philadelphia, Pa.).

13. Daisy Dwyer, *Images and Self Images* (New York: Columbia University Press, 1978); Fatima Mernissi, *Beyond the Veil* (1975; Bloomington: Indiana University Press, 1987).

14. In addition to common religious beliefs, the long period of living in Moslem countries resulted in cultural borrowing. The Islamic influence is particularly strong with regard to folk beliefs and the status of women. See Raphael Patai, *The Seed of Abraham* (New York: Charles Scribner's Sons, 1986).

15. Abundant examples can be found in printed collections such as: Louis Brunot and Elie Malka, *Textes Judeo-Arabe de Fes* (Judeo-Arab Texts of Fez) (Rabat: Ecole du Livre, 1939); David Cohen, *Le Parler Arabe des Juifs de Tunis* (The Arab Speech of Tunisian Jews) (Paris–La Haye: Mouton, 1964); Jean Quememeur, *Enigmes Tunisiennes* (Tunisian Enigmas) (Tunis: Publications de l'Institut des Belles Lettres Arabes, 1944).

16. Cf. James Fernandez, *Persuasions and Performances* (Bloomington: Indiana University Press, 1986), pp. 23–25.

17. Forouz Jowkar, "Honor and Shame: A Feminist View from Within," *Feminist Issues* 6 (1986): 45–65; Moshe Shokeid, "Continuity and Change among North African Jews in Israel," *Jewish Folklore and Ethnology Newsletter* 5 (1982): 1–3, and "Transformation in Family Life during Cultural Changes," in Shlomo Deshen and Moshe Shokeid, eds., *The Jews of the East* (in Hebrew) (Jerusalem: Schocken Books, 1984), pp. 61–70.

18. See the critique by Michael Herzfeld, "Honor and Shame: Problems in Comparative Analysis of Moral Systems," *Man* (n.s.) 15 (1980): 339–51.

19. David D. Gilmore, "Introduction: The Shame of Dishonor," in David D. Gilmore, ed., *Honor and Shame and the Unity of the Mediterranean* (Washington, D.C.: American Anthropological Association, 1987), pp. 2–21.

20. Noy, "'Animal Language' Folktale."

21. Mernissi, *Beyond the Veil*, p. 4.

22. See Judith R. Baskin, "Silent Partners" (in this volume), for rabbinic ideas about the complementarity of maleness and femaleness in marriage.

23. Carol Delaney makes this point regarding women in Turkey, but it is valid in other Mediterranean areas as well. See Delaney, "Seeds of Honor, Fields of Shame," in Gilmore, ed., *Honor and Shame,* pp. 5–48.

24. See Richard Bauman, *Verbal Art as Performance* (1977; Prospect Heights, Ill.: Waveland Press, 1984).

25. Sabra Webber, "Local History Narratives in a Tunisian Mediterranean Town" (Ph.D. diss., University of Texas–Austin, 1981); and "Women's Folk Narratives and Social Change," in Elizabeth W. Fernea, ed., *Women and the Family in the Middle East* (Austin: University of Texas Press, 1985), pp. 310–16. See also note 3 above.

· 10 ·

Seasons of the Soul:
Context and Meaning in
an Orthodox Girls High School

SALLY CHARNOW

Sunday, March 9, 1986. There was no advertisement for Shevach High School's music and dance festival, *Seasons of the Soul*, on the door of Stephen A. Halsey Junior High School. If your daughter was not in the performance or you had not read the ad in the *Jewish Free Press* (an Orthodox Jewish English-language weekly), it would never occur to you to go in.

Women and young children poured through the entrance: this performance of adolescent girls was off-limits to adult men in accordance with the Orthodox interpretation of Jewish law (halakah). The students of Shevach High School, an all-female institution with a scholarly curriculum split between religious and secular studies, created and performed *Seasons of the Soul*. I saw the ad in the *Jewish Free Press* and came to the performance to consider *Seasons of the Soul* as a theatrical representation of the community.

Ticket and refreshment tables flanked the school's entrance. The music of the Sephardic singer Chiam Moshe echoed in the background. The music, the posters, the kosher refreshments, and the girls in costume and make-up rehearsing last-minute lines and dance routines around the chaotic entranceway transformed this gray anonymous public school space in Queens into a place filled with backstage vitality. The Shevach community was taking time out from textbooks and lessons to celebrate itself.

In this chapter I will examine three different social and political contexts of the performance, each of which represents a different set of meanings embodied in *Seasons of the Soul*. These meanings are both implicit and explicit in the Shevach girls' construction and presentation of themselves. While in my analysis I juxtapose the three perspectives in a discontinuous and contradictory narrative, perching each context uneasily beside the next, the disjuncture in the text allows us to experience problems in the relationship between meaning and context: one context may obscure or deny one meaning or set of meanings while another may suggest only one possible interpretation. This approach is needed to unravel the plurality of meanings attached, in Jewish culture, to femaleness. These meanings are often at odds with each other, always problematic, and inevitably linked to power relationships.

I rely upon Bakhtin's concept of "heteroglossia" in relation to language and context. Bakhtin uses the term "heteroglot" to describe the multiplicity of meaning in language. "Language is heteroglot from top to bottom," he explains, "it represents the co-existence of socio-ideological contradictions between the present and the past, between differing epochs of the past, between different socio-ideological groups in the present,"[1] The concept of heteroglossia—varied voices—is not new in the discipline of anthropology. In fact, the recognition that fieldwork is significantly composed of language events and that the ethnographic text treats many voices, those of different informants as well as that of the ethnographer, has led to a major rethinking of the role of ethnographer as "author" and the necessarily subjective character of the fieldwork experience. (See the introduction in this volume.) By placing side by side three contradictory contexts—the performers envisioning themselves, the embodiment of gender constructions, and the politics of the discourses of Judaism—my analysis of *Seasons of the Soul* reveals Bakhtin's concept of heteroglossia in both language and form.

The First Context: Through the Eyes of the Performers Themselves

The festival director and Shevach alumna Devorah Ochs explained that *Seasons of the Soul* evolved from "wanting to do something poetic that would also have meaning in the Jewish religion." It is important to note that this Orthodox teacher very casually incorporates into her own self-image the right and ability to generate

Jewish meaning. "There would be two dimensions. So the seasons, what about them? We didn't want to just do the Jewish holidays— that's boring. So we combined the religious with nature and emotion. Each season would have a dance dealing with nature and emotion. The music and drama would be the religious part."

The range of musical style and genre chosen for the festival spans the religious and the secular worlds, including traditional Jewish and Israeli folksongs, rock 'n' roll, soul singing, the blues, classical music, and Broadway show tunes.[2] The song I examine here, "What Page Are You On in Prayer Book Blues," is composed by the Diaspora Yishiva, a group of "returnees"[3] who gear their music to the younger generation.

The festival song "What Page Are You On in Prayer Book Blues" exemplified artistic syncretism. Two girls dressed as hillbilly yeshiva boys in flannel shirts, jeans, caps, sidelocks, and prayershawls are sitting in chairs in front of the curtain, center stage. As hillbilly yeshiva boys in drag, they sing the following lyrics in a twang, quasi-country blues style:

> I've got the what page are you on in Prayer Book Blues
> Am I to sit or stand in Synagogue Blues
> Oh, my folks sent me to *cheder*
> When I was just a child
> Instead of learning *aleph bes*
> I was out there running wild.
>
> And the guy right next to me is taking a snooze
> I don't know what I am reading
> I don't know what to speak
> God spoke to us in Hebrew
> But to me the thing is Greek.
>
> I've got the kid knows less than me Blues
> And its not nice to sit and sing the Blues
> So its *cheder* for you young man
> Learn your *aleph bes*
> Don't you dare take after me
> With egg all on your face
>
> I guess I'll see you later
> 'cause I'm going back to *cheder*.

This song satirizes the need of many unobservant Jews for page numbers to be announced in synagogue during services, thereby acknowledging the girls own perceived superiority and knowledge of the holy text. It also refers to an internal Jewish discourse: in the less Orthodox congregations, page numbers often are called out, continually helping the participants locate the correct place in the service. As a representation it unites contradictory elements in a cohesive system. The women clearly identify themselves with the knowledgeable Orthodox branch of American Jewish practice, distancing themselves from their less learned and nonpracticing "sisters." The costume, musical form, and accent foreground everything that is not Jewish, yet the lyrics and the moral would only be understandable and humorous to this particular audience.

A feeling of security and community solidarity emerged from this performance; as one student explained, "We don't want to be isolated or sheltered. It's not like the *Goyim* are living in our world—we live in theirs. We have to strengthen ourselves, keep our identities, but you can't stifle yourself, or put a force field around yourself. We know we will be affected. It's important to know what's happening in the Jewish and non-Jewish world."

The dichotomy between the secular and religious is experienced and recognized by the insiders themselves. The tension is exemplified throughout the interviews I conducted. Speaking with great integrity, pride, and clarity, the students divide the world into two spheres: the secular world and the Orthodox Jewish world. Within the context of the secular world, the sky is the limit. They articulate plans for attending university, receiving advanced degrees, and working in professional careers such as medicine and law. Each girl sees herself as both a mother and a career woman. The school is proud of its students' academic achievements and encourages the young women to work hard and develop their scholarly abilities and resources. Education is highly regarded in the community. Yet, in the religious context, these young women define their gender roles clearly by the Scriptures (in their Orthodox interpretations), and are ready and willing to completely comply with these restrictions. For example, when asked if any of them are interested in becoming rabbis, they respond in unison, "The only way to become a *rebbetzin* [rabbi's wife] is to marry a rabbi." "It's not a woman's purpose to be a rabbi," one girl added. "We have to support the family (meaning financially and emotionally) and don't have time to study; we have too much work to do."

The tightly knit community of Shevach High School creates and maintains its identity by not limiting the girl's creative choices to a "traditionally" Jewish world. It seems that the girls embrace both secular and religious sources of authority. When one is dislodged from the center, the other comes into focus, allowing for a certain flexibility in their cultural repertoire. As consumers in the material world, the girls actively reproduce and shape meaning within the Orthodox context. "Prayerbook Blues" is a representation of how the Shevach High School community constructs its identity by choosing comfortably from both secular and religious worlds.

The Second Context: An Analysis of Gender Roles and Relationships

The girls dressed as young yeshiva *bochers* in "What Page Are You On in Prayer Book Blues" provoke another set of questions with regard to women, girls, and performance of self-identity. Aside from the obvious transgression of halakic prohibitions of cross-dressing, there are broader implications in the portrayal of boys by young girls, contributing both to the cultural significance and theatrical success of the song. Recent gender analysis sheds light on the use of drag as a convention. Within the dominant culture, it is very rare that a woman will impersonate a man at all, even rarer that it will appear amusing. In the theater, drag works when men play women, the marginalized Other, because the audience always knows that men are creators and controllers of the discourse. It then becomes humorous for the one in power to portray the Other on the margins of society. When a woman plays a man, she is miming the subject, and unless the intended audience is entirely female—as in the case of most lesbian performance—it often is not funny, and most probably not even attempted. However, by addressing an audience of women only, the girls of Shevach High School can laugh and poke fun at their male counterparts. They are able to create a sense of themselves as girls and to feel their own power—a power confined to the private sphere of the women's community.

"I guess we have become more liberated," one student remarked; "we can do things that men can do. There is even a feeling that women are sometimes superior to men [they giggle]. We can entertain for women who usually get nothing. It feels great. There is even a 'famous' women's singing group called Ashira. They record tapes that are sold only to other women. It says on the tape that men shouldn't buy it. If they do, it's their problem."

The girls of Shevach neither self-consciously portray themselves as feminists nor accept sex roles as anything but God-given.[4] The feminist critic Edith Diamond argues that it is only by telling the "stories which bear all too painfully the inscriptions of history, that we find the female subject, not transcended yet not erased, but rather carefully, subversively at odds with what exists."[5] It is my belief that the Orthodox girls have not in fact assumed their identity as women within the dominant Orthodox community, nor have they placed themselves at odds with it. Their self-image relies on patriarchy, which presumes a separate female-centered sphere, distinct from, but not equal to, the male-centered one. The separateness of the female domain obscures, for the girls, the power relations that are based on gender distinction. In other words, as also represented in Kaufman and Sered in this volume, it is precisely through a differentiation by gender—literally, a spatial separation between men and women—that an Orthodox Jewish woman finds her sense of self.

For this audience the actual presence and experience of social power dynamics are not erased but are temporarily transcended in a sex-segregated society. Composed of women from the community, including mothers, grandmothers, sisters, and cousins, the audience is enraptured by the girls' performances. Riveted to their seats, the audience members eagerly await the final section, entitled "The Story of Karen," in which the girls tell the story of the sustenance and rejuvenation of their community.

The Third Context: Judaism as a Political Discourse

As the "The Story of Karen" begins, two narrators are sitting stage left. Most of the action is in pantomime except for one interaction between Karen and an Orthodox man. This genre is commonly referred to as story theater: there is no scenery; a backdrop is painted verbally by the narrators. The sacred Western Wall of the temple in Jerusalem is etched out across the back of the stage by two Orthodox characters, a man and a woman, both praying rhythmically throughout the piece.

"The Story of Karen" revolves around the "return" of an assimilated Jewish girl to the Orthodox fold. During a summer vacation in Israel, she experiences a spiritual revelation at the Western Wall that opens up a newly found path for religious renewal. In analyzing the text, we recognize the form as a psychoanalytic fantasy. After Karen's transformative experience, caressing the warm stones of the Wall and then leaving a note in its crevices as she sees those around her do, she literally bumps into an Orthodox man also leaving the Wall. This Orthodox man, the prince of the fantasy, breaks the previously silent pantomime and introduces language into the skit. And he introduces Karen to the whole new language of Jewish spirituality.

A Lacanian psychoanalytic approach, based on the recasting of the Freudian model in linguistic terms, seems particularly apt to describe the classical Jewish patriarchy represented by the male role in this scene. Through access to language the Orthodox man at the Wall expressed the *patriarchal symbolic order,* the prevailing cultural norm. He immediately offers to find Karen a home within the Orthodox community of Jerusalem. At this moment, the second narrator raises her eyebrow knowingly and says, "Most of you know how the story ended." Yes, we do. Once again the male presumptively fills the girl up with identity, religion, and community. Again, in Lacanian terms, he fills up all that she supposedly lacks; he fills her void with his socially sanctified dominance. He brings her a father and a husband rolled up in one; he returns her to the community from which she has strayed. "The Story of Karen" is a romantic, erotically signified fairy tale. The girl, Karen, is spiritually exiled; her prior, independent identity is lost forever. She is led back to the construct of "woman": wife and mother, for the Orthodox community.

From another perspective, "The Story of Karen" represents the essence of the entire festival, and to take it further, the community as a whole. The drama critiques the dominant American culture while celebrating Orthodoxy. One audience member, a mother of one of the girls, said, "On the continuum of observance, I think there is a whole movement to the right, the less Orthodox are becoming more and more and the more are becoming even more. American culture is so empty, there is a feeling of emptiness: it is spiritually bankrupt; it is controlled by Madison Avenue." As the festival director explained, "This movement is growing. There are kids at Shevach who are 'returnees' and those who have been religious for generations."

The focus of "The Story of Karen" skit is not Israel as the spiritual homeland of the Jews but the building of the Orthodox community in Rego Park, Queens. In fact, Israel, as a nation-state riddled with political crises in 1986, was not mentioned; nor were Palestinians, Arabs, terrorism, or the internal economic disorder and antagonism among Jews. Most aspects of Israel that appear in the mainstream press were eclipsed. Israel was seen in a religious, not a geo-political, context. As the director clarified, "The Middle East is not a particularly hot topic at school. They learn about it in Social Studies, a secular subject. The girls don't know the politics. We establish a difference between the holy *Eretz Yisroel*[6] and Israel, the modern state—and the emphasis is on the holy *Eretz Yisroel*."

This emphasis reflects the fact that Shevach High School is part of the Beth Jacob school movement, which has a direct affiliation with the political party Agudat Israel in Israel. The platform of Agudat Israel calls for the observance of halakah in every sphere of public and private life.[7]

Currently, in Israel, Agudat Israel supervises independent educational institutions, refusing to be included in the secular state educational network. Through their ties with Agudat Israel, Shevach High School and the other Beth Jacob schools influence the tide of Israeli politics—whether this role is fully acknowledged or not. In a sociological study of Agudat Israel and the ultra-Orthodox in Israel, Rita Simon explains that even though they comprise a small percentage of Jewry, the sects exercise a distinctive and important weight on the character of Israeli society. They have set themselves apart, and in their separateness they establish a moral hierarchy in which they place themselves at the top. They believe they have been chosen for a special kind of existence. As an international network, Agudat Israel is supported by Orthodox Jews worldwide. Funds are raised in North America, Britain, Australia, and South Africa to maintain educational, health, and welfare institutions in Israel; it is clear that this community could not exist on such a large scale without substantial support from the Orthodox centers around the world.[8]

This conflict between the sacred and the secular, Eretz Yisroel and Israel, the nation-state, persists. In fact, according to some it is the major source of social unrest in the Jewish world today. While "The Story of Karen" shows the religious aspect of the community's relationship to Israel, it hides the political. The official connection between Beth Jacob and Agudat Israel and the profound implications for both the state of Israel and this community are obscured.

However, for the young women of Shevach, there is no contradiction. In this context, Israel is a stopover on the way to building Jewish life in Queens. For Karen, Israel is the symbolic call of *teshuvah,* of return, "her road back to her roots, her religion, and her self." The play serves to legitimize and celebrate the beliefs and values of the community. It speaks to its members of expansion and rejuvenation. By acknowledging their strangeness—"imagine, in the heat of an Israeli summer, Orthodox people are wearing long pants, shirts and socks, how weird"—they accept it as their norm and place it "center" stage.

What they claim to be doing is not engaging with the dominant society but rather maintaining an enclosed, intact community in order to resist the trend of spiritual impoverishment in the United States and create meaning and expression in daily life. As we have seen, they paradoxically use and incorporate the secular world in expressing their traditional values. These girls have the best of both worlds: they actively consume in the secular world without falling prey to the alienation of this consumer-based culture. As the creation of "The Story of Karen" illustrates, they also understand what their community provides. Karen is responding to the feelings of warmth and cohesiveness of this group. In reaction to an all-too-well-documented alienation of American society, Karen's "return" to her faith is seen from the Orthodox perspective as an effort to seek comfort and reassurance in a sense of community solidarity.

Conclusion

Seasons of the Soul earnestly celebrates the lives of the student performers and the Orthodox Jewish community of which they are part. As a folk performance, it transmits the lore, sacred material, stories, traditions, history, and ideology of the community that created it. It enhances a feeling of social solidarity, of working and sharing as a group within the school and in the larger community.

Contextualizing the event in three different manners allows us to see the disparity between the possible meanings that insiders themselves acknowledge and those that we, as outsiders, may interpret.

Although the community defines itself as separate from mainstream culture and as a close-knit, intact group, allowing for a small degree of "seepage" from the secular world, I would suggest that the Shevach women are instrumental in "managing" a greater degree of "seepage" than they recognize consciously. Like Schely-Newman's Jula in this volume, these girls incorporate modernity into their traditional representation of Judaism without being aware of their own syncretistic and creative role. Along with Davis's bar mitzvah mothers, they produce and direct a performance that publicly affirms their version of Jewish womanhood. Further study would reveal a dynamic relationship between Jewish women and the secular world.

The structure and content of the fairy story of Karen is merely a spiritualized version of a standard narrative that remains similar to "mainstream" stories of "origin" and renewal. A religious context to the tale in no way subverts it. On the other hand, the song "What Page Are You On in Prayer Book Blues" is an authentic parody in which the performers express their position in three worlds: as women-girls, as Orthodox Jews, and as Americans; but simultaneously they gently question all three. Perhaps it is in this gentle rebellion and resistance that we find the girls pushing their definitions of self a bit further on every side.

NOTES

1. Mikhail Bakhtin, "Discourse in the Novel," *The Dialogic Imagination* (Austin: University of Texas Press, 1981), p. 291.

2. This combination of the most diverse styles and genres in the same artistic product, in one and the same narrative and in one and the same song, illustrates what the semiotician Petr Bogatyrev describes as the syncretic essence of a folk dramatic form. See Petr Bogatyrev, "Semiotics of Folk Theatre," in Ladislav Matejka and Irwin R. Titnik, eds., *Semiotics of Art* (Cambridge: M.I.T. Press, 1976), pp. 33–50. This mixing and matching of genre and style continues throughout the festival. Most of the English-language musical pieces in the festival are taken from an album entitled *Journeys,* by Moshe Tess. Tess, a *ba'al teshuvah,* or "returnee," to the Jewish faith, features songs that are concerned with the experiences of the rebirth of Jewish spirituality and observant life.

3. A "returnee" is a Jew who has rediscovered spirituality and joins an Orthodox community. The students of Shevach High School were both "returnees" and traditionally Orthodox Jews.

4. The notion of a "feminist sense" is quite problematic. Claire Duch-

en, in *Feminism in France: From May 1886 to Mitterand* (London: Routledge and Kegan Paul, 1986), suggests that feminism is a somewhat undefinable multiplicity of organization, practice, and theory. See Hélène Cixous and Catherine Clement, *The Newly Born Woman* (1975; Minneapolis: University of Minnesota Press, 1986), and Luce Irigaray, *Speculum of the Other Woman* (1974; Ithaca: Cornell University Press, 1985), for a discussion of female subjectivity and the cultural construction of gender.

5. Edith Diamond, "Refusing the Romanticism of Identity: Narrative Interventions in Churchill, Benmussa, Duras," *Theatre Journal* 37 (1985): 8.

6. *Eretz Yisroel* refers to the spiritual home of the Jewish people as it is expressed in the Bible and other religious texts. It is not *necessarily* directly connected to Israel, the modern nation-state as conceived in 1948. There is often an overlap, especially concerning rationales of settlement of the West Bank by Orthodox and ultra-Orthodox groups.

7. Many of the political parties in Israel today have their roots in the late twenties and thirties in Eastern Europe, where numerous schools and cultural activities of the Jewish community were run by the hand of Jewish political parties. In 1929 the ultra-Orthodox Agudat Israel took over the sponsorship of the Beth Jacob schools. For further information on the founding of the Beth Jacob schools, see the chapter on Sarah Schenirer, "The Mother of the Beth Jacob Schools," in L. Dawidowicz, *The Golden Tradition* (New York: Schocken Books, 1984), pp. 206–9.

8. Rita Simon, *Continuity and Change: A Study of Two Ethnic Communities in Israel* (Cambridge: Cambridge University Press, 1978).

· 11 ·

Women's Roles in
Judeo-Spanish Song Traditions

JUDITH R. COHEN

Judeo-Spanish ("ladino") song has always been acknowledged as a repertoire sung, transmitted, and, to a certain extent, shaped by Sephardic women, although men have also played positive roles in the Judeo-Spanish song tradition.[1] Until very recently, however, scholarship addressed to this repertoire tended to focus on the songs themselves, paying little, if any, attention to the women who have kept them alive. This woman-as-vessel approach, regrettably, is hardly unique to ethnomusicology. The content of a song can reveal values and roles perpetuated by women through their traditional performance. However, women's impact on the history of Jewish cultural practice is better understood through the study of the *processes* through which women pass on cultural content, particularly during times of social change. Women express themselves not only through song but also by developing new strategies and contexts for transmitting traditional materials.

Although a few recent studies have begun to examine traditional women's roles in Judeo-Spanish song, most fail to address the new roles women are in the process of developing as the repertoire and the contexts of its performance undergo profound changes. Judeo-Spanish Jews coming of age today in the new Sephardic Diaspora have had to find new ways to learn the musical traditions of their ancestral culture.

Women have taken significant initiative in creating novel roles and venues for transmitting Judeo-Spanish song. For example, some of the older generation have undertaken new roles as tutors to outsider performers who have taken an interest in acquiring parts of the repertoire. Additionally, scholarship—particularly women's scholarship—in the field of Judeo-Spanish song has recently increased significantly. In this chapter, I would like to present an introductory exploration of women's roles in transmitting traditional repertoire, changing contexts of performance, and creating a body of scholarship on Judeo-Spanish song. This work is based on a survey I have administered to thirty-eight female and twenty-six male respondents located in North America, Europe, and the Middle East, whom I identified as performers and scholars working with Judeo-Spanish song.[2] Women have shaped and continue to shape Judeo-Spanish song, which has played a central role in Sephardic culture. My research further corroborates that Sephardic song tradition, including its content and contexts, have largely under womens' guidance become an important genre in the folk-music circuit, providing pleasure to many listeners and fruitful work to a number of scholars.

An Introduction to the Genres of Judeo-Spanish Song

To understand the evolving roles of women in perpetuating Judeo-Spanish song traditions, I feel that it is necessary to present a survey of the forms and content of the tradition we are addressing. Judeo-Spanish song is the heritage of the descendants of the Jews exiled from Spain in the late Middle Ages. For five centuries—albeit ever more precariously—Sephardic Jews, as they are known, have continued to speak and sing in the language known variously as "ladino," "Djudezmo," and "Spaniol," in Eastern Europe, and "Ḥaketia" in Morocco. Recently, scholars have used the compromise umbrella term "Judeo-Spanish" to refer to all the regional variations.[3] Many song texts, particularly romances (ballads), can be traced to early Spanish sources. Others, along with most of the melodies, are of more recent composition and reflect their various host cultures: Morocco in the western Mediterranean and the former Ottoman Empire lands in the East, often referred to as Western and Eastern traditions, respectively.

The main genres of Judeo-Spanish song may be briefly summarized as: romances, life cycle, calendar cycle, lyric, and locally composed songs. Images of women vary in these songs, and women attribute meaning to each of the genres.

Romances

In the romances women have shaped a repertoire of stories that serve many functions besides the not inconsequential one of sheer entertainment. The majority of the romance narratives feature women—either as main or accessory characters. Some of their powerful, often contradictory images of women lead one to wonder why women themselves have chosen to perpetuate and transmit them. The *romancero*'s portrayals of women range from the passively victimized to the dynamic, articulate, and inventive.[4]

Though the songs may originally have been composed by men, women made the corpus their own by selecting their favorites and adapting them over the centuries to their own sensibilities. An example of how this is done occurred during a rehearsal of Gerineldo, a group with which I perform. The Moroccan Sephardic singer Kelly Amar felt uncomfortable singing the words "and for company, I'd like Jesus Christ and my mother," which appeared in the ballad "La mala suegra." She proposed a change to "my father and my mother," which maintained the original scansion and assonance. Although Kelly had never heard the term "dechristianization," a term used by scholars to describe the process through which performers transform Christian references in the repertoire to lyrics more compatible with their own Jewish values, she was following in the footsteps of generations of Sephardic women in making this change.

In my study, tradition bearers discuss the activities of medieval characters as if they constituted the latest episode of a soap opera. My informants know very well that the lives and deaths of Ximena, Urraca, and Melisenda of the songs are not their lives. They are not going to kill off a hundred suitors like Gallarda or sing about going to sea to rescue their lovers while embroidering nighties for the queen's latest offspring, as do some of the *romancero* heroines, but they nevertheless derive much pleasure from their intimacy with these ladies. Romances also serve as a vehicle for validating and transmitting to their daughters and young sons Sephardic women's own codes of morality and honor, and they provide escape valves for frustrations and fantasies.[5]

Life Cycle Songs

In Judeo-Spanish tradition, songs of birth, courtship, marriage, and death are largely the domain of women. In terms of song repertoire, the most important life cycle category is the wedding. Wedding songs and their themes are described at great length elsewhere.[6] Here, it may be noted that the images of the bride are a mixture of the idealized and the practical. Always beautiful, for once she may be seductive, even entertain erotic daydreams, with no censure ("with love I'll go to share his bed"), as they are directed toward her husband and can be seen as part of her upcoming duties as a Jewish wife and mother. Bawdy wedding songs sung by women among themselves can be seen as an extension of this notion. At the same time, the bride may have practical concerns ("in my father's house I looked in the mirror, in my husband's I look in his wallet"), again, part of her duties to her future family. She also expresses spiritual sentiments: "I come and go, enamoured of the Holy Law." The new bride's understandable fears are hinted at rather than clearly expressed in songs where she delays the proceedings by making endless adjustments to her appearance. As a genre, the wedding songs present a more realistic picture of women's roles in Sephardic culture than the romances. The bride knows that her role includes her obligation to her husband to "set his table, pour his wine and lie down next to him. " (See Baskin in this volume for rabbinical views on the wifely role.) Being the center of attention, in semi-seclusion with women family and friends, gave the bride a one-time-only hiatus, a brief chance to be the delicately blooming "almond tree" in the ephemeral space "between the sea and the sand."

Calendrical Cycle Songs

Calendrical cycle songs in Judeo-Spanish tradition constitute an area where women's and men's singing overlap to a greater extent than in romances or life cycle songs. When women appear in these texts it is mostly as characters in biblical narratives or as archetypical heroines. For example, in the much-loved nineteenth-century narrative of Sol Hachuel, a Moroccan Jewish teenager is executed for refusing to abandon her faith.

Lyric and Locally Composed Songs

Lyric and local songs are the genres most likely to reflect women's recent historical experiences and express individual creativity. Most of these songs are from the Eastern European repertoire. Although they are the songs best known to the general listening public, they have been relatively neglected by scholars.[7] Here, performance does not seem to entail specific gender role division, at least at present, partly because these songs are not generally linked to specific social functions.

Songs of recent composition in these genres might reflect the "new" urban woman of the 1920s and 1930s: "I want a woman of good family, well-dressed, with *sex appeal* [sic], a good pianist and like a flame in bed." Actual women's names may be mentioned. "Good-bye, Rachel Levy, I'm off to Africa," or "Esterina Sarfaty is making love." Occasionally, cruder allusions are directed at women: "La Senyora Rigoleta" is "asking for it," and "Sara la preta" ("the black one," referring to an unattractive character) has "lost her breast." Even when romanticized and sentimentalized, these are not the stories of long-dead nobility but slices of life close to home.[8]

The majority of lyric songs dwell on relations between the sexes. The images they present of women are by and large far less dramatic and powerful than those of the *romancero*, and less tied to Jewish ritual life than the life cycle songs. Boy-meets-girl, boy-abandons-girl, boy-sighs-for-beautiful-girl, and other clichés of twentieth-century "romantic love" abound. ("As trees cry for rain, my heart weeps for you"). Or, less romantically, "Hey, Sarah, get me some water, I'll buy you new shoes." To which request Sarah responds, "My father's an important businessman, who needs you?"

Lyric and local songs are still the ones most often heard on commercial recordings and in concerts today, and this more contemporary, familiar image of women has informed whatever public consciousness there is today of Judeo-Spanish folksong, more than the complex forms of the *romancero* and the wedding songs. Not coincidentally, these lyric and local songs are often sung by men as well as women.

Contexts

In Eastern Europe and North Africa all the genres mentioned above were associated with cultural contexts, places, and occasions at which the songs were sung. Many of the contexts were typical of preindusrial circum-Mediterranean cultures in the late nineteenth and early twentieth centuries. Many of the traditional domestic and life cycle song contexts were modified as the home countries of the Sephardic Jews underwent political and economic upheavals during the twentieth century. The same dislocations that changed local cultural configurations in which Sephardic song flourished led to massive migrations of Jewish communities from Eastern Europe and North Africa to Europe, North America, and Israel. In these new homes, the contexts in which Sephardic women traditionally sang all but disappeared. First-generation immigrants, tradition bearers who had learned the songs in their original cultural contexts, nevertheless continued to value their song traditions. "Our people, we sang everywhere . . ."; "they can take everything from us except our songs"; "I sing downstairs waiting for the taxi."[9]

One example of a lost context is the Moroccan *matesha* (Arabic, swing). The *matesha* was a swing set up in the interior courtyard of a typical Mediterranean house around the time of Passover. Girls took turns swinging and singing *cantares de matesha* (swing songs), sometimes romances, sometimes light verses, sometimes with built-in instructions for the girl on the swing to relinquish her place to another.[10] This was a time for relaxation and, away from parents' close surveillance, an opportunity for courtship.

Highrise apartments do not lend themselves to *mateshas*, and singing romances over a dishwasher instead of a cradle is not an inviting prospect. The week-long Mediterranean wedding with several stages, each with its own set of songs, has, in North America, gone the way of the *matesha*. If Sephardic song traditions are to be preserved, then, either traditional contexts need to be re-created or new ones invented that will support performance of the songs. Home videos, senior citizens' club meetings, community-sponsored concerts, all involve some group participation, and Sephardic women have learned to transfer their singing activities to such contexts. Recently, the interest of scholars and outsider performers—as well as some members of new, transplanted generations of Sephardic Jews—has encouraged singing in the context of field recordings. Recordings, in turn, find their way into still other contexts: documentary recordings and radio broadcasts, scholarly conferences or performances by musicians who diligently comb archives hoping to augment their repertoires. In these new contexts Sephardic song takes on a life of its own, in a way actually creating its own new contexts.

New Contexts, New Roles

In the late 1980s, Spanish Television produced a series called "Voces de Sefarad" ("Voices of Sepharad," not to be confused with the American ensemble of the same name). The series consisted of seven hours of performers and scholars of Judeo-Spanish music around the globe. Almost all the performers chosen, male and female, were depicted in romantic natural or "medieval" settings that, for some mysterious reason, were seen as appropriate to this predominantly urban musical tradition. The women, in particular, were shown in romantic settings often more evocative of the characters in the ballads than of the performers themselves; they reclined in rowboats, peeked winsomely from casement windows, or, in the case of more robust divas, strolled majestically in sumptuous formal gardens. Whether these stereotypical images represent the past, or the director's fantasies about the past, they do not reflect today's realities.

As we examine new contexts for Sephardic song repertoire, we become aware of newly constructed roles such as coach, educator, consultant, public "outsider" performer, and scholar. While both men and women are involved in these roles, women appear in the numerical majority in all of these roles. Sephardic song remains, then, in several different aspects, a "women's tradition."

Women Performers

Since I include all types of performers of the Sephardic repertoire rather than only tradition bearers in my discussion, a word about such paired opposing concepts as amateur/professional and insider/outsider is in order. The line between amateur and professional can be difficult to draw; and insider/outsider differences may not be as obvious as in the past, as outsider performers become more sophisticated in their approach to source material, while young people born into the culture grow up increasingly unfamiliar with the language and songs of their grandmothers.

Currently, *insider* and *outsider* refer simply to people born either into or outside the tradition, respectively. Insiders will include Sephardic-born persons who learned the language and songs only as adults. Amateur/professional is tricky: knowledgeable tradition bearers whose singing is respected in their own community can hardly be called amateurs. I will refer to people who may not think of themselves as singers but who did provide me with songs and/or information as *tradition bearers*. I refer to insiders who also perform for a wider public as *insider performers*.[11] Finally, the phrase *outsider performers* refers to performers from outside the tradition, most of whom earn (or try to) their living from music. However, as with other paired opposing terms, it may be more productive to view insider and outsider as points along a continuum rather than as opposites.

In table 1, I summarize the contexts in which singers in each of these categories is likely to perform. In figure 1, I show a sample continuum of performer types. Similar figures could apply to other common distinctions, such as *amateur* and *professional*.

Table 1. Performers and Contexts

	Tradition Bearer		Insider Performer		Outside Performer	
	Female	Male	Female	Male	Female	Male
Informal/Community						
Home	X	X	X	X	(—)	(—)
Fieldwork session	X	X	(—)	(—)	—	—
Community	X	X	X	X	(—)	(—)
Synagogue	—	X	—	X	—	—
Women's songs	X	(—)	X	(X)	(—)	(—)
Formal/Stylized						
Live concert	—	—	X	X	X	X
Radio and television	(—)	(—)	X	X	X	X
Documentary recording	X	X	(—)	(—)	—	—
Commercial recording	—	—	X	X	X	X
Women's songs	(—)	(—)	X	(X)	X	X

Key: X = standard context; (X) = occasional participation; — = not applicable; (—) = not usual context but may occasionally occur.

Tradition Bearers

While some women have lost their motivation to sing along with their old familiar surroundings, others display the ability to transfer

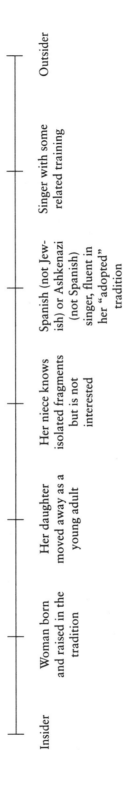

Figure 1. Sample Continuum of Performer Types

singing to new contexts such as those provided by their new surroundings. Whether they regularly sing or not, many tradition bearers offered me not only songs and stories but homemade pastries, invitations to community events, and even a feeling of having been adopted into a family. Creating a family-like context for discussion of the songs was important to the women, and I may have become a substitute for children to whom the songs had not been transmitted.

Some tradition bearers provided songs more or less at random; others, as they got to know me, prepared quite deliberately for our interviews. In Montreal, Hanna Pimienta used to happily save up long versions of rare Moroccan romances for my visits, and Buena Sarfatty Garfinkle wrote out unusual topical songs and proverbs culled from her memories of pre–World War II Salonica. Alicia Bendayan sang for researchers in Morocco in the 1950s; thirty-five years later in Israel she is regularly sought out for her melodically intricate renditions of ballads and life cycle songs.

Other women have assumed teaching roles. Emilie Levy and her daughter Gloria, in New York, performed a great service for Judeo-Spanish song in the 1950s by recording an LP of songs, which inspired many performers. Now in her eighties, Emilie told me of having coached outsider women performers such as Isabelle Ganz, who directs the group Alhambra. Rachel Amado Bortnick, in San Francisco, narrates the video *Trees Cry for Rain,* and in one sequence she painstakingly corrects the singer Judy Frankel's pronunciation. When Ms. Frankel responded to my questionnaire, she was one of the very few outsider performers who echoed tradition bearers' emphasis on pronunciation as a key criterion for evaluating Judeo-Spanish song performance. Rebecca Amado Levy's home video re-creates traditional song settings; Mrs. Levy gives copies to those she feels will use them and has provided information for various student projects. Encouraged in turn by some of those she has helped, and by her daughter Mati, she also wrote an informative and evocative book in English and Judeo-Spanish, *I Remember Rhodes.* The list could go on; yet what is important is that women have adapted their roles as singers, guardians, and transmitters of Judeo-Spanish songs to new circumstances, extending their nurturing role from the family to a wider context. The very notion of "family" has been perhaps extended to include outsider researchers whose desire to preserve the repertoire and keep it alive coincides with the goals of the insider women. Furthermore, the women have maintained criteria for the evaluation of Sephardic song performance that, through their interactions with researchers and outsider performers, may continue to serve to control and assess the quality of Sephardic song performance.

The idea that women are illiterate or disinterested in the written word is belied by the notebooks treasured by many Judeo-Spanish families, full of long ballad texts painstakingly copied out by their mothers, aunts, or grandmothers. Tradition bearers may refer to printed anthologies to refresh their memories during field recording sessions, or pass around scraps of paper on which they have jotted down words for friends. In a senior citizens' home near Tel Aviv, I watched the residents' choir read from songsheets written out for them in the Cyrillic alphabet. Tradition bearers, both women and men, are more interested in learning or relearning songs than in worrying about the authenticity of their sources. To the dismay of some scholars, insider women may even learn new repertoire from outsider recordings, just as they did traditionally from visitors. In this way women keep alive the tradition that, like all folk traditions, was always fluid.

Insider Performers

Insider performers are performers from the tradition who have adapted their performance roles to accommodate popular audiences. Insider performers are relatively recent and scarce in the Moroccan Judeo-Spanish tradition; most are women. The Eastern European tradition, on the other hand, has seen several decades of professional insider performers since the early days of the recording industry. Most of the early insider performers were men, with a few notable exceptions. The best-known, indeed legendary, example of these women is Victoria Rosa Hazan. In her nineties and in a Brooklyn nursing home at the time of this writing, this prolific recording artist of Turkish and Judeo-Spanish song continued until recently to sing, play her *oud* and *chumbush,* and help seekers of songs and information.[12]

Of the thirty-odd contemporary insider performers I have been able to identify, about two-thirds are women; all but six are from the Eastern tradition. While most work as soloists, or soloists with (mostly male) instrumental accompanists, two have formed internationally recognized ensembles: the Moroccan Gerineldo, based in Montreal, and the Turkish Los Pasharos Sefardíes, based in Istanbul. Both founders, Oro Anahory-Librowicz and Karen Gerson, were born into their traditions, though the latter had to learn much of it as a young adult. Both have carried out formal academic research on Judeo-Spanish language and literature, and Gerineldo's director is widely recognized for her scholarly publications on Sephardic song tradition. Avoiding whatever they identify as "modernization" and "westernization," both women have shaped ensembles recognized as authentic by their own communities, and respected and enjoyed outside them as well. And both can and do use their community standing, continually learning from, in Karen Gerson's words, "our grandmothers and our grandmothers' grandmothers."[13]

Women have become role models for both insider and outsider performers. Victoria Rosa Hazan has already been mentioned. Ester Roffé, in Caracas, is almost universally considered by Moroccan tradition bearers to be the best performer of their songs. The chamber music style accompaniments on her records may be scorned by scholars but are enjoyed by many tradition bearers; in any event, no one quarrels with her vocal style. Henriette Azen, in Paris, has recorded the only albums of Moroccan songs sung entirely a cappella[14] and is regularly consulted by performers in the Paris area. Her recent compact disk, dedicated to her late husband, includes an *endecha* (lament) sung in his memory and can almost be seen as a long and complex *endecha* in itself. Flory Jagoda, probably the best-known insider performer, has composed a few songs that have entered the traditional canon as far as performers and audiences are concerned, whatever scholars may think. She performs with her adult children, moving traditional transmission into concert and studio-recorded settings. Many outsider performers cite her as their ideal performer, as well as a helpful consultant, though tradition bearers' reactions are mixed.[15] Other insider performers, less well known, work in their own ways to reappropriate and disseminate their Judeo-Spanish song heritage.

Outsider Performers

Outsider performers have become increasingly important in Judeo-Spanish song. Until recently, most concentrated on the Eastern repertoire. Several outsider performers are now exploring the

Moroccan repertoire. An increasing number consult with scholars and have done some work with documentary recordings and even with tradition bearers.

At the time of this writing, about two-thirds of the outsider performers I have identified are women. Ensembles usually employ more men than women instrumentalists; as in most other performing groups, a woman solo vocalist with male instrumentalists is common, the reverse and all-women groups almost nonexistent.

According to the questionnaires completed for this study, outsider performers, male and female, see themselves as creative artists approaching the Judeo-Spanish song with both respect and innovation. However, one facet of the responses of these performers that strikes me is the imagery used by women outsider performers to describe their relationship to Judeo-Spanish song.

Judy Wachs, director of the very successful group Voice of the Turtle, introduced a concert with a mildly confused but evocative metaphor of Judeo-Spanish song as a five-hundred-year-old tree transplanted to different soils and watered by different rains, and whose branches are sometimes pruned. Esther Lamandier, in Paris, links spirituality, instinct, and sensitivity to the courtly poetry whose beauty has "conquered" her. Marcela Neil, of Germany's Mangrana group, sees Judeo-Spanish song as "being thrown out of its sleep . . . quite roughly." Jacinta writes, "it was the repertoire which chose *me*"; Letizia Arbeteta, in Madrid, spoke of "incorporating [the songs] into my soul and my body."[16] Repeatedly, women performers' remarks suggested an image of the repertoire as an almost animate entity, demanding of the singer a personal, nurturing relationship with songs among which they have chosen to work and live.

Several women founded and direct ensembles, and their responses often reflect their concern with working out their leadership roles, resolving tensions between leader and group, and between group and audience. Asked who made the decisions, most said their groups work by consensus, but they themselves have the final say. Rosa Zaragoza, of Barcelona, grinned at me and wrote down, "I pay my musicians to play the way I like them to." Then she passed the pen to the guitarist Francisco Tomás, who added, "If I don't like the arrangements, I protest." Judy Wachs, in concert, introduced herself as "director." The only other woman in the group, Lisle Kulbach, winked at the audience and added in a pseudo-aside, "And I make all the decisions." These data suggest that women performers, while they may change traditional performance styles considerably, retain a primary interest in human relationships that is not at odds with traditional values.[17]

Scholars, Writers, and Consultants

The role of scholars has been crucial to the reshaping of the Judeo-Spanish repertoire, perhaps in ways they did not originally envision or even welcome. Its relative popularity would not have happened without the published anthologies of Isaac Lévy and, to a lesser, but still important extent, those of Manuel Alvar, Leon Algazi, Arcadio de Larrea Palacín, and others. Commercially available documentary recordings are, though less sparse than they were a decade ago, not that easy to come by, and resourceful performers have made their way to official archives and/or to scholar-collectors for source material.

The early Judeo-Spanish scholars, from the late nineteenth to the mid-twentieth century, were mostly men. They usually concentrated on texts rather than music, with some exceptions, and tended to privilege the romance over other forms. While scholars such as Samuel Armistead and Joseph Silverman, Manuel Alvar, and Paul Bénichou produced now-classic editions and analyses of the texts, disproportionately few musical transcriptions and little or no discussion of performance practice was provided. Isaac Lévy's anthology, until very recently the most widely used by outsider performers, has no documentation beyond an indication of the city of origin. Israel Katz's monograph was the first devoted to Judeo-Spanish music. While it is a pioneering study, it treats only the ballads, giving barely any attention either to other genres or to social context and the lives of the women who sang the songs. It was as if tradition bearers existed solely as convenient vessels harboring treasures to be sought and claimed by ballad hunters intent on clarifying possible links with Spain's long-past Golden Age.

The 1970s and 1980s saw not only a growth in the number of Sephardic "revival" performers but a dramatic increase in the number of women scholars in the field. Their work reflects the general movements of what seems to be a "kinder, gentler" ethnomusicology, revealing a deep interest in the social context of the songs, in the lives and thoughts of the singers, and in what the music means to them.[18] Such issues as women's concepts of honor and sexuality and their self-images have been explored, and the neglected area of dance has been opened up. Most of us have been seriously concerned with social context, and in some cases have balanced the attention given to various genres, displacing the paramount position accorded to the ballad by most early scholars. The studies by Judith Etzion and Shoshana Weich-Shahaq, which do focus on the ballad, confront, in a more systematic way than had been done before, the question of their musical relationship to early Spanish music.

Just as the lines separating amateur from professional and insider from outsider are not always easy or practical to draw, so the lines between scholar and performer, scholar and collector, and scholar and disseminator are not always definite. For Pamela Dorn Sezgin the most rewarding aspect of her years of work with Turkish Sephardim was the extent to which they adopted her into their lives. She, in turn, learned and practiced their speech and song patterns and was told, as a compliment, that over the telephone she could be mistaken for a member of their own, older generation. One question in my scholar's survey was, "What is your most important role?" Answers varied, but Shoshana Weich-Shahaq's was unique in specifying "consulting"; many performers, indeed, acknowledge her help. Kamelia Shahar, in Jerusalem, and Matilde Gini de Barnatán, in Madrid, are not academic scholars, but their work in radio and their own backgrounds give them unique vantage points from which to put people interested in Sephardic song in contact with each other, and to act as consultants on repertoire and performance style.

Women have played important roles in Judeo-Spanish song traditions. They sing the songs, transmit them, participate in changes shaping new repertoires and variations of specific songs, and enjoy many, though not all, innovations from outsider performers. They collect, write, analyze, advise, and set standards. Women's role as tradition bearers has been the crucial one in preserving the repertoire. Among outsider performers women outnumber men, and they tend to speak of their work in affective terms. In scholarship, women tend to be concerned with understanding the songs within the context of their singers' lives. While in the early days of the "re-discovery" of the Sephardic repertoire, it was clear that women sang and men analyzed, today both men and women sing and analyze. However, as my research indicates, women currently outnumber men in all categories of roles associated with Sephardic song except instrumentalist. Women's voices are heard, not only through their renditions of the songs, their manipulation of the lyrics and content of the repertoire, but also through their new roles, such as those of consultant, scholar, insider and outsider performer, and musical director of groups that perform commercially. Fortunately, in everyday life, women singers and scholars are stepping out beyond stereotypical boundaries to play their part in whatever conservation or re-creation may yet be possible of an old tradition as multifaceted as are the women themselves.

NOTES

1. Men have also played positive roles in the Judeo-Spanish song tradition. However, acknowledging men's contributions to this women's tradition, rather than looking for women's contributions to men's traditions, reverses the usual approach to women's roles in Jewish studies and underscores women's ongoing achievements in the area of Judeo-Spanish song.

2. This represents a 71 percent response rate from my total population of ninety identified soloists, group members, and scholars working with the targeted song traditions. My current work on innovation and reactions to it in Judeo-Spanish song, including this study, has been made possible through a fellowship from the Social Sciences and Humanities Research Council, Canada. I prepared questionnaires for outsider and insider performers, scholars, and the public, and used a sample excerpt tape for tradition bearers to comment on. At the time of writing, I have identified about sixty-six performers, including those who perform with groups. Thirty have completed questionnaires. Of the twenty-eight men identified, only soloists and group leaders were targeted; seventeen have answered questionnaires. Nine of ten women scholars contacted returned questionnaires; seven of ten men scholars contacted answered. Tradition bearers who listened to sample tapes number twenty, more or less evenly divided among men and women. Unless otherwise specified, quoted comments are taken from written and tape-recorded questionnaires, interviews, and conversations.

3. The most popular term, "ladino," technically refers only to literal translations of Hebrew liturgical texts into Spanish. Moroccan Sephardic Jews use only the term *Ḥaketia* for their vernacular. "Sefarad" is a biblical term traditionally interpreted as meaning Spain, though its use has been popularly extended to various Jewish groups of non-Ashkenazi origin. The new Sephardic Diaspora refers to Jews who left their North African and Eastern European homelands during and after World War II.

4. It has been suggested that men devalued or downplayed the *roman-cero* as a women's repertoire. It could be that modern men are more comfortable with the images of women in lyric and local songs than with passionate, larger-than-life *romancero* heroines or realistic brides, whose power and pain they cannot translate into terms compatible with their ideas about the nature of women.

5. Oro Anahory-Librowicz, *Cancionero sephardi du Quebec*, vol. 1 (Montreal: Fonds FCAR, 1988).

6. For wedding songs, see Alvar López, *Cantos de boda judeo-españoles* (Madrid: CSIC, 1971); Oro Anahory-Librowicz and Judith Cohen, "Modalidades expresivas de los cantes de boda judeo-españoles," *Revista de Dialectología y Tradiciones Populares* 41 (1986): 189–209; Judith Cohen, "*Ya Salió de la Mar*: Judeo-Spanish Wedding Songs among Moroccan Jews in Canada," in Ellen Koskoff, ed., *Women and Music in Cross-Cultural Perspective* (1987; Urbana: University of Illinois Press, 1989), pp. 55–68, and "Judeo-Spanish Song in the Sephardic Communities of Montreal and Toronto: Survival, Function, and Change" (Ph.D. diss., Université de Montréal, 1989 [UMI #8918229]), pp. 145–51. See also A. de Larrea Palacín, *Cancionero judío del norte de Marruecos. Canciones rituales hispano-judías* (Madrid: CSIC, 1954); Shoshana Weich-Shahaq, "The Wedding Songs of the Bulgarian-Sephardi Jews," *Orbis Musicae* 7 (1979–80): 81–107, "Childbirth Songs among Sephardic Jews of Balkan Origin," *Orbis Musicae* 8 (1982–83): 87–103, and *Judeo-Spanish Moroccan Songs for the Life Cycle* (Jerusalem: Hebrew University, Jewish Music Research Centre, 1989), with cassette.

7. For discussion of songs in these categories, see Judith Cohen, "The Lighter Side of Judeo-Spanish Traditional Songs: Some Canadian Examples," *Canadian Folk Music Journal* 15 (1987): 25–34; Edwin Seroussi, "The Growth of the Judeo-Spanish Folksong Repertory in the 20th Century," *Acts of the 10th World Congress of Jewish Studies* (Jerusalem, 1990), pp. 173–80. See also Maria Teresa Rubiato, "El Repertorio musical de un sefardi" *Sefarad* 25 (1965): 453–63, for an earlier study.

8. For discussions of gender, love, and gossip in the Turkish Sephardic song repertoire, see Pamela Dorn, "Gender and Personhood: Turkish Jewish Proverbs and the Politics of Reputation," *Women's Studies International Forum* 9, no. 3 (1986): 295–301, and "Songs of Love, Songs of Desire: The Notion of Romantic Love in the Music and Traditional Life of Turkish Sephardim" (paper presented at the Second International Symposium on Sephardic Studies, State University of New York at Binghamton, 1991).

9. From conversations with Buena Sarfatty Garfinkle, Montreal, 1982; Berta Levy, Rishon letsion, Israel, 1990; and Alegría Benhamron, Montreal, 1990, respectively.

10. Gladys Pimienta, "Las kantes de matesha" *Aki Yerushalayim* 4 (1982): 13–14, 30–32, 77–79, and informal conversations, Jerusalem, July 1990; interview with Julia Edéry, Montreal, January 1990; interview with Hannah Pimienta, Montreal, January 1991. See Weich-Shahaq, *Judeo-Spanish Moroccan Songs,* for full transcriptions of some *matexa* songs and chants.

11. "Performance" here is used in the sense of formally "putting on a show," whether or not they receive payment for doing so.

12. See David Bunis, *Sephardic Studies: A Research Bibliography* (New York: Garland Press, 1981), pp. 120–24, for a discography. A reissue of some of Hazan's 78 rpm releases is being prepared by Global Village Music in New York City. An *oud* is a Middle-Eastern stringed instrument, and a *chumbush* is a stringed instrument similar in shape to a banjo.

13. Interview with Karen Gerson, questionnaire cited.

14. Another important new group that sings a capella was recently organized in Israel by the ethnomusicologist Edwin Seroussi. The group, made up of three women from Bulgarian, Moroccan, and Turkish traditions and one man who learned his repertoire from his Greek and Turkish grandmother, was organized by Dr. Seroussi to accompany him on lecture tours.

15. As this study focuses on women, and for reasons of space, I have not discussed men's contributions here, but in the area of insider performers they are equally valuable. The early performers—Yitzhak Algazi, Haim Effendi, Jack Mayesh, and others; Yitzhak Levy, E. Abinun—and, more recently, Yehoram Gaon, Nico Castel, Joe Elias, Jak Esim, Avner Perez, Solly Levy, and others have made inestimable contributions.

16. Quotes from questionnaires submitted by Marcela Neil, Letizia Arbeteta, and Pamela Dorn-Sezgin (1991–92).

17. Editor's note: For women's concerns with relationships cross-culturally, see Carole Gilligan, *In a Different Voice* (Cambridge: Harvard University Press, 1982); and Nancy Chodorow, *The Reproduction of Mothering: Psychoanalysis and the Sociology of Gender* (Berkeley: University of California Press, 1978).

18. Quote from Judith Wachs and Lisle Kulbach from my notes on spontaneous comments during their concert for the International Symposium on Sephardic Studies, State University of New York at Binghamton, May 1991; quote from Rosa Zaragoza and Francesco Tomás from interviews, Barcelona, July 1991. For works by the main women scholars in the field, see Oro Anahory-Librowicz, *Cancioner séphardi du Québec I* (Montreal: Fonds FCAR, 1988); Rina Benmayor, "Social Determinants in Poetic Transmission: The Judeo-Spanish Romancero," in Issachar Ben-Ami, ed, *Studies in the Oriental Jewish Heritage* (Jerusalem: Magnes Press, 1982); Pamela Dorn Sezgin, "Gender and Personhood: Turkish Jewish Proverbs

and the Politics of Reputation," *Women's Studies International Forum* 9, no. 3 (1988): 1–37; Judith Etzion, "The Music of the Judeo-Spanish Romancero: Stylistic Features," *Anuario Musical* 43 (1988): 221–55; Weich-Shahaq, "The Wedding Songs of the Bulgarian-Sephardi Jews"; and Henrietta Yurchenco, *Ballads, Wedding Songs and Piyyutim of the Jews of Tetuan and Tangier* (Morocco: Folkways, 1983). See articles by Letizia Arbeteta and Maria-Teresa Rubiato and the M.A. theses by Marcia Barryte (dance), Carol Merrill-Mirsky, and Michelle Shallon; see also J. Cohen, "Sonography of Judeo-Spanish Song: Cassettes, LP's, CD's, Videos, Film," *Jewish Folklore and Ethnology Review* 15, no. 2 (1993): 49–55.

·VI·

AN ANTHRO-
POLOGICAL
VOICE

·12·

Toward an Anthropology of Jewish Women: Sacred Texts and the Religious World of Elderly, Middle-Eastern Women in Jerusalem

SUSAN STARR SERED

In 1984 and 1985 I conducted fieldwork among a group of elderly, Middle-Eastern Jewish women living in Jerusalem. My objective was to study the meaning of religion for women who conduct fairly autonomous, female-oriented religious lives within the constraints of male-oriented and male-dominated culture.[1]

The population with whom I worked consisted of women of a number of ethnic groups: Kurdish, Yemenite, Turkish, Persian, Iraqi, and Moroccan. The women ranged in age from fifty-eight to ninety (few knew their exact ages), and most had come to live in Israel as teenagers. Many of the women were widows at the time that I met them. Most of their husbands had worked as laborers or vendors, and they had worked as housewives, with occasional stints at factories, farms, or in domestic service at times of financial hardship. For the most part, they are poor and depend on small pensions from the National Insurance. I met them at a municipal Senior Citizens' Day Center, and in the course of the fieldwork accompanied them to synagogue, on visits to holy tombs, to celebrations, and to mourning rituals, and spent time with them while they prepared for holidays. I describe the religious world of the Day Center women in detail elsewhere.[2]

The Day Center women represent a population that has been considered marginal in almost every way—poor, female, old, illiterate, unemployed, ill, non-Western, and powerless in terms of the formal political and religious establishments. Yet, when they speak about their beliefs, their customs, and their worldview, they and their concerns stand at center stage. Not surprisingly, many of the themes that I found central to the lives of the Middle-Eastern women have also been noted in studies of Hindu, Islamic, and Christian women. Interpersonal relationships, the well-being of family members, fertility, and death are central religious concerns for women cross-culturally.[3] On the other hand, both the context and the particular manifestations of these themes are unique to Jewish women. As an outgrowth of this project, I began to recognize the need for a model of religion that could be of more general use in the anthropological study of Jewish women.[4]

The Day Center women perform few of the ceremonial acts that many of us associate with normative Judaism. They do, however, participate in numerous religious rituals each day—they recite blessings, donate small sums of money to charity, kiss sacred objects, purchase amulets, light candles, attend Judaica lessons, prepare for the Sabbath and holidays, frequent holy tombs, and pray in the local synagogues. They direct a substantial portion of their meager financial resources toward supporting religious institutions and funding religious rituals. The sacred permeates all aspects of their lives— nearly every conversation ends with someone looking upward and saying, "Everything is in God's hands," or "God is great, and everything will turn out for the best." Time, for these women, is marked off by the Sabbath and holidays. Birth, marriage, and death are surrounded by hundreds of rituals imparting the message that life is not a random, natural process but a significant part of a divinely created and ordered universe.

None of the women know how to read, and only a very few received even the most limited formal education. Their religious knowledge is a combination of rituals and beliefs learned from their mothers, from their children (who are literate and many of whom attended religious schools), and (quite recently) from local rabbis who teach special weekly classes for women.

The women's experience of religion is highly gender-specific; they conduct their religious lives mainly among other women, and they talk about their religious concerns and behavior from a gynocentric perspective. For example, the women describe a "religious person" in the same way they describe a "religious woman," while their description of a "religious man" is very different. According to the women, the perfectly religious woman/person is someone who helps others; they say that the greatest mitzvah (divine commandment, good deed) is to give cooked food to a hungry beggar. Conversely, the perfectly religious man is someone who correctly performs appropriate rituals; a truly religious man wakes up at midnight to study Zohar.

The religious world of the women centers around networks of relationships: with children, ancestors, extended family, saints, and the poor. Relationships within each category are made sacred by numerous halakic (legally required) and extra-halakic religious rituals. The women believe that their female religious world is just as holy, traditional, spiritually powerful, and important to the continued existence and well-being of the Jewish people as the religious world of the male rabbis, cantors, circumcisers, scholars, judges, exegetes, poets, writers, priests, and teachers.[5] Although in fact most of their rituals are extra-halakic, the women are unaware of such distinctions; they do not believe that their female rituals are superstitious, optional, local, magical, syncretistic, or in any way tangential to Jewish life.

Anthropology, Religion, and Women

The study of women and religion encompasses three rather different fields: (1) the study of female symbols, (2) the study of official (which is usually synonymous with male) definitions of the religious role and status of women, and (3) the study of the actual religious lives of real women. The last of these fields is of prime importance to the anthropological study of Jewish women.

Unfortunately, studies of women and Judaism have tended to confuse these inherently distinct approaches. The first two types of studies typically approach women as objects of men's perception. Within traditional Judaism, texts written by men legislate women's status (halakah) and elaborate upon female symbols (midrash and kabbalah). Through study of these texts one can learn a great deal not only about men's view of the role of women in the family and society but also about men's use of "the feminine" as a cultural symbol. To the anthropologist, however, it should be clear that feminine symbols are not real women. Feminine symbols may in some more or less (in)direct way reflect real women, they may be projections of male wishes or fears, they may be concise ways of expressing the various existential dilemmas that grow out of gender distinction, they may explain certain rituals, they may be a number of other things, but they are not real women, and the anthropological study of Jewish women must clarify that point from the outset.[6] Similarly, laws made by, expounded upon, and enforced by men should not be treated as expressing women's worldviews, women's moral voices, or even women's wishes. In cultures that emphasize gender difference and sex segregation, one cannot assume that men speak for both men and women.

In contrast, the anthropological study of Jewish women looks at women as subjects, as actors, not as symbols or objects that are acted upon. Thus, the anthropological study of Jewish women is first and foremost the study of specific women in specific times and places, specific women who through words and actions explicate and interpret their own life experiences.

That this point needs to be made at all is itself worthy of comment. Masculine symbols and real men are rarely confused in the way that feminine symbols and real women are. The reasons for this difference are various. First, as the earliest feminist critiques of anthropology have shown, anthropologists in the field have too often spoken primarily to men—in other words, they received male explanations of various cultural items. They saw the culture through male eyes. And if the anthropologist were a man, he saw the culture through double male eyes—his own and those of his informants. In a typical situation, women's religiosity was studied from a double distance, through two pairs of tinted glasses. Therefore, instead of learning about the religious lives of real women, we learned about how male fieldworkers understood the male informants' interpretations of women. Because so much of the study of Jewish women has been textually oriented, this problem has been unusually severe. Jewish women, then, are seen not only through male eyes but also through the eyes of what is most likely the male elite—rabbis, scholars, and *poskim* (legal decision makers).

The second reason for the confusion of women with female symbols is related to the androcentric perspective pervasive in the social sciences. In the words of one feminist scholar, within an androcentric perspective the male norm and the human norm are collapsed and become identical. So it is assumed that the generic masculine habit of thought, language, and research is adequate. To study males is to study humanity. Finally, and this is the relevant point here, when women, per se, are considered, they are discussed as an object exterior to humankind, "having the same ontological and epistomological status as trees, unicorns, or deities."[7]

The androcentric perspective assumes that men somehow create religion. One result of this perception is that religious symbols are studied either as projections of male psyches or as outgrowths of men's cultural needs. While one may choose to argue that in patriarchal culture men do indeed create military or political institutions, it would be difficult to convincingly argue, based on empirical evidence, that men alone create religion. However, only a few scholars explicitly state that they believe that men create religion. Instead, we find studies of religion that assume that where women's explanations of religious phenomena differ from men's, men's explanations somehow came first and women's are a sort of feminization of the male-created cultural norm. Unless such a sequence can be convincingly proven in a specific case (and it rarely can), this type of assumption has a deleterious effect on the study of Jewish women.

The first steps in avoiding the trap of androcentrism must be conscious and concerted efforts to see women as normative rather than as exceptions, as actors rather than objects acted upon. In cultures (such as many traditional Jewish cultures) where men and women concentrate on different activities, priorities, and norms of behavior, we can expect to find that men and women see the world somewhat differently: a given phenomenon may quite naturally look very different from an androcentric and a gynocentric perspective.[8]

A *Dynamic* Model

Because both academicians and Jewish *poskim* tend to reify women, we must emphasize the need for a dynamic model: women change throughout their life cycles and as a result of their individual and unique life experiences. While the religion of Jewish women has often been described as home-oriented and the classic image of the Jewish woman shows her lighting Sabbath candles surrounded by her young children, this sort of model may have relatively little meaning for very young, very old, and childless women.

Women's religiosity may drastically change over the course of their lifetimes. The elderly Middle-Eastern women of Jerusalem explain that when they were younger they were too busy with the home to attend synagogue. As old women, they do so daily. When their husbands were alive they could not visit the holy tombs because their husbands demanded that they be home to prepare meals. As widows, they go to the holy tombs as frequently as they can arrange transportation. When they were busy wives and mothers, they never had the opportunity to expand their knowledge of Jewish tradition, history, and law through attending classes. As middle-aged women many tried to attend literacy classes, and as old women they regularly attend Judaica classes given by local rabbis and *rabbaniot* (learned women). As active mothers they dedicated an enormous amount of time and energy to cleaning, cooking, laundering, and physically caring for their children. Now that they are too old to engage in much physical work, they care for their children and grandchildren through prayers and ritual.

The religious concerns of elderly women clearly differ from those of middle-aged women, young women, and girls. When the women of this study reminisce about their own lives, different types of religious activities and concerns emerge for various life stages. They remember dancing at picnics during Passover as young girls; they remember having no time for religion as young married women with small children; and they recall beginning to learn about Judaism, perhaps attending literacy classes, as middle-aged women. Now, as old women, they have developed a vibrant, innovative, communal public religious life. Clearly, then, a static model is of little use for understanding this sort of religious development.

Another way in which a static model has served to inhibit the serious study of Jewish women is through placing disproportionate emphasis on menstruation and menstrual taboos. Yet, empirically, women do not menstruate for most of their lives. Most women spend most of their lives premenstrual, postmenstrual, or amenstrual as a result of nursing, pregnancy, or (unfortunately) malnourishment. From a female perspective, menstruation is a poor explanation for women's religious concerns, participation, and emphases. For example, the elderly Jerusalem women began attending synagogue not when they ceased menstruating (which happened decades ago) but when their husbands died and their children no longer made demands on their time (which happened more recently).

From a Gynocentric Perspective

In the Mishna there is a well-known saying that there are certain deeds for which one is rewarded both in this world and in the next. These deeds are enumerated: honoring one's father and mother, practicing loving kindness, and making peace between a man and his neighbor. "But the study of Torah surpasses them all."[9] Implicit in this statement are the words "for men." The writer of this aphorism most likely did not expect that women would be Torah scholars.[10] For men, literacy stands at the center of the meaning of Jewishness. A "Jew" is a "person" who reads certain prayers, who learns from certain books.

Illiteracy has been an integral part of women's role in many Jewish societies. In certain Jewish communities and at various times women have been prohibited from studying Torah and even from learning how to read.[11] Questions of interest to the development of the anthropological study of Jewish women are: Where does an illiterate group fit into the "People of the Book"? How does literacy look from a gynocentric perspective? What theoretical tools should be used to study the religiosity of a category of people who are by definition illiterate but who exist parallel to or in conjunction with a group that is literate? From a gynocentric perspective, literate Judaism cannot be defined as normative with illiterate women relegated to the status of a minor subset of Jews who do not quite fulfill all the obligations of the religious system. From a gynocentric perspective, nonliterate Judaism is also normative, mainstream, and legitimate. Women are not a fringe group; women are 50 percent of the population.

One way in which women relate to a religious system that commands Torah learning for half of the population while forbidding it to the other half is through the ritualization of literacy; that is, through emphasizing the ritual rather than the literary value of the written material.[12] Not only do women ritualize literacy, but the ritualization of literacy does seem to function on two different levels, one for men and one for women. Many Middle-Eastern men sit in synagogue and study the Zohar, reading it quickly and understanding almost nothing of what they read. The women, who barely have physical access to the holy books at all, cannot even sound out the holy letters. In fact, it may be more appropriate, from a gynocentric perspective, to talk about the "mystification of literacy."[13]

For the elderly, Middle-Eastern women of Jerusalem any type of religious literature or object with religious writing is sacred. And, since they are not able to distinguish sacred literature from profane, any paper with Hebrew words may be treated as a ritual object. At the holy tombs in Meron (to which I accompanied the women on a pilgrimage), a man was selling photocopied papers with a great deal of printing. Several women bought and kissed the papers, only afterward asking me what was written on them (they were amulets). Many women have pages with Hebrew printing hung on walls of their house. Very few have any idea of what is written on the pages, but they know that the pages guard their homes.

During a trip to a local yeshiva the women were shown into the room where the young (male) students sit to study. Several women randomly picked up books from the bookshelf in the back of the room and kissed them. One woman also kissed the bookshelf itself. For her, the holiness of the books penetrated even the wood of the shelves. Another woman remembers how her saintly father-in-law would visit sick people in the hospital and bless them and bring "the book." When asked what book, she answered "big like this" and made a rectangular shape with her hands. From her tone it was clear that even the shape and size of this book were significant.

Simha, an extraordinarily articulate informant, was born in Israel and raised her children in Jerusalem during years of famine, war, and, finally, independence. She told the story of how one time many years ago a chicken to which she was especially attached disappeared from her yard. She searched for it everywhere, but it was nowhere to be found. As a last resort, she opened a prayer book at random and asked her husband to read what was written on that page. He told her that the words "walk in the path and you will find it" appeared there. The next morning, after dreaming that she found the chicken, she went to the market. On the way home, as she was walking along the path, she saw the chicken at the house of an acquaintance (who had apparently stolen it).

For these women, the written word takes on an increased value. To describe something she believes to be absolutely true, Simha says, "It is written." To describe something the truth of which she is unsure, she says, "So people say." All of the women attribute to the written Torah any important belief or custom. For example, according to one woman, there is a certain weed that cleans the blood and so is healthy to eat twice a year. The women say, "It [this herbal remedy] is written in the Torah, in the Sefer [the Book], my father said." Or, "God is everywhere. It says so in the prayerbook."

Simha explains that she is careful to always kiss the mezuza because "it is the Ten Commandments, written in the Torah. If one letter is damaged, it is forbidden for the mezuzah to be in the house. Harmful spirits can come in if no mezuzah is up. We say the '*Shma*' everyday and that says to put up mezuzot. It guards you and your children." She went on to relate that one time many years ago there was much illness among the people living in her courtyard (here she used female pronouns, so it is not clear if only the women were affected or if her grammar was faulty.) One person/woman would recover and another would get sick. It turned out that the mezuza was damaged (*pasul*). Another woman tells me that she does not know what is written inside the mezuza, but she would not let her daughter move into her new house until she put one up. She describes how rabbis in Iraq wrote amulets, just "scribbling something" (*le-kashkesh mashehoo*) on a piece of paper. But these papers were effective, both for Jews and for Arabs, "because we believed."

The women's ritualization of literacy looks quite different from the Torah study that most of us consider to be "normative Judaism." We may even be tempted to treat the ritualization of literacy as a corruption of "true Jewish values," or as a pathetic attempt on the part of a fringe group to compensate for their own inadequacies. The study of Jewish women must avoid these androcentric and ethnocentric interpretations. For the elderly, Middle-Eastern Jewish women of Jerusalem (and for millions of other Jewish women of other places and centuries) the ritualization of literacy is normative Judaism. When the women treat texts as ritual objects, they incorporate the texts into their interpersonal, relationship-oriented religious world: books, mezuzot, and pages with Hebrew writing guard over one's home and loved ones.

The Little Tradition

Within a system that defines male as normative, women frequently deviate from the norm.[14] Within a system that is sexually segregated and in which the male world is defined as the official world, the content of the women's world needs to be examined by a different set of tools. The question that seems most interesting to me as an anthropologist studying Jewish women is not whether a women's brand of Judaism exists (I think it can easily be shown that it does) but how the two religious systems (the male and female, the great and little, the halakic and extra-halakic) interact. Women's Judaism can only be understood in relationship to the male-dominated and male-oriented institutions that sometimes suppress, sometimes ignore, and sometimes encourage women's religiosity.

Male culture can sometimes out and out suppress women's rituals simply because men have more institutionalized power. An example of this power would be the building of metal enclosures and the prohibition on (women's) candle lighting at an increasing number of holy tombs in Israel today. For many women, physical contact with dead saints is a crucial form of religious expression. Similarly, leaving candles at the tombs of saints ensures that the saints will continue to concern themselves with the needs of their descendants. Preventing women from touching the tombs and from lighting candles are serious attacks on women's traditional religious rituals. Elderly Middle-Eastern women have no input into the decisions of the Israeli Ministry of Religion, and rules outlawing their rituals can easily be implemented.

An unanticipated side effect of suppression can sometimes be the creation of new rituals to circumvent the oppressive situation. For example, at the holy tombs at Meron women can be seen throwing unlit candles through the metal grating that closes off the tomb from the hands of visitors. It is the dynamic described here that is of particular interest to anthropologists. Women have a religious concern—protecting their families through enlisting the aid of dead saints and ancestors. Their concern is expressed through certain rituals—lighting candles and touching the tombs. The political/religious establishment does not allow the women to practice these rituals. The women necessarily find another way of expressing the same religious concern. The fascinating twist here is that once candles are thrown into a closed-off area (rather than placed on an officially approved shelf), the women's traditional ritual becomes transformed into a ritual of rebellion.

Male and female religious rituals sometimes exist parallel to each other, with occasional, significant meetings. For example, women of most Jewish ethnic groups light candles in a variety of non-halakically ordered situations. These candles are generally lit for the welfare of living descendants or as a way of signaling deceased ancestors. The situations at which such candles are lit include, for one elderly Yemenite informant, a daughter's giving birth, a grandchild's ride in an airplane, a neighbor's illness, and a husband's death. Simultaneously, candle lighting is required by halakah in certain other situations. That candle lighting is required at such times as the Sabbath Eve and Hanukkah strengthens women's perception of the efficacy of candle lighting at the non-halakically required times. That the official religion endorses candle lighting increases the women's perception of candle lighting as a holy and efficacious religious ritual. The great tradition sometimes gives the outside form to a more female content. Many elderly Middle-Eastern women attend synagogue because they believe that the time when the Torah is held up is particularly efficacious for making personal petitions on behalf of their families. In other words, women who are not required by halakah to attend synagogue, who take no part in the official synagogue service, who perhaps can barely hear or understand the formal service from their seats in the ladies' gallery, come to synagogue regularly on Mondays, Thursday, and the Sabbath to make petitions when the Torah is raised. In this case a male ritual—synagogue Torah reading—has given the outside form to a female religious activity—that of making personal petitions on behalf of family members.

Insidious Terminology

Anthropologists studying women have unfortunately inherited a corpus of terminology that too often serves to obscure the reality of women's lives. The literature abounds with words like "superstition" and "old wives' tales." When we look more closely at what these words are used to describe, we begin to suspect that women's beliefs and rituals are frequently dismissed as not-really-religion.

The anthropological study of Jewish women must recognize the insidious implications of treating religion and magic as if they stand in a dichotomous relationship. As Robert Fornaro has convincingly shown, in what the scholarly world calls "religion" women generally appear subordinate, while in "magic" women seem to perform evil witchcraft. If we reject this artificial division of the ritual-spiritual map, we discover that women are very active indeed in supernatural matters.[15]

When a literate Jewish man listens to the Torah reading in synagogue he is obeying a divine law, learning about the history of the Jewish people, and participating in the life of the community. When an illiterate Middle-Eastern Jewish woman listens to the Torah reading in synagogue, she is waiting for the Torah to be raised up because at that moment she has the best chance of convincing God to grant her a personal favor on behalf of a particular, beloved individual. A pervasive problem in the academic studies of religion and Judaism is the tendency to treat the first set of motivations as more noble, beautiful, important, eternal, or true than the second set. This sort of treatment is ethnocentrism and androcentrism at their worst: there is no reason to assume that the experience of the holy is any more immediate to a Torah scholar in a yeshiva than to a woman pinning on amulets to protect her family. Crucial to the development of the anthropological study of Jewish women is the realization that relationship-oriented, dynamic, extra-halakic Jewish religiosity is as worthy of study and respect as text and halakah-oriented Judaism.[16]

Toward an Anthropology of Jewish Women

I chose to study the women described in this essay because of their illiteracy. Scholars of Jews and Judaism have traditionally been so attracted to (blinded by?) texts that the world described by the texts has come to be seen as the only—as the real—Jewish world. By working with illiterate women, I purposely sought to distance myself as much as possible from texts. However, at risk of confusing the issues a bit, I suggest that those very texts that all-too-often exclude and demean women also define the parameters of the anthropological study of Jewish women.

Even in this one volume, the reader has seen juxtaposed Moroccan, Eastern European, Central and Western European, American, Babylonian, Kurdish, and Tunisian women. The cultural differences, the time spans, the geographical distances are immense. Some of these women would probably be unrecognizable to others of the women as Jewish. As anthropologists, we talk about cultural contexts: the experiences of Jewish women in Tunisia surely are not so different from the experiences of Muslim women in Tunisia, the development of Jewish feminist rituals has undoubtedly paralleled the development of Christian feminist rituals, and women cross-culturally are active participants in their children's rites of passage. It would be simple to argue (as Debra Kaufman indeed has argued in her wonderful book *Rachel's Daughters*) that particular groups of Jewish women can be best studied in the context of non-Jewish women of the same time and place (Kaufman, for example, looks at the newly Orthodox Jewish American women against the background of newly religious Christian American women and twentieth-century American feminists).[17]

In the beginning of this essay, I warned against trying to understand the lives of Jewish women by reading texts written by Jewish men. Yet, it is these very texts that provide connecting links among Jewish women of various times and places. Often, only by virtue of their relationship to sacred texts does the notion "Jewish women" have meaning. Even if most Jewish women cannot read or understand them, it is the texts that legislate who is Jewish; it is the texts that lay out the general shape of the Jewish liturgical calendar; it is the texts that define and enhance the power of certain men to lead the Jewish community; it is the texts that preserve the reservoire of stories, images, symbols, and rites that Jewish women cross-culturally draw upon; and it is the texts that institutionalize male dominance and female subordination.

Not surprisingly, how Jewish women relate to the great tradition has begun to emerge as a key issue for feminist Jewish anthropologists. And indeed, a number of contributors to this volume stress this theme. Debra Kaufman, for example, explains that newly orthodox women present a "'graceful' interpretation" of the laws of menstrual purity—an interpretation that they, as women, find empowering. In a very different context, Judith Davis studies contemporary bar mitzvah's from a gynocentric perspective, and she discovers that the "ritual ordeal" for mothers is not the official synagogue ceremony but the organizing of a communal celebration. Penina Adelman shows contemporary Jewish women creating new rituals that draw upon traditional images and symbols. Dianne Ashton argues that because Jewish women (unlike Jewish men) were not indoctrinated in Judaism through mastery of Jewish texts, they may have been freer to express innovative and unusual ideas and to find their own personal meanings in biblical narratives. Her conclusion—that Jewish women shape their own spirituality while simultaneously reaffirming the Jewish great tradition—resonates with my own work and with most of the studies in this volume.

The anthropology of Jewish women is the anthropology of women who stand in relationship of some sort (worshipful, antagonistic, creative) to Jewish texts. The anthropological challenge, as I see it, is to explore the nature of that relationship. For the women among whom I conducted fieldwork, that relationship is ritualistic, dynamic, ambivalent, and somewhat manipulative. Yet my work with those women has convinced me that without reference to the texts, one may speak of an anthropology of women who happen to be Jewish—not of an anthropology of Jewish women. An anthropology of Jewish women cannot ignore texts, but neither can it be limited by them.

NOTES

1. The cultural context of the women is male-oriented and male-dominated in the sense that Israeli political and economic institutions are disproportionately ruled by men; that Israeli society is on the whole structured to meet male rather than female needs (for example, the school day ends at twelve noon, interfering with the work lives of mothers of young children); that the women's natal and marital family groups emphasized the male as the "head" of the family; and in that sense that within the Jewish religious tradition the deity is addressed in the masculine gender, God's message is portrayed as conveyed through men (Abraham, Moses, etc.), institutionalized leadership is almost always male (the Sanhedrin, the priesthood, the rabbinate, the courts), and that most (or perhaps all) laws and prayers have been written by men.

2. In *Women as Ritual Experts* (New York: Oxford University Press, 1992), I present in detail the religious rituals and concerns of the Day Center women.

3. See Margaret Alexiou, *The Ritual Lament in Greek Tradition* (Cambridge: Cambridge University Press, 1974); Lois Beck, "The Religious Lives of Muslim Women," in J. I. Smith, ed., *Women in Contemporary Muslim Societies* (London: Associated University Presses, 1980), pp. 27–60; M. H.

Beech, "The Domestic Realm in the Lives of Hindu Women in Calcutta," in H. Papanek and G. Minault, eds., *Separate Worlds: Studies of Purdah in South Asia* (Columbia, Mo.: South Asia Books, 1982), pp. 110–38; Lucy Rushton, "Doves and Magpies: Village Women in the Greek Orthodox Church," in P. Holden, ed., *Women's Religious Experience* (London: Croom Helm, 1983), pp. 57–70; C. Thompson, "Women Fertility and the Worship of Gods in a Hindu Village," in Holden, *Women's Religious Experience,* pp. 113–31; Susan Wadley, "Hindu Women's Family and Household Rites in a North Indian Village," in Nancy Falk and Rita Gross, eds., *Unspoken Worlds: Women's Religious Lives in Non-Western Cultures* (San Francisco: Harper and Row, 1980), pp. 94–109.

4. While the particular examples that I cite below are drawn from my own work on religion, the issues that are raised are equally applicable to the study of other aspects of the lives of Jewish women.

5. They are aware, however, that men have a monopoly on institutionalized power.

6. I am not trying to discredit the legitimacy of the study of symbols; I am simply trying to distinguish between the study of symbols and the study of real people, a distinction that is taken for granted in the study of men but that is somehow glossed over in the study of women.

7. Rita Gross, ed., *Beyond Androcentrism: New Essays on Women and Religion* (Missoula, Mont.: Scholars Press for the American Academy of Religion, 1977), p. 10.

8. See Edwin Ardener, "Belief and the Problem of Women," in Shirley Ardener, ed., *Perceiving Women* (London: J. M. Dent and Sons, 1974), pp. 1–18; Ashton, "Grace Aguilar and the Matriarchal Theme in Jewish Women's Spirituality," in this volume.

9. Mishna "Peah" 1:1. This phrase is also in the prayerbook (weekday morning service), so it is very well known.

10. In the Talmud "Sotah" 20a, it is written that is forbidden for a man to teach his daughter Torah. While this is not the only opinion expressed in the Talmud, this is the formulation most known in the Middle-Eastern Jewish community.

11. Jewish women in Yemen were actually forbidden to read because it was believed to be against Jewish religion, that rain would pour for days on end and crime would flourish if they were to learn, and that a woman should never be higher than her husband. See Lisa Gilad, *Ginger and Salt: Yemini Jewish Women in an Israeli Town* (Boulder, Colo.: Westview Press, 1989). Rhonda Berger-Sofer, who conducted fieldwork among the ultra-Orthodox Ashkenazi women of Mea Shearim, quotes an informant who told her the story of a great rabbi who said that his very righteous mother did not know how to pray, learn, or read Hebrew. The only prayer that she

knew was the Grace After Meals. The rabbi felt that if she had not known the Grace After Meals she would have been even more holy. Berger-Sofer found that nowadays most girls know how to pray from the prayerbook, but the older women are proud that they do not know (Berger-Sofer, "Pious Women: A Study of Women's Roles in a Hassidic and Pious Community: Mea She'arim" [Ph.D. diss., Rutgers University, 1979], pp. 56–57).

12. Shlomo Deshen, "Ritualization of Literacy," *American Ethnologist* 2, no. 2 (1975): 251–60.

13. Daphne Izraeli suggested this formulation to me.

14. The anthropologist Robert Redfield, studying peasant society, coined the term "little tradition" to refer to the culture of the unreflective many (as opposed to the "great tradition" of the reflective few). The Jewish anthropologist Barbara Myerhoff defines the little tradition as the local, folk expression of a group's belief. It is an unsystematized, not elaborately idealized oral tradition practiced constantly and often unconsciously by ordinary people without external enforcement or interference. See Redfield, *Peasant Society and Culture* (Chicago: University of Chicago Press, 1956); Myerhoff, *Number Our Days* (New York: E. P. Dutton, 1979).

15. Robert Fornaro, "Supernatural Power, Sexuality, and the Paradigm of 'Women's Space' in Religion and Culture," *Sex Roles* 12, nos. 3–4 (1985): 295–302.

16. The reader may be tempted to argue that the religious mode described in this essay is limited to uneducated, elderly, primitive, old-fashioned, or simple women. However, fieldwork I am now conducting among young mothers in Israel indicates that extra-halakic, interpersonally oriented rituals are the most persistent of Jewish rituals. There is no indication that these rituals are disappearing now that most women are literate (although some rituals have changed their form, even acquiring literate elements). See Susan Sered, "Religious Rituals and Secular Rituals: Interpreting Models of Childbirth in a Modern, Israeli Context," *Sociology of Religion* 54 (1993): 101–14.

17. Debra Renee Kaufman, *Rachel's Daughters: Newly Orthodox Jewish Women* (New Brunswick: Rutgers University Press, 1991).

Contributors

PENINA ADELMAN is a social worker and folklorist living in Boston. She is the author of *Miriam's Well: Rituals for Jewish Women around the Year* (Biblio Press, 1986) as well as a forthcoming children's Bible. Her work on women's ritual continues among observant Jewish women in the United States and Israel.

DIANNE ASHTON is an assistant professor of philosophy and religion at Glassboro State College, New Jersey. She researches women in Jewish history. In addition to her work on Grace Aguilar, she is co-editor, with Ellen Umansky, of *Four Centuries of Jewish Women's Spirituality: A Sourcebook* (Beacon Press, 1992).

JUDITH R. BASKIN is the chair of the Department of Judaic Studies at the State University of New York at Albany. She is the author of *Pharoh's Counsellors: Job, Jethro, and Balaam in Rabbinic and Patristic Tradition* (Scholars Press, 1983) and the editor of *Jewish Women in Historical Perspective* (Wayne State University Press, 1991).

MICHAEL BERKOWITZ is an assistant professor of modern Jewish history at Ohio State University, Columbus. His book *Zionist Culture and Western European Jewry before the First World War* was published by Cambridge University Press (1993), and *Zionism between the Wars: Western Jewry and the Zionist Project, 1914–1993* is forthcoming from Cambridge University Press.

SALLY CHARNOW, a Mellon Fellow in Interdisciplinary European Studies, holds an M.A. in performance studies from New York University, where she is pursuing a Ph.D. in history and researching French Jewish identity after 1945.

JUDITH R. COHEN is an ethnomusicologist associated with the University of Toronto and a performer of Judeo-Spanish song—as well as French Canadian, Balkan, medieval, and other traditions—focusing on women's repertoires and performance styles. Her recent publications include "Sonography of Judeo-Spanish Song (Cassettes, LP's, CD's, Video, Film)," in the special issue on "Sephardic Folklore" of the *Jewish Folklore and Ethnology Review* (1993).

JUDITH DAVIS is a family therapist practicing and teaching at the University of Massachusetts, Amherst. She has a private practice, continues her research on ritual, and is currently writing a book for bar/bat mitzvah families tentatively titled *Mazel Tov: Mining the Magic of Your Child's Bar/Bat Mitzvah.*

MYRNA GOLDENBERG has been teaching literature and composition at Montgomery College, Maryland, since 1971, where she is also the coordinator of women's studies. In addition to her family, teaching, and civic responsibilities and pleasures, she has a full schedule of researching, lecturing, and writing on Jewish women, particularly on Jewish women's experiences in the Holocaust.

DEBRA RENEE KAUFMAN is a professor of sociology at Northeastern University in Boston. She has published numerous articles and chapters on women and work, family, feminist theory, and fundamentalism and gender identity. She is author of *Rachel's Daughters: Newly Orthodox Jewish Women* (Rutgers University Press, 1991) and coauthor, along with B. Richardson, of *Achievement and Women: Challenging the Assumptions* (Free Press, 1982).

PAMELA S. NADELL, associate professor of Jewish studies and history at the American University, Washington, D.C., has published widely on Jewish immigration and Jewish women. Her book *Conservative Judaism in America: A Biographical Dictionary and Sourcebook* (Greenwood Press, 1988) was hailed as a major contribution to American, Jewish, and religious history. She is currently researching women in the American synagogue.

MAURIE SACKS, associate professor of anthropology at Montclair State University, New Jersey, publishes on Jewish women, ethnic education, and American folk art. Her publications include "Computing Community at Purim," in the *Journal of American Folklore* (1989); "Some Problems in the Study of Jewish Women's Folk Culture," in *Contemporary Jewry* (1989); and "An Anthropological and

Postmodern Critique of Jewish Feminist Theory," in the *Jewish Political Studies Review* (1994).

ESTHER SCHELY-NEWMAN received her Ph.D. from the University of Chicago. She is a faculty member of the Department of Communication and Journalism at the Hebrew University in Jerusalem. Her publications include "The Woman Who Was Shot: A Communal Tale," in the *Journal of American Folklore* (1993).

RITA J. SIMON is University Professor at the School of Public Affairs and Washington College of Law at the American University, Washington, D.C. Author of twelve books and editor of ten in the areas of ethnicity, law, and women's studies, she has also served as editor of the *American Sociological Review* and *Justice Quarterly*. Her current research interests include a study of women rabbis and ministers.

SUSAN STARR SERED is the author of *Women as Ritual Experts: The Religious Lives of Elderly Jewish Women in Jerusalem* (Oxford University Press, 1992). Her current research is a cross-cultural study of women and religion. She lives in Jerusalem with her husband and four small children and serves on the faculty of Bar-Ilan University.

Index

Aaron, 116, 117
Abraham, 83, 88
Academic disciplines, 15*n*21
Adam, 26
Adelman, Penina, 215
Aggadah. *See* Rabbinic Judaism
Agudat Israel, 178–79, 181*n*7
Aguilar, Grace, 9, 73*n*6, 79–93, 104;
    on Jewish women's moral and spiri-
    tual power, 80; literary clubs and li-
    braries, 86
Agunah, 7, 15*n*27
Alhambra (musical ensemble), 191
All but My Life (Klein), 103
Alliance Israelite Universelle, 158
Alvar, Manuel, 195
Amenorrhea, 97, 101, 102
American Anthropological Associa-
    tion, 2
American culture: spiritual impoverish-
    ment of, 177, 179
American Folklore Society, 12–13*n*1;
    Jewish section of, 1, 12–13*n*1
American Israelite, 87
American Jewess, 87
American Jewish women. *See* Jewish
    women: American
Amulets, 211, 214
Anahory-Librowicz, Oro, 193
Angelou-Osmond, Matia, 113
Androcentrism, 7, 205, 207, 211, 214
Anthropology, 2; approaches to study
    of human behavior, 2, 6, 215; con-
    cept of tradition in, 109, 111–12;
    ethnographic texts in, 172; and
    feminist theory, 3–6; heteroglossia
    in, 172; positivism in, 3; public and

private domains in, 21 (*see also* Pri-
    vate domain; Public domain); and
    ritual, 126, 203–18; scientific mod-
    el of, 3; and study of Jewish wom-
    en, 150, 203–18; training in, 5;
    wholism in, 3
Antisemitism: in England, 80; stereo-
    type of Jewish men in, 44
Ardener, Edwin, 3
Armistead, Samuel, 195
Ashira (musical ensemble), 176
Ashton, Dianne, 104, 216
Association for Jewish Studies, 15*n*21
"At Haran's Well" (Skinner), 87
Athens: Nazi prison in, 96; Red Cross
    in, 96
Auschwitz, 96, 97, 101, 102, 103. *See
    also* Concentration camps, Nazi
Authenticity: of Judeo-Spanish songs,
    192, 193; of Kos Miriam ritual,
    120; of tradition, 109, 110

Ba'alot teshuvah, 10, 142–154, 180*n*2;
    attitudes toward gender roles
    among, 144, 145; family values
    among, 144, 145; improvement of
    heterosexual relations of, 145;
    movement in America, 144; music
    of, 173, 180*n*2; rejection of secular
    culture, 144; ritual and sexuality
    among, 148; roots in counterculture
    of, 143; search for moral guidelines
    among, 144; at Shevach High
    School, 177; in "The Story of
    Karen," 177, 179; worldview of,
    149
Babcock, Barbara, 123*n*10